ROADIES N ROCK

This book is my honest recollection

I knew when I was just a kid that I want concert business.

I worked my first show when I was 11 years old, and as I write this, that was 49 years ago.
This book is my story of how I was a kid who wanted to work concerts for the rest of my life and that is exactly what I did.

Roadies n Rockstars is all I have ever really known my whole life. The early morning load ins, the late-night drives, doing the impossible then getting up and doing it again.

The thing about working concerts, is that I never had that sensation of "What are we doing tonight?".
I always knew what I was doing, I was working a show.

This book is my story of how I went from a kid working in the bars of Ohio to making the jump to lightspeed all the way to Radio City Music Hall & Madison Square Garden.

I dedicate this book to everyone that knows what it's like to get up early in the morning, go to work, put in a tough day, run on little sleep, and come back for more.

ROADIESNROCKSTARS.COM

HOW I MADE IT TO NEW YORK CITY

Raised by Beatniks..7
Coco...9
Cleveland Municipal Stadium...11
Bob Seger & The Silver Bullet Band....................................12
The Union..14
Return to the Land of the Posers.......................................22
Warcylde..23
Maleki..28
Return to Cleveland...30
Cleveland Music Center...31
The Motion..34
How not to grow marijuana 39
Jeff Healey...43
Harvest..45
Richard Elliot...46
2 Nice Girls..47
Pop Will Eat Itself..48
The Henry Rollins Band...49
Napalm Death...50
The Fixx...51
The Spudmonsters..52
The Bo Deans..53
Mark Cohen..55
Kings X..61
Primus...62
Kix...63
Kansas...64
The Bullet Boys...66
The Sun Rhythm Section...67
Trixter..68
Tribe Called Quest...69
The Bobs...70
Pere Ubu...70
Murphey's Law..70
Nirvana..71
The Exploited..73

Tito Puente	76
Zaza	77
Helmet	79
The Royal Crescent Mob	79
L7	80
The Impotent Sea Snakes	81
Pearl Jam	82
Luka Bloom	84
Henry Rollins	85
Integrity	86
Gary Richrath	87
Kings X	89
Goober and The Peas	90
The Dead Milkmen	90
Tori Amos	91
The Zoo	93
The Byrds	94
Front Line Assembly	95
Odd Girl Out	96
Screaming Trees	98
Ween	98
The Twist Offs	99
Warrior Soul	99
The Toasters	100
Compton's Most Wanted	100
WTF is a Rave?	101
Right Said Fred	103
The Wallflowers	105
The Tragically Hip	105
Pat Benatar	106
The Average White Band	107
Toto	108
Flipper	109
Mark Cohen	113
X	114
Southside Johnny & The Asbury Jukes	115
Polka Festival	119
Chris Isaak	120

Urge Overkill	120
The Reunification of the Hopi and Navajo Nations	121
Robin Trower	129
Penn & Teller	130
White Zombie	132
Greenhouse 27	134
Sheryl Crow	135
The Genitorturers	136
B Stage	137
Stuttering John	138
Chuck Mangione	140
The Neville Brothers	142
The Pepsi Country Music Festival	143
John Mellencamp's Birthday Party	148
Margaritaville	149
Ronnie Milsap	150
George H. Bush	150
Moonwalk 94	151
Dion, Sarah McLachlan	151
The Green Day Riot	152
Tony Bennett	156
Hal Ketcham	158
Afternoon Riot	159
Endfest 94	160
Bad Company	162
America, Overkill	162
Nine Inch Nails	163
Blue Oyster Cult	164
Green Day	165
Joe Cocker	166
Plant Merger Announcement	167
Los Lobos	169
State of the Division Meeting	170
Drew Carey	171
Entombed	173
The Smithereens	173
311	173
State of the Division Meeting	174

Bone, Thugs & Harmony	175
De La Soul	178
Olga Tanon	178
Nine Inch Nails	179
Sons of Elvis	181
Ned's Atomic Dust Bin	196
Stanley Clark	197
Helmet	197
Thrill Kill Cult, Lords of Acid	198
Engelbart Humperdinck	199
Worst Show Ever	201
Concert for the Rock n Roll Hall of Fame	209
Alanis Morrissette	211
Truck Driving 101	213
Alanis Morrissette	217
Morris Day & The Time	218
Little Richard	220
Bob Dylan	232
WMMS Buzzard Fest	224
Chuck Berry	226
Southern Comfort Blues Festival	228
Akron Rib Cook Off	230
The Monkees	235
Busted	237
Maple Fever	240
The Plumbers	245
The Experts from New York	246
Eddie Money	247
Peter, Paul & Mary	248
The Sex Pistols	250
Todd Rundgren	251
Another Bad Idea	256
Bob Dole Tour	260
Jesus Christ Superstar	262
New Edition	274
Johnny Mathis	286
Tony Bennett	289
50th Anniversary USAF	291

The Bee Gees..293
The Fossil Rock Tour...295
A Chorus Line...310
MTV Video Music Awards..312
West Side Story..313
Jingle Ball...325
Escape from Cleveland..329
Looking Back..331

Raised by Beatniks

My parents were beatniks making the scene in between Boston and San Francisco in the early 60s.
I can't confirm it 100%, but I truly believe that my father was patient zero of the hippies.

My father had gotten out of the army by spending every moment searching for the forms that could get him out.
Finally, he discovered a stipulation, that said you had to be a certain weight if you were a certain height, and he just starved himself until he got out.

As two penniless beatniks traveling across the country, whenever my parents needed a reference for anything, they would say "Just call Professor Ghoulardi at MIT, He will vouch for us".
My parents had a friend who had broken into the MIT system, and assigned himself a laboratory, a secretary, and a salary.
All under the name, Professor Ghoulardi.
Legend has it, that the best LSD that saturated the East Coast of the United States in the early 60s came from that laboratory at MIT.

By 1962, my parents had me and a guitar store in Boston's, Harvard Square.
At that time there was no other place to buy quality acoustic instruments.
My father was traveling back and forth from Spain to Boston bringing back custom guitars.
Business was booming for them, and they had captivated the attention of what was happening with the folk music scene.
At some point, my father figured out that it was much more profitable to bring back guitar cases full of hash without guitars in them.
My mom wasn't down with this program, so she took me and split and my father returned to Africa to learn the ancient ritual of proper hash making.

When my father returned from Africa, he became the musical director for Timothy Leary and his LSD parties.

He went on to do several albums for Vanguard Records when everybody thought that sitar music was gonna take off.
He spent the rest of his life as the Forrest Gump of the hippies, blindly walking through every amazing situation completely oblivious to what's going on around him yet shockingly actually in the middle of international conspiracies.
His story is a book all to itself.

My mom was a nurse in Cleveland, and I grew up as a latchkey kid coming home to an empty house every day.
it's just how it was.

My after-school ritual consisted of feeding myself by making my own pot pies and teaching myself how to play guitar.
One Gilligan's Island, one McHale's Navy and the food was ready.

We lived in Cleveland Heights in 1974 and two interesting things happened to me that changed my life forever that year.
I got my first job, and a rock band moved in across the street.

We lived in a duplex, standard for working class Cleveland style neighborhoods.
After the rock band moved in across the street, a guy named Steve moved in upstairs that owned a portable sound system.
He would become my babysitter when my mom worked a double shift, and I would go out with him and the band to do shows in local biker bars.

Coco
The Flipside, Cleveland Heights Ohio sometime 1974

After many nights hanging out sitting in the corner in the basement when they were practicing, I finally got the chance to go and roadie a show with the guys.
Mom was working a double shift, and these were the only guys to watch me, so they took me with them.

I had an aunt in Youngstown OH that loved riding motorcycles and hanging out in biker bars and would always take me with her.
When she would be too drunk to ride the Honda back home, I would sit in the front and ride the bike and she would put her feet down at the stop signs.
My feet could reach the pegs but not the ground.
I was ready for some more adult adventures.

I was 11 years old and unloading the van and bringing the gear into the club.
It's been almost 50 years since I loaded that show into that nightclub and I could still remember the smell of the room when we walked in.
Every little detail from the checkerboard floors to the dark wood bar, the two pinball machines in the corner and on the opposite side is where we set up the sound board.
The Flipside was a rock'n'roll punch palace at the corner of Cedar and Taylor in Cleveland Heights.
Years later two guys named Pete and Dewey would buy that place, cut a hole in the floor, and started serving wine and turned it into a fancy place.

When I was there in 1974 with Coco It was a shot and a beer kind of place with nothing but motorcycle parking out front.

The guys played three one hour sets that night, I spent a lot of time playing pinball and accepting alcoholic beverages from adults.
Nobody cared that I was in there underage, I was a roadie for the band and that's all that counted to anyone.

At some point, my official babysitter Steve the sound man passed out behind the mixing console.
I scooted right in and started grabbing some knobs.
My first show and I was mixing.
The mixing console did not have faders, it had control knobs the size of a baseball.

I don't even have a memory of being nervous about it, I just kind of stepped up.
The show was over at 2:00 AM, we loaded it out and put everything back in the van.
I was so high on adrenaline, and some other substances when I was standing on the sidewalk, and I watched the bass player from the band leave.

He walked out of the club, handed Steve his base and after he started his Harley a beautiful woman with long jet-black hair, got on the back of his bike and they rode off into the night together.

At that point it was just me and Steve standing on the sidewalk next to the van, he said to me" Are you ready to go"?
Looking right at him I said" I'm ready".
I was ready to do this for the rest of my life.

Cleveland Municipal Stadium
1974-1980

In 1974 one of my best friends lived next door to me and we were constantly in trouble.

John and I were rowdy, breaking things, skipping school constantly and we could not be trusted.

The only solution was for John's father, Mr. Artzner to take us both to work with him so he can keep an eye on us.

He was the manager for the commissaries at Cleveland Stadium and we worked boiling hot dogs, pouring sodas and stealing beer.

Minimum wage at the time was $2.25 an hour, I was thrilled to be there, and I was thrilled to have it.

Every baseball game and every football game, we were there.

And eventually that would turn into every concert.

We were there June 4th, 1974, for the riot that ensued from "10 cent beer night".

I wasn't even 12 years old yet, and I got to experience my first riot.

My two favorite memories of working there before being fired in 1980 as one time as the players were warming up, I sat over the dugout and just watched the guys hit balls.

There was a player on the Cleveland Indians at that time named Buddy Bell, and I watched him hit seven in a row into the bleachers.

My most favorite, was using my employee ID to go on to the field in the afternoon and watch "Pink Floyd" sound check when they came in 1977.

I was the only one on the field, with my ID clipped to my shirt.

It was surreal, standing in that exact same spot 4 hours later surrounded by 80,000 other people.

Bob Seger & The Silver Bullet Band, The J. Geils Band, Eddie Money, Def Leppard
Cleveland Stadium, 7-19-80
This was the day I was fired from Cleveland Stadium.
Like all good things, everything comes to an end.
From 1974 to 1980 I had a good run.

The thing about the big concerts, was since they were so rare, we needed a lot of extra help.
We were encouraged to bring people in that wanted to work.
I brought in my buddy Mr. Caris who had worked with me before during games.
At this point I was done with this job in so many ways and I had zero intention of actually working the show, my plan was to punch in and then disappear out into the crowd.
Mr. Caris and I we're interested in girls and weed, not hot dogs and brown sugar water.

Before we disappeared, I had keys to a storage room that was up on the upper balcony.
We discovered a box about the size of a stove, and it was filled with white "Cleveland Indians" frisbees.
Hands down the find of the century.

We dragged that box to the edge of the upper deck and threw every one of those frisbees in the crowd.
I couldn't even guess to how many it was, the way they were stacked in the box it was in the hundreds.

The crowd was cheering as we were throwing these frisbees, some of them floating hundreds of feet across the stadium.

Of course, we got busted and before security could get their physical hands on us, we disappeared into the crowd.

That was it for the World Series of Rock at Cleveland Stadium.
Was it because it was my last day?
I can't say for sure, but I had a good run there.

To this day, I meet people who were at that show and remember those frisbees.

Two weeks later I went and picked up my last check from Cleveland Stadium.
Now when I look at my Social Security statement, it shows my 1974 income.
On the page it's just a number, but those numbers represent a lot of memories for me.

The Union
Athens Ohio 1980-1982
In 1978, I had just started high school 10th grade.
The last grade I had graduated was the 8th grade, the school system refused to have me because of my "behavioral issues" for the entirety of the 9th grade and they just pushed me through.

My only goal, for attending the 10th grade was in hopes of stealing a triple beam scale from the science department.
Like my father before me, I was only interested in guitars, drugs, and girls.
I had zero intention of attending any of the scheduled activities that were laid out for me.

It's funny that I recently found a psychological report that my mom kept from when I was 14 years old.
It reports "Peter does not want to do his work, because he feels that it interferes with his free time. Peter feels like the questions from his teachers are stupid and everything is irrelevant because he's going to be a musician".
How intuitive.

I remember it was November, about a week before my 16th birthday and I met an 18-year-old senior that was blonde, beautiful and she had her own apartment.
She invited me back to her apartment that afternoon, and that was the last the time I was ever at that high school or any other high school ever again.

Her and her roommate had sex with me for three days.
Once I recovered enough body fluids, I went back to my mom's house got my stuff and I officially moved in with the chicks.

We had an apartment on Coventry Road above the cool record store called Record Revolution.

By the springtime I had a job selling hot dogs out of a cart downtown.

My boss only counted the hot dogs, but he didn't count the buns, so I would feed the homeless people in the area with chili sandwiches.

My job at the stadium was only part time whenever there was a game and the pay sucked.
Usually after spending all day downtown in the rain selling hot dogs, I would go to a second job washing dishes at a restaurant down the street from our apartment.

Another job that I was qualified for, was pumping gas at a gas station.
Pumping gas and changing flat tires.
This was a time before the self-service gas station, some guy like me would come out there, rain and snow, pump the gas, check the oil, check the air in your tires and then not get a tip for any of it.

When you worked at a gas station in the winter, the worst sound in the world was the sound of a flat tire bumping down the street.

I was 16 years old when I worked at Cedar Taylor Sunoco.
The place was owned by a Russian guy named Sam, who had been in three different armies during World War 2.
He started in the Russian army, was captured by the Germans, escaped, and fought for the Hungarians and then the Polish resistance.

He worked in a ladder factory for 20 years, saved his money and bought Cedar Taylor Sunoco.
One thing about Sam, is that he didn't give a fuck about anything, including his customers.

I worked there six days a week, 7:00 AM to 5:00 PM for $86 a week.
At some point I got my buddy Spek a job there with me and they would leave us there alone on the weekends.
On the weekends one tire repair was enough money for two corned beef sandwiches and a six pack, that meant everything to us.

I was 16, running a gas station on the weekends, going home to my two hot girlfriends, as far as I was concerned everything was awesome.

I'm at work one day and a woman asked me if I would put the license plates on the car for her.
She was parked right in front of the office.
I grabbed a screwdriver and installed the rear plate first.
As I was crouched down in front of the car installing the front license plate, the engine started.
I immediately stood up, and I was looking at the woman right through the windshield and she was looking right at me as she popped the clutch and drove right over me into the gas station.

Old school gas station style, we had that pyramid of oil cans stacked in the windows.
She drove me through that plate glass window, through the oil cans and I ended up underneath her car inside of the office.

My boss and his son-in-law come running in from the garage, and as I'm lying under the car, the first thing my boss said to me was "Goddamit Charlie, what the hell did you do now?".

They pulled me out from under the car, and I had a big piece of glass sticking out of my left shoulder.
The woman was screaming hysterically, not helping.

I looked down at my left arm, and there was a big open gash.
When I turned my arm the other way, I could clearly see white bone and I had an immediate sensation that I was really in trouble.
I remember saying, I think I need to go to the hospital.
What did my boss do?

He sent me next door to the vet.
Of course, the vet was horrified and immediately demanded that somebody take me to a proper hospital.
They put me in the front seat of the tow truck, and took me down to the closest hospital on Euclid Ave.

A couple minutes after I got there, some guy came in with a shotgun blast to the chest and my priority status moved way down the list.
At some point I felt I was going to release myself on my own recognizance, I got off the gurney started making my way up the hill and a couple men in white uniforms came and got me to take me back inside.
To be fair, I was leaving a considerable trail of blood.

This had happened around 10:00 o'clock in the morning, and by the afternoon I was back at work pumping gas with a cast on my arm.

When one of the girls I was living with went off to college at Ohio University down in Athens OH, I went with her.
For a while I got away with living in the girl's dorm for several months, then I finally rented a trailer out of town on a dirt road.

During the day I worked at a pizza place called "Angelo's" and at night I worked at the bar right next door called The Union.
My boss at Angelo's was a complete dick to me and the people at the Union were totally cool, but I needed both incomes to survive.

At Angelo's I was hired as one of the prep cooks, dicing ingredients all day. There was somebody else that made the dough, and an old woman that had been there forever that made the sauce.
The sauce had been a recipe from her family, and we followed it to the letter every day.

One day for reasons I'm not clear of, they fired the guy that made the dough and told me from now on I would also be doing that job.
They weren't even nice about it.
My workload was being doubled, while the pay stayed the same. The whole thing was worse because the owner was just such a dick all the time.

So, I come in for work one morning, and I'm informed that the woman that has been making the sauce forever had a stroke and can't come into work.
She's out.

Now they want me to make the sauce too.
Again, the guy was a complete jerk about it, and when I raised the issue about getting all this work done in an 8-hour shift, he started spitting in my face yelling at me.

That day I did all the prep work, I made all the dough, I made all the sauce, and I burned the recipe for the sauce and the dough.

The next day when I came in, the first thing I did was I went to the owner, and I asked for a raise because of the extra workload.
He said to me point blank "I don't need you, get out of here".
So, I left.

A couple hours later, the manager shows up at my trailer.
I didn't have a phone out there, no way to get a hold of me but to show up.
He starts explaining to me that they can't find any of the recipes for the dough, or for their special sauce.
I told him that, I couldn't find them either I was just making it all from memory.

Surprisingly, I got my job back and now instead of $4 an hour I was making $8 an hour.
The owner kept insisting that I write down all the ingredients and I kept refusing.
I even refused to make the sauce or the dough in front of anyone else.
Suddenly, the same guy that was spitting at me just a couple weeks earlier now had to kiss my ass and he was pissed.
He hated every minute of it, and I loved every minute of it.

I still had my job at The Union working the door and doing sound for the bands coming in.
The most popular band we had was" Mark Markham & the Bogus Brothers"
Mark had been the rhythm guitar player for Chuck Berry at some point, so he was like a local celebrity.

I was on top of the world with my big raise, and with some money I had saved up I bought a bitchen Camaro.

It was a Saturday afternoon that my girlfriend and I were driving from town to my trailer.
We took a left down the road I lived on and there was about a half dozen people blocking the road.

We came to a stop, I put my car in park and before I could roll down the window to ask what was going on, a rock came right through my side window.
I was covered in glass and was being punched in the face repeatedly and simultaneously being dragged out through the window at the same time.
My girlfriend was screaming, as they were dragging her out of the car on the passenger side.
I tried to pull myself up level with the hood of the car, when I saw some woman punch her in the face and tear her blouse off her with some man holding her by the hair.

I was being stomped out on the gravel road when one of the guys throwing punches at me missed and hit the dirt and that's when I grabbed him and bit him.
I bit him in the face from his eye socket to his jawbone, I had so much of his face in my mouth it took two attempts to spit it all out.

The moment he started screaming, him and I were both covered in his blood.
In that moment, everyone was kind of stunned, I picked up a rock and slammed it across the face of the guy standing in front of me. With that rock still in my hand, I broke the face of the woman that was punching and stripping my girlfriend.
The rock made its way up against the skull of the man holding my girlfriend's hair, and now everyone else was now stepping back.

At this point, her top and bra were gone, and she had her pants around one ankle.

I grabbed her by the arm, and we ran through heavy pricker bushes that had one-inch thorns.
After about an hour adrenaline run through the woods, we finally found a farmhouse and used their phone to call the sheriff.
When the sheriff came out there, I was informed that we were in the next county over, and the county I was assaulted in was looking to ARREST ME!!
The sheriff had found my car in a ditch with all the windows broken.
Law enforcement went with us as we went back to my trailer to discover that had been riddled with bullet holes.
Thankfully my dog was still alive.

I was thankful to have my Camaro, even with all the windows broken, but they had destroyed the transmission doing God knows what and now it only had first gear.
After they dragged me out of the car, they broke my glasses so now I couldn't see anything.

I drove that car 300 miles back to Cleveland, 35mph in first gear unable to read any of the road signs.
But I had my dog, my girlfriend, my guitar and that's all I really cared about.

I had zero expectations of any justice in this situation.
When I was 14 years old, I was abducted by a group of men that were looking for somebody to torture and kill.
They spent the day beating me, and when they thought I was dead, they put me in a ditch, poured lighter fluid on me and set me on fire.
The Sheriff's Department reported that I was throwing up so much blood I put my own fire out.
In the following months that I spent in the hospital, my family had made my Funeral arrangements twice.

When we wanted to press charges against the people that had done that to me, the sheriff told my family that if we did that they would come back and kill us all.
In the eyes of law enforcement, it was better just to let it go.

It was a valuable lesson for me, and that lesson was that if you are poor in Ohio there is no justice for you.

Return to the Land of the Posers
Cleveland Ohio 1982-1985

All I wanted to do at this point was play in a band.
My girlfriend and I had split up, I was renting a room in a house with a ridiculous amount of people in it and my job was cleaning nightclubs.
We would go in at 3:00 o'clock in the morning, right after the clubs had closed and we would clean the place.
One of the places we cleaned, was a club down in the flats called "Peabody's Down Under".
It was a 500-seat venue that had national acts coming through multiple times throughout the week.

I had a small sound system that consisted of an 8-channel powered mixer and two speakers.
My new girlfriend was doing an acoustic solo act, and I would provide the audio.
One of the few times that I got to sleep with the talent every night.

I went on a lot of auditions, and every original band in Cleveland all had the same plan.
The plan was to stay in the basement and rehearse 11 months three weeks out of the year, do one show and wait for the record company to show up and give you a contract on the way to the limo.

I thought that plan sucked.

There was plenty of great cover bands playing around town, and for the guys with their arms folded in the back of the room playing with their hair they had nothing but snide attitudes about it.

I put an original band together called "Deceiver", and although we had some good originals, I knew the truth of it all, that being a local band didn't matter, you had to go on the road.

Warchylde
National Tour 1985/1986
I answered an ad in the local" Scene Magazine" for a band that was looking for a sound man to go on the road with them.
These guys had already been on the road for several years perpetually and they were 100% self-contained.
They promised $50 a week and $3 a day for food money.
I was in.

With my BC Rich bass guitar, my bag of clothes I met up with the group in Canton OH.
The show was a motorhome, a 24-foot truck full of sound, lighting, back line, and the world's most dangerous pyro system.

Although these guys were from Canton OH just an hour south of Cleveland, there was no band in Cleveland that was set up like these guys.
The two brothers Cal and Casey, bassist and guitarist had built the entire show from the ground up.
The rest of the band consisted of The Florida Boys, all from the Tampa Bay area.
Butch Whitney on guitar, his brother Michael on drums, and the late great Joe Irby on lead vocals.

The" Rude Crew" consisted of a sound man, lighting/pyro guy, someone to deal with the back line and a warm body to run the spotlight.

There was an entire rock and roll club scene that was happening on the East Coast of America that featured touring club bands.
These were groups that did not have a record label, did not have any kind of real management but we all had a booking agent, and that agent was John Titak, from Southern Talent International.

The standard gig was Wednesday through Saturday.
We would roll into small town America, mostly military towns and as John would say "You get to be a rock star for the weekend".

My first night with them was in Newport News VA.
I was excited, and now it's all about taking notes and paying attention from the guy that had been mixing them who was leaving.
His name was "Pops", he looked like one of those guys from a World War Two movie that had been in combat too long.
The band was great, and their set list was pure classic rock.

That night after the first show, the tour manager wanted to see me in the motorhome.
He gave me 1/2 gallon of Jim Beam and dumped up pile of cocaine in my hand.
He said to me "Besides making us the loudest band everywhere we go, we expect you the fuck as many girls as possible, drink as much alcohol as we do, commit random acts of vandalism and you have to let everybody know that you're with us",

It's been almost 40 years, since I sat with him in that motorhome and to this day, I have never encountered a group of people that partied harder than these guys.

I walked out of that motorhome, and a car filled with strippers that just got off work pulled off with the drummer Mike, and he said, "Get In".
I'm barely 24 hours out of Cleveland, and I'm in the back seat of a car with three strippers smelling my hand.

We got to some apartment complex, and it seemed like everybody from the club was here.
There were some other band members and the other crew guys were already there.
I didn't see it the moment it happened, but for some unknown reason Our lighting guy "The Germ", dumped over the refrigerator in the kitchen with the door open.
As if there was a psychic connection between the two of them, our spotlight guy "Somebody", picked up a phone off a table and threw it through the front picture window.
The Rude Crew was in full swing.

A bunch of people started cussing Somebody, it was getting heated and the moment the fight broke out one of the girls who had been smelling my hand asked me if I wanted to get out of here and go back to her place.
Sure, let's go.

I get in the passenger seat of this girl's car, and we swerve our way out of there.
By this time the sun was starting to come up and we were driving through some forest, it looked to me like a park.
I had no idea where I was, I had no idea where I was going, I didn't even know who I was with, and I was having the time of my life.

As she was driving, I had my hands all over her, and her free hand that was not on the steering wheel was shifting me into 4th gear.

She wasn't looking at the road when we both felt a bump.
We both spin around, and she had just driven over a bunny rabbit.
To this day, I don't know why, but I just busted out laughing.

Immediately, she downshifts me into reverse.
Now she has both hands on the steering wheel, and she is pissed.
She's cussing me out, I'm still laughing and trying to put my dick away when we suddenly feel "bump bump bump".
As she was cussing me out, she ran over a family of ducks that was crossing the road.
I was laughing so hard I started crying, it was difficult for me to breathe.
She slammed on the brakes of the car, and screamed at me, "GET THE FUCK OUT OF MY CAR!".

As I was standing there, watching her taillights disappear into the horizon, there were still duck feathers everywhere.
It took me hours, to find our motel by the only landmark I knew.
Our white 24-foot truck was the only one flying a pirate flag.

That was the first night, of a year that I spent with these guys.
Our level of debauchery was just on another level altogether.

I admit that we were heinous.
Our level of indifference was so far from the standards of civilization. This was a time in America, when the "Moral Majority" was running around the country screaming about satanic music and here we were showing up in their town bringing everything they feared.
Sex drugs and rock'n'roll.

We were everything small town America did not want.
There was a wake behind us filled with broken relationships, alcohol poisoning and poor decisions.
I could not count how many nights that a couple would come to party with us, and the guy would be leaving alone without his woman.

However awful you think we were; we were worse than that.
The only thing I could honestly say, is that I never saw anyone have sex against their will and I never knowingly had sex with anyone that was under 18.

It was just not unusual, to have a half dozen naked women in the motel room every night.
The thing about groupies in the 80s, was that in the smaller markets there was only so many big concerts that came through per year.
If you were a hot woman who wanted to throw your body at some Rockstar, there was only so much opportunity throughout the year. Mötley Crüe, might come to your town once a year, but there is a new group down at the rock club every week.

I once hooked up with a woman who was thrilled to tell me that she had sex with Vince Neil from Mötley Crüe whenever he was in town. When we got back to her place, there was an 8 by 10 of him in a frame next to the bed.
I picked it up to read the inscription, and it said, "Can't wait to see you again so I could slap your tits and spit on you...Vince".
I always knew he was a romantic.

The closest I had to a near death experience with these guys that didn't involve electricity usually involved a vagina that I should have stayed away from.

I seem to develop a pattern, of attracting women that got excitement from putting me in a dangerous situation to make their husbands/boyfriends jealous.
In my year with that band, I survived several near misses with husbands, boyfriends, and the Sheriff of Nottingham West Virginia.

In all honesty, my behavior was atrocious and I'm lucky to have lived through it.

The rest of my thoughts on this matter are all laid out in my previous book, "The Book of Maleki".

Maleki
Semi National tour, 1987/1988

My primary reason for bringing my bass guitar with me, was because I was determined to find a band that was already established and had something going that needed a bass player.

I had seen first-hand the process of starting from scratch and that wasn't what I wanted to do.
The other reality was that I was having a good time and I didn't want that to end.
The only way I saw that I could keep this up, was to find another band in the same circuit doing the same thing.

One of the towns that Warchylde played quite a bit, was Huntington WV.
For a small college town, the level of outrageous partying there was just off the hook.
Another bizarre aspect of the town, I don't know if it was the water, the coal dust, but all the local women were beautiful.
When you go from town to town, club to club you get a good view of the average women.
This place was way above average.

I met a local band there, that had some great originals and was looking for a bass player and a singer.
There was a local guy named John Taz Compton that had just returned from Los Angeles, and he looked like he he was carved out of Mount Rockstar.
He became the singer, and I became the bass player.

The two guitar players, Brian Lusher and Ron Weatherall had the guitar styles of KK Downing and George lynch.
It was a great combination.
The drummer Darrell Starkey, behind a giant blue sparkle drum kit, he went fast and furious all night long.

Our original plan was to rehearse for a month in their buddy Ricks garage, and then do some shows out of town to work everything out.
Six days into practicing our show, we got a call from the guy who owned the big rock club in town, Big Dan.

Big Dan said he just had a band cancel, he didn't have a group for the weekend, and he needed us to come in tomorrow, load in and do a show for the weekend.

This was kind of worst-case scenario for us.
Exactly what we did not want to do, go out unprepared.
We pieced together a sound system; some stage lighting and we made it happen.
For sure there was plenty of rough spots, but we did the gig and we played to 1/2 filled club.
The club owner was happy that we came in, made it happen and he felt that there was a lot of potential for our show.

After going on the road for six weeks, when we came back to play that same club it was standing room only for four days.
Over a period of 22 months, we headlined clubs in 17 states.

For the most part I really said everything about this period of my life in The Book of Maleki, but I will say that the survival skills that I obtained during this period of my life prepared me for everything I was going to encounter in the concert business.
In the future I would work on the biggest shows in the world, and there is nobody that I work with that could possibly comprehend what I lived through on the road with Warchylde and then my own band Maleki.

Return to Cleveland
Fall 1988

I fell in love with a girl from West Virginia and adopted her two-year-old daughter as my own.
I wanted a normal life.

I wanted to sleep in my own bed every night and I wanted just to go to work and have a life away from all this insanity that I had been living for the past decade.
It was just really taking its toll on me.

From the age of 16 to 26 I had a solid 10 years of drinking, drugs, what could best be described as sexual mayhem and just overall weirdness and debauchery.

After my band was over and I came back to Cleveland with my new bride and adopted daughter in tow and $0.50 in my pocket.
I was starting life all over again fresh and new.

We moved back into my mom's house in Cleveland Heights OH and with a marriage down at the courthouse and a trip to the Rent A Center for a new stereo that I couldn't afford the weekly payments on, our new life was ready to start.

Now that I was instantly married with children, I needed a job.
I was 26 years old fresh off a decade of drunkenness with my number one qualification in life was playing bass guitar at high-volume, high-speed, high with an erection.

Initially I had a hard time getting hired for those three special skill sets, so I had to revert to what I knew best, and that was working concerts.

Cleveland Music Center 1989.
Cleveland music center was a huge store.
We had 100 pianos in the store and 1000 guitars.
At the time a store with 1000 guitars was just incredible, it was part of Akron Music Center.
 If you lived in Ohio, the Music Centers were a big thing, and they were owned by these two brothers.
The store I worked at was ran by Bob, who had a thing going on with his brother, so it was definitely a competitive sales environment.

I was paid not by the hour at that job, I was paid on percentage of the gross profit, not percentage of the sale or percentage of the profit percentage on the gross profit.
 I don't even know how that could be considered legal or if it was ever legal at all but it was definitely shady and I was definitely there for days at a time all day long making nothing, zero, nada penny.
Meanwhile during the day if there's no customers there, it's not like I'm just sitting around staring at the wall.
I'd be stringing guitars up or dusting stuff off or doing a little bit of this or that.

The owner of the store Bob had to be the greatest salesman that I've ever known in my entire life.
 Bob was in his 50's, thick glasses, thick white hair, always had a big smile and a sharp looking suit on.
If you made eye contact with Bob you were buying something, it was that simple.
Like a predator in the wild man once he locked eyes on you, that was it there was no escape.
There was nothing that you could say to him that would make him back away from you.
Outside of saying "You know what Sir I'm just 100% full of crap I have no intention of buying anything", that was that was your only escape.

Once a poor guy locked eyes with Bob when he was looking at a keyboard and Bob went up to him and said, "Well you ready to take it home?" and the man replied, "You know I am I'm just gonna go down to the bank and get some money and come back and I'm going to take it home with me today".

Bob said to the guy "Oh that's great, hey I'll give you a ride I got a kick ass van with an awesome stereo man you're going to love it".

The guy says "Yes well uh I've got other things to do today and I've got some stops to make" and then Bob says "Hey I got all day we'll go out for lunch I got a cooler in the van would be great you know the guy the guy was just so embarrassed because there was nothing he could say to back away from bobby's mental grip, I mean he just had like some grip on people, it was it was really amazing.

But the only way I made money is if I sold stuff, and it made you be unscrupulous.

We had we were a Kramer dealer, and we had this one blue Kramer that I sold five times because it was repossessed four times.

The store had a rent to own program for young musicians out there and you know for a guy with no credit if you wanted to buy a nice guitar it was a path forward to do that and that was the good news, the bad news that we had a repo guy whose nickname was Rambo, and he was completely serious about getting the gear back.

If you've missed a payment Rambo is knocking at your door at 3:00 o'clock in the morning with a serious face and no smiles.

I thought that I could work at a music store and share my experience of audio equipment and my perspective from being a musician on stage. None of that mattered at all, it was just a "Cha Ching" used cars salesman vibe that I was completely not into not into at all.

On top of that I wasn't making any money, I was putting in a lot of hours there and not making any money.

One of the most interesting days we had at the Music Center was we had some guy comes in and he was just kind of muddling around and he wanted to try a guitar.

After plugged it into an amp, he tried another amp, and he was playing this Hendrick style stuff and it was kind of loud

11:00 o'clock in the morning, and you know it's like just do we really need this this volume?

I approached the guy and I said "Hey man this is great, but can I get you to turn this down" and goes "Yeah no problem man" and it turns out that the guy is Noel Redding from the Jimi Hendrix Experience.

He was in the area because his fiancée or his wife or whatever had family in the area, so it was kind of funny that you know I'm the guy that told Noel Redding to turn it down.
 My boss was immediately flipped around and went from telling me to go tell that hippie to go turn it down to him getting his picture taken with him.
This place was killing every soul I had my rock'n'roll soul my scrupulous soul I had to get out of here.

I was bouncing back and forth between them and a band that was doing weddings, corporate events, night clubs and bar mitzvahs. They were called, "The Motion".

The Motion
Cleveland Ohio 1989

This group was a Motown review with male and female lead vocalist, full horn section, great band.
They were the premier group in town for this genre of music.
And honestly, they were great.
Their sound man at the time was a guy named Steve who had a bit of a crack problem.
The thing that was trippy, was that Steve was probably 15 years older than me, and one day we were talking about some of the places he used to live.
He said to me, "I used to live on Idlewood in Cleveland Heights in the early 70's".
I said wow that's crazy because I used to live on Idlewood in Cleveland Heights in the 70s.
He looked at me for a minute and said "2644?"
My mind was totally blown.
That was my address.

In 1974 my mom worked nights and the guy that lived upstairs from us owned a sound system and would babysit me.
 A rock band lived across the street.

These guys would take me out with them to do shows in local biker bars.
The guy that looked out for me was named Steve, and here it is 15 years later and I'm doing shows with Steve again.
It was really mind blowing for me.

Steve was mixing the band and I was doing the lights.
The lighting for the band consisted of four stands with four lights per stand.
Not exactly an epic show but it's what we had.

And just like when I was 12 years old, Steve would pass out drunk behind the mixing console and I would take over.

The sound, lights, back line all lived inside of the "Motion Van".

The van had never seen 5 minutes of maintenance an oil change or a trash bag.
The band worked several days a week, so the van was always on the move.

At some point the band fired Steve, moved me over to the audio position and I hired my old lighting guy from my band Maleki, to come up to Cleveland and be the new lighting guy for the Motion.
75 bucks a night was big money and there was nothing to it.
When we played clubs, the place was packed.

As easy as the gig was my buddy dropped out and went back to West Virginia.
My buddy Larry did it for a while, but the band fired him when he refused to cross water to do a gig on an island.
Larry said it wasn't his fault it was just a matter of fact that Jews don't cross water.
Larry was the only person I ever traveled with who once got into an argument with a waitress at a diner because the pancakes came as a set of three and he was only willing to pay for one pancake.
Shockingly he did negotiate his way to only paying for one pancake.

My buddy Mr. Helle, and his new bride moved in with us and we were both doing local shows together.
I was mixing The Motion and he was mixing a band called The Dinosaurs.
By any standards the neighborhood we lived in in Cleveland Heights was not a very good neighborhood.
One night during a snowstorm Mr. Helle asked me if he could use the Motion Van To go down to the store to get some cigarettes.
It was only a couple blocks away and even though it was snowing heavily outside it was a short trip.

He takes the keys, him and his wife head out the door.
It was probably 11:45 at night almost midnight.

According to him he gets to the gas station and some guy asks him if he "Wants to buy a VCR for $4?"

Since he wasn't thinking clearly, he agreed to this proposal.
The caveat was the guy said you had to come to my house which was about a block away and down a side street.
So, this guy is walking down the street and they're slowly following him in the van, the snows coming down hard, sideways.
Get to a house, the guy says wait here and he walks up the driveway.
Rob pulls into the driveway.
The guy walks back walks up to the van, opens the driver's door and starts hitting Rob with a baseball bat.

Since the floor of the van is filled with empty beer bottles, Rob's wife starts picking up beer bottles and pinging glass off this guy.

Rob has a seat belt on, he's got his arm up trying to defend himself and the only move he's got is he puts the van in reverse.
The problem now is the guy is trapped because the door is open, now he's going backwards with the van.

Rob goes into the street backs right up into the driveway on the other side of the street and pins the guy in between the door of the van and a tree that's on the tree lawn.
Folded the door right up.

Rob puts it in drive punches it out of there, straight back to the house which was only a couple blocks away.
We call the fuzz, they come and go check out the scene, they find blood where the impact was but no guy.
This was on a Friday night.
The very next day, Saturday, Larry, and I had to take the van down to Youngstown to do a gig and I couldn't close the door on the van.

It was horrible.
I had it Bungie closed, but it wasn't closed at all.
There was a big gap, it was snowing, and it completely sucked.
Of course, the band was all pissed off about it, that van was living on his last days and that folded up door fit it perfectly.

On the way home after that gig the alternator died, and I lost the headlights on the van.
I got Larry hanging out the window on the right side with the flashlight trying to identify what is the side of the road, it's a full-blown Blizzard, my door is open, his window is open, we can't see shit, it was horrible.

We get the van back to my house and we had a gig the next day somewhere on the West side out in Berea.
The next day I go out and the van won't start.
So, what do you think I do?
I have it towed to the gig.
Instead of paying whatever it costs to fix that van we towed it from gig to gig for the next two weeks.

Finally, we got to some gig we were doing at a mall somewhere and I flat out refused. I said I am not having this van to do one more gig, this is ridiculous you gotta do something you gotta buy something rent something you gotta do something but I'm not doing this.
After the show that night, they got a van from somewhere and we loaded out into the new van, and we left the old van in the parking lot of that mall.

Over the course of the next two years whenever I drove by that parking lot, there would be something new missing off that van.
First to go was the tires, then the rest of the doors, then the glass.
It was stripped down to nothing still on blocks and still in that parking lot right where I left it over two years later.

The band cared less and less and so did I.
The last show I did with them was at somebody's house for some private function.
I remember being all by myself and the woman who owned the house wouldn't let me drive the van up the gravel driveway to where the house was, because she claimed I would "spin the gravel" so instead I had to leave the van at the bottom of the hill and drag everything up a gravel driveway up behind the house where the performance area was.

It was tenfold the work; it was stupid, and I put big groove marks in her driveway dragging some of those cases that only had three wheels because the band refused to spend a penny on anything.
I don't know, the band was playing, and I just felt like I had enough of everything.
I was just so sick of everything all at once that I decided that this show is over.
I picked up my full Coca-Cola and I poured the entire thing into the mixing console.
The audio system made a horrible sound, and the show was over.
I had had enough.
There were a great band but being a great band sometimes isn't enough, you also must do great things and must have some consideration for the people in your employment.

How not to grow Marijuana
Cleveland Heights 1989

My buddy Rob and I had a lot of things in common.
We lived in the same house, we both were mixing local bands, we both smoked pot and neither of us had any money.
The logical conclusion that we came to was that since we can't afford marijuana, we should grow our own.
Rob had discovered an ad in the back of a High Times Magazine where we could order seeds from Amsterdam, and that's what we did.

The first hurdle was now over, we needed the second key element which was proper lighting.
Somebody told us that the same kind of lights that illuminate the billboards on the side of the highway was the same kind of lights that you needed to grow marijuana.
With this information we did what anybody else would do and we went down to E 55th St. Climbed up on top of a billboard and removed one of the lights.
I certainly wish it would have been as easy as that.

The first problem was that we had to disconnect it from live 220 Volt power.
Problem #2 is that it was bolted in there pretty tight and the entire apparatus, the housing was huge, and it was much heavier than we had anticipated.
We got everything to the ground, all three of us survived.

We get the giant light hooked up in the basement we use two-liter Pepsi bottles to grow the plants and to keep the root base small and we were ready to go

90 days later we had a full crop, and we were thrilled.
Mission accomplished.
We were so happy to have weed that we just gave it to our friends.
out of that entire first crop we didn't sell a penny's worth to anybody we just smoked it and gave it to our friends.

We were just getting ready to harvest the second crop when we got a phone call on a Saturday afternoon.
It was Ohio Edison the electric company calling to inform us that since there was excess electrical usage from our house that they were going to send somebody over in the morning to inspect our breaker box in the basement.

The problem with that, is that's where all the weed was.

I remember that we had been doing bong hits all day long, a real wake n bake and kept it going kind of day.
When I got off the phone with the electric company, I was 100% panicked.
It's one thing to make decisions when you're high and it's another thing to make decisions when you're panicked but when you're high and you're panicking that is not the time to be making decisions.

What we decided to do was to immediately cut down all the plants and burn everything in the fireplace.
Horrible idea but that's exactly what we did.
After we get the fire going well, I went outside for something I don't know I don't remember why I went outside.
I remember the sensation I had when I realized that the entire neighborhood smelled like marijuana, and I had the only house on the east side of Cleveland with a fire with smoke coming out of my chimney in the middle of July.
Let alone a thick cloud of marijuana smoke.

Immediately I run back in the house panicked and we start filling up pans of water and throwing that into the fire.
Of course, that made it completely worse and now the house is filled with it.

Since we decided that burning it might not be the best option, we thought we should just get rid of it, all of it.

We started stuffing it in these little Baggies and I was like why are we doing this this looks like we're trying to distribute it?

We switch to just filling garbage bags.
I think we filled six garbage bags.
We took the garbage bags full of weed out to my car and put him in the back seat.

Our brilliant plan was to drive down to a junkyard that we knew, and we were going to throw the bags over the fence.
Our pothead mentality had convinced ourselves that the only thing that was important was not having the weed on our person or on our property.

To this day I don't know what possessed us to do this but we just started throwing bags of the weed out the window as we were driving.
My partner wanted to throw the weed out the window I wanted to wait till we get to the junkyard and as we were arguing about it like two pot heads do, I ran through a stop sign.

Cleveland Police officer puts his lights on and pulls us over.
I remember being unable to swallow, my mouth was so dry, and I was so horrified because I was so busted.
Just as a almost ready to bust out in tears, out of nowhere a white Cadillac came down the street and side swiped the police car, the parked car in front of me and kept on going.

It was the miracle we needed.
We both got out of the car and through all the weed on the sidewalk and split.

We went back to the house and spent the rest of the day and into the night cleaning up the mess upstairs and downstairs.
by the morning we were ready for the electric company to come and inspect the property.

The next morning, the electric company never showed up.
They never showed up.
They never came to the house, they never sent us a notice, they never called again, and we never heard any more about it.

Five years later I was loading out a show at the Cleveland agora on east 55th St. And I met a guy who told me an amazing story.
he said he was walking down the street one day on E 55th St. And he found a trash bag full of marijuana.
said it was the best thing that ever happened to him.

Jeff Healey, The Thieves
Peabody's Downunder, April 2nd, 1989

At that time so many of the local sound companies just wouldn't give me the time of day.
If nobody knew you directly and personally, they didn't want to deal with you at all and that's just how it was.
You had to know somebody to get into anything because nobody was trusted and that's just how it was.

1990 I weasel my way into getting hired to be the sound guy for one night at Peabody's Downunder in the Cleveland flats.
I don't even remember who hired me or how I got hired, but I remember this, I remember that in the early 80s I worked with a janitor crew cleaning that nightclub.

We were part of the crew that went in at 3:00 o'clock in the morning 4:00 o'clock in the morning after the place was closed and go up and clean up the disaster that happened the night before.
I spent many an early morning sweeping, cleaning, mopping and the inevitable, the vomit in the urinals.

Cleaning bars and nightclubs and now almost a decade later to be there as the sound guy, and not being the guy with the tongues cleaning the vomit out of the urinal, it was a big step up for me and I was excited.
As the house sound guy my job was to mic up both bands, facilitate the set change and be the monitor mixer for both acts.

The problem for me at that time was that system they had was really convoluted, and they had a rack mount mixer that didn't have faders only dials, and it was some scenario where you couldn't land every input that was happening, you had to you had to mix and match and choose the patch that you needed.

The bands crew came in aggressive, and I was nervous.
I remember that I had a heavy sweatshirt on, I was just suffocating, from the heat.

I just wasn't ready for the gig, hands down I was in over my head. With nobody there to help me and nobody to turn to, I got to a point where I got the first band going.
But when it came to the set change and the repatch, man that is where I fucked everything up and I couldn't recover from it.

I couldn't figure it out and we had to call somebody from the sound company to come down there and rescue me while we had five 500 people whatever standing outside in the freezing rain.

To say that everybody was mad at me was putting it lightly.
It was brutal and the person the sound company sent down was this super tough monitor mixer named Mariam and she ripped me up and down a new one.
And you know what, and I stood there, and I took it and I took it and I took it
I put my tail between my legs, and I took it.
it was a very tough learning experience. It's rough when everybody in the room including the audience is mad at you and you're the reason this whole thing went wrong and you're the one responsible for this disaster and that cannot be pinned on anybody else, that's just you.

It's a great character-building experience, that's for sure.
I was un-politely told to never come back there again.

Harvest
Classic Rock/Pink Floyd Revue 1989/1990
I will tell you straight up I was emotionally exhausted after ruining that show.
I had met a band that was doing a classic rock show and then a one-hour Pink Floyd set they were looking for a sound man and I was ready to jump back into my element.
My comfort zone was nightclubs and not dealing with national acts.

For the year that I was with the band we mostly played college towns.
Some point the band bought an old school bus and now I really felt like I was back home.
We played as far as Vermont when I was with them.

For this amount of stuff that we had, it was a great show to bring into a nightclub and the band was terrific.
What really made it for me, was everybody in the band was just so cool. They were the nicest guys to hang out with, it was always fun.

Today that same band is now called "Wish You Were Here" and they are one of the premier Pink Floyd tribute shows in the country.
I loved my time with these guys.

Richard Elliot
Empire Club 4-14-91

I get hired by a sound company that has several club installations in Cleveland.
Two of the clubs were "Peabody's Down Under" and the "Empire Club".
Each had their own installed audio system and how it worked is that the boss would make a schedule of who is going to be at what venues, and we would show up and do it. The pay at that time was $50 per gig.

Harvest had been paying me $80 per show, and now for the luxury of doing national acts so I'd be getting paid $50 a show.
That $25 a day was going to hurt, but it was the price I was willing to pay to prove that I could do these shows and move up the ladder.

These clubs were referred to as roadhouses, places where touring bands would come through and play and have local live entertainment.

I get my first big chance working at the club called the Empire Club and my first show there was Richard Elliott.
Some saxophone dude that I had never heard of before, but I know he was some big deal to somebody, and I know that I was nervous because I didn't want to mess this up.
It was a lot of pressure on me to make sure that this was right.
I was given the same opportunity almost one year earlier and I completely effed it up, it was worst-case scenario.

On this night, everything went great, everybody was happy, and I nailed it.
The very next night, we did a band called Saigon Kick, I also did monitors for them, and everything went great.

2 Nice Girls
Peabody's Downunder, 4-16-91
My triumphant return to Peabody's.
The last time I was here, I left with my head down in shame.
This time, things are going to be different.
My first gig there was interesting, it was a group called 2 Nice Girls.
They came up on stage, and they would grab their breaths and move them in a rotating fashion and scrunch down and yell "Breast exam".

That's what I remember about that show. It's not meant for me, but the audience seemed to enjoy it.

The only thing I cared about, was that in my eyes I had broken the curse.
I had three successful shows in three days, it felt like ruining that show a year earlier was ancient history.
My time cleaning the vomit out of the urinals in that very same club seemed even farther away than that.

Pop Will Eat Itself & The Limbomaniacs
Peabody's Downunder 4-17-91
This was a radical transition, from lesbians having a Johnny Cash look like contest to these guys.

The Limbomaniacs were fun.
They bring out a high energy show that is like high funk with samples and this crazy front dude that's playing the bass making it all happen. I think they're a San Francisco band, but I'll just say it again, they were a lot of fun.

Pop Will Eat Itself was some digital dance group thingy from England. What I remember about them, is that we had an old school two track or four track reels to reel tape deck up on stage that was the bulk of their show.
Most of the show was coming off that tape track.
Once again, I was responsible because for a power source for that thing, I plugged it into a waiver strip that had other things plugged into it.
I should not have done that, but I did that nonetheless and during the show whatever fuses in that crappy little thing popped and the tape deck stopped playing.
Those two guys in that group we're just up there with their heads bopping back and forth and no music coming out.
The lights flashing and me scrambling with their tech trying to figure out what's going on.
 I trace it back to that stupid power strip.
That was in 1991 and ever since then I have never once ever plugged anything important in a crappy power strip.
It was a valuable lesson at their expense, but everyone loved the show, and everyone lived.

The Henry Rollins Band
Peabody's Downunder 5-6-91

I would be lying to you if I said that I wasn't a little intimidated by Henry Rollins.

He came in for sound check and I was the monitor mixer and although he was very professional and polite with me, he was a tense dude.

I could tell that he was wrapped tight and or it was the most amazing person fake persona of all time, but I was certainly taken aback by how serious he was about what he was doing.

Before the show I had to go upstairs to the dressing room and I don't even remember like what the reason was, I think I was looking for the sound guy.

I go upstairs and there's Henry Rollins in the dressing room and he had that "part animal part machine" tattoo on his back.

Two hot chicks rubbing oil on him while he was lifting weights, I was like man that's the way you do it.

When I think about when I was in the 80s getting ready for the show what were we playing the instrument, doing some shots doing some blow, some weed.

I was not getting some oiled-up titties rubbed on me while I was lifting weights.

I obviously handled it all wrong, Henry had it right.

The show was great.

Henry just out there with his black shorts just crushing it, there was no doubt about who was the star of that show was, it was Henry Rollins.

Napalm Death, Godflesh & Nocturnes
Peabody's Downunder 5-9-91

What can you say about a nice group of boys like Napalm Death that hasn't already been said?
I don't remember 5 minutes of the first two bands, but I remember Napalm Death.

The monitor console at Peabody's at that time was up on stage left, physically up on the stage level all the way on the left-hand side.
 It was so tightly packed back there, that you could barely turn around, barely slide in and out and you had to hang off the edge of the stage to swing yourself around the console to get onto the stage.

Napalm Death starts and about 30,40 seconds into the show the crowd rushes the stage and just dumps everything down.
Marshall stacks go down, drum kit goes down, everything goes down and its total chaos.
 The show stops and now everyone's just trying to get everybody off the stage and trying to get this thing back together.

 I had to mic everything back up, get everything back up and running again.
We get all the gear back up, get everything working again, and then I don't remember how long this show lasted after, that but it was not long. A wave came from the middle of the room, like a tsunami of humans and again rushed the stage, took everything down and it was show over.
 I remember pulling the drummer up from underneath the pile.
There was no room for a barricade downstage front, there was just no room at all. People just right up against the stage. How many security guys could you have in in the front being pummeled by the crowd?
We had some rough ones.

The Fixx
Empire Club 5-13-91

There was a time in the early 80s when this band was all over MTV. this band was huge they had a lot of hits and because of their MTV exposure you know every member of the band was certainly instantly recognizable.

I was the monitor mixer for that day, and the guys came in for a sound check.

I was a little stressed, but everyone was just so cool and laid back that it really made the day very relaxing. I was very appreciative of that.

The support act we had that day according to my book was an artist named Greg Tripp and Greg I'm sorry, but I just don't remember anything about your show.

But I remember The Fixx.

I remember being so blown away that every song they played was a hit,
"Red skies at night", "Saved by zero", "One thing leads to another", the entire crowd was singing along.

It was like the ultimate 80s party.

Obviously, I was not a fan of them at that time because I was into rock and metal but being on stage with those guys for those songs I couldn't help but be part of the audience well and part of the fandom.

It was just really a good time; it was like goodbye to the 80s but glad it was there all the same time.

It was a great show.

The Spudmonsters
Empire Club 5-18-91
The Spudmonsters were a local hardcore band.
 One of the guitar players in the band owned a local record store so they had a little more our resources and I want to say professionalism.
You could tell they were a little bit more organized than some of the other local bands of that caliber that were playing around Cleveland at the time.

They were a great band, and they had some great gimmicks.
One of the things that they would do during their show, is they would throw these bags of instant mashed potatoes into the audience and then start throwing pictures of water onto the crowd and as the mosh pit was raging on the crowd was making mashed potatoes.

 If you're thinking that it must have been a tremendous mess, you're right. It was.

The Bo Deans
Empire Club 5-20-91
I had never heard of the Bo Deans.
They brought with them a very colorful production manager, and there was no doubt who oversaw that show.
For that show I was just a loader they brought in their own monitor rig and their own lighting rig and since the empire was up two flights of stairs.

Loaders were needed, and when I wasn't mixing that's what I did.
I remember specifically that we took our lighting rig down, and we installed 12 intelligent lights, eight on the upstage and four on the down.
This was the first time ever that I'd ever seen what they call moving lights.
hey were the Intelabeam 700 HX, and they were about 3 1/2 feet tall looking cylinders and instead of having a moving head, it had a mirror that would move and the light would hit the mirror reflect off that and that's how it would get its effect.

We get all this set up and the guys are playing with the lights, and they look amazing.
The support act was the Gear Daddies, and I don't remember anything about but I'm sure they were awesome.

When the show started, the lights were just white and on.
They didn't move, they didn't focus in their out, they just stayed white and just stayed on.
By about the 3rd or 4th song now the lights are moving, just making very micro moves but it's up to this point it's still stayed the same color white.

By the song "Black, White & Bloodred", now it's changing colors and now it's moving and now the show is building.
It looked amazing by the time they were at the end of it.

What we call slicing and dicing and doing all the effects that you would see at any nightclub or within the first one minute of any popular show today.
What made it interesting is that it was something that no one had ever seen before, now every time I go to work and see a show, the show opens every light moves everything wiggles you everything has been seen and there's no place to build from them from there.

At least these guys knew what they had they knew it was different, and they really knew how to use it.
Whoever their lighting director was, he was somebody that knew what he was doing because the show looked great.
I always tell everyone to this day that the best moving light show I ever saw in my life was the first moving light show I ever saw in my life and that was at the Empire Club with the Bo Deans.

Mark Cohen
Empire Club, The Coffee Break Concert 5-23-91
OK, growing up in Cleveland I enjoyed a local tradition that was known as the coffee break concert.
The local radio station WMMS would promote a free concert every Wednesday during the afternoons at a local venue.
When I was growing up it was the Cleveland Agora on 24th St. that they used to have these concerts and man I saw a lot of great concerts at the coffee break concert one of the reasons that I saw many is because they were free and that worked in my budget but also broadcast live on the air so if you couldn't come down and see it you know you could just listen to it and I saw it and heard many great shows at the coffee break concert.

Well, being a kid from Cleveland you can imagine how excited I was when I was as an audio person in my 20s and I got to work the coffee break concerts.
At that time in the early 90s we were doing the coffee break concerts at the empire club on E 9th St.

My employers considered this a one-man job.
And by today's standards even low budget broadcast that would be considered outrageous and unprofessional.
Usually when the group would come in, they would bring their own sound guy to mix the front of house and me being the house guy I would then mix monitors for the stage and then WMMS would bring in some van that would park on the on the street.
I don't remember how they did the broadcast, but they had a split and it was always a much simpler package, the band was usually doing the shows acoustic.

The load ends for these kinds of shows were usually 8:00 o'clock in the morning because we were alive at noon and since we weren't bringing in a lot of gear for usually it wasn't a big deal and we always had plenty of time.

We get this guy coming in and his name is Mark Cohen and he's got some hit on the radio and they bring in a grand piano for him.

The piano had to be carried up the stairs, so I was involved in that I got a little extra loader money for that and for a guy making 50 bucks a show a little loader cash went a long way.

We get the piano on the stage, and I get it mixed up and I put a wedge in front of them and put a vocal mic out there this industry standard sure SM58 which you've seen a million times on every stage around the world to this day we still use the SM58.
I was told by the production by the club and by WMMS that this guy was going to come in sit at the piano sing his songs and telling answer some questions from the DJ and that would be it and the show usually lasted an hour on the air from 12 over at 1:00 PM.
9:00 o'clock rolls by 10:00 o'clock rolls by 11:00 o'clock rolls by and still no Mark Cohen.
 At this point the audience is lined up outside waiting to get in but we can't open the doors because we don't have an artist.

I want to say it was about 11:20 when the entourage finally showed up and it was a bunch of people but not one of them was a sound person but and they were carrying a lot of gear.
They had guitars and they had electronic keyboards with them and somebody from their camp came up to me and said "OK, Mark is going to stand over here and play acoustic guitar and then this other person's going to come over here and play keyboards and then he's going to go over there and then this guy's going to do and:.
I stopped the guy I said "Whoa, I'm prepared for one man to sit at a piano and we're on the air in 40 minutes. Whatever we're doing we gotta get on it".

Now instead of this being 3 inputs 2 for the piano 1 vocal mic, now it's almost 20 inputs.
 I'm running cables all over the stage and now I'm putting wedges all out and now we're behind and this is a real problem.
We still haven't let the audience in yet.

That they don't have a sound guy to mix the show, means that I must get the monitors set with nobody to be the monitor mixer.
Set everything as what we call it "set it and forget it".

I go to the front of house and mix the show.
This mark Cohen fellow sits down at the piano looks at the microphone. The SM58 and before he says one word into that microphone and before he touches the piano, he looks at the radio station people and he says" Do I really have to sing through this? don't you have anything more expensive?"
I couldn't believe what I was hearing.

We use these mics for every show with name acts certainly bigger than him and nobody ever once ever complained about the type of microphones that we were using.

This microphone was already as we call wrung out" and we were show ready and I didn't have to EQ it or do anything else to it because I had already done that before he showed up.

So now instead of anybody telling him no, the radio station guy says I'll go get something from the van and disappears and comes back with this thing that is the Sennheiser 441 and the only time I had ever seen it used as a vocal mic was with Stevie Nicks.
I plugged it in, swapped it out with the 58, turned it up and immediately it sounded like shit. It had what we call zero rejection, and it was feeding back.
It sounded like shit and feeding back, two things I did not want to deal with.

Now the best thing that I could do is make this thing not feedback, pray for the best and go out to the front of house, mix this show and try to survive this as best as we can.
The doors are open the crowd is in, everyone's ready for and we have like 3 minutes before the show starts.

One of the people with mark Cohen stops me before I go to front of house and grabs one of the radio people and says" Who is going to do monitors for the show?"
And I politely responded the answer is "nobody".

The guy insisted that somebody had to do it I insisted that there was no time and that there was nobody here qualified, so the radio station said we have somebody we'll bring up from the van.
I ask the all-important question "Has he ever done monitors before?" They said I didn't know, I said that's not a good enough answer.

So, they bring up this kid out of the truck and I say a kid he's like maybe late teens early 20s and at the time I'm in my late 20s, but I have an F load of shows behind me, and he did not.
I asked him the direct question "Have you ever done this before?"" To his credit he gave me an honest answer the one I was ready for "no".

At this point we're about a minute from air and I still have not been to the front of house mixing console.
I looked at them point blank and I said to him "This side of the mixing console we are not using, this side of the mixing console we are using.
Under No Circumstances, under any threat, do I want you to touch the side that we're using at all for any purpose. No matter what they ask you, no matter what they request I'm begging you please touch nothing.
Just nod your head smile give him the wink but please touch nothing. if I see you touch one knob on this mixing console, I'm going to come up here and beat you with a mic stand".

I fight my way to the front of house console, and I get there just in time to turn up the number one microphone which was the host who was the DJ, I think it was this guy named Matt the Cat.

From where the front of house mixing council was in that venue it was up against the wall in the right-hand corner of the room and from where the monitor console was up on the stage, I could look straight up from my perspective and clearly see the monitor mixer standing there.

Physically on the stage behind the monitor console, semi hidden by the PA and by the side fills but I could see him.
The DJ introduces the artist and the first thing the artist says is "Hello check one to turn up my microphone".
And what do you think happens?

What was that one thing that I said that kid not to do?
There I was at the front of house console completely helpless as I watched that idiot reach down grab a knob and the entire stage started feeding back.
It sounded like a spaceship was landing, taking off and mutilating cows all at the same time.
That wonderful sound is also regenerating through the house audio system since I have that up.
Now I must turn off the entire sound system, fight my way through the crowd to get to the stage, push that idiot away from the console, figure out what he did and then restore it back to the way I originally had it.

I again told him touch nothing and I told the exact same thing to that stupid manager that was that insisted that he did it in the first place that unless he knew what he was doing touched nothing.

So now I fight my way back through the crowd I make it back to the mixing console and I start turning everything up again and now the shell continues.

The artist gets up from the piano picks up an acoustic guitar goes down stage to a new position and what's the first thing he does?
He turns his head and says to the monitor guy I need you to turn this up I need more before he hears anything he asks for more.
Reminds me of my wife today when she asked me to turn the TV up before we've heard it.

Shockingly that idiot behind the console again started touching knobs by his request and again the entire stage starts feeding back and again I've got to shut down the entire system fight my way back to the crowd get back to the stage push that moron out of the way and again restore it back to the way I originally had it.

The show was a disaster by any scale, anywhere you look at it and I don't even think the show lasted for 40 minutes.

I do remember being chastised by my employer over it, that this was somehow my fault.
I was completely pissed off about it because it was so shitty to put me in that situation and expect me to, I don't know hit people with a tranquilizer dart.
How is any of this fucked up plan my doing?

That said it was the last time we ever did a coffee break concert with one technician.

Kings X & The Eric Gales Band
Empire Club 7-19-91
We get King's X and the Eric Gales band.
As a Kings X fan and I was thrilled that they were there.
During the day I spent a lot of time with the bass player Doug during the sound check it really worked with him on getting the sounds that he needed. he was very particular about his vocal content as with many artists art and I was thrilled to have the time with a bass player that I really looked up to.

After sound check I go get the Eric Gales band together get them on stage.
At that time Eric was 16 years old and his brother was up playing bass and I don't remember who the drummer was.

One of the things that could really piss off a sound guy is when you're miking up the band and the band is playing and noodling. The drummer is hitting the symbols like right in my face like it was really irritating me and then when I was miking the guitar rig up every time I'd bend over to put the mic in front of his cabinet this kid would like hit it really loud cord it was like right in my face I'm like finally I said "hey hey hey can you just give me a minute dude, could you just give me a minute to mic this up and then you know you could do your rock'n'roll thing man but I need a minute".

The kid obliged; I mean I could tell that he was oblivious of his actions. He was just a kid, and I really blew it off and thought no more of it and then we started the sound check.
The band kicked into Jimi Hendrix 's Spanish Castle Magic and I was blown away.
To this day could be one of the most explosive renditions of that song that I have ever heard a band play live, and they were fantastic.

That night Kings X did not disappoint, they were amazing.
My favorite part of that show was that from my perspective from the monitor console across the stage, off stage right was a young couple watching the show and they had the biggest smiles on their

faces from the moment the show started to the moment the show stopped.
 I mean if you could imagine holding your face in a frozen smile for an for 90 minutes two hours what however the show long the show was I mean it was really impressive.

Primus, Tad
The Babylon a Go Go 8-8-91
For a while the company I worked for had an installation at a nightclub called the Babylon a Go Go.
One of the unique features of the club was previously it was a gay bar so all the beer spigots behind the bar we're all shaped like penises.
To be fair they were tremendous penises.

This was my first show at this club, and I don't want to guess what the capacity was, but it wasn't a lot it had to be maybe if you put 3-4 hundred people in there like that is that seemed like jam packed.
We got these two bands one is called Primus and the other is Tad and they were both traveling in vans.
At that time, I had not heard of either of these groups.
Tad goes on, I was the monitor guy, and I don't remember anything out of the ordinary for them.
We do the set change, and we get Primus up there.

When Primus started the energy in the room completely changed.
First off it was a fair statement that the venue was oversold.
 More people had showed up for this thing than anyone anticipated.
I couldn't take a guess at how many people were in the venue but the correct answer is definitely too many.
The crowd was pogoing up and down with the band and I could feel the floor flexing.

I went downstairs in the basement with the club owner and the promoter of the show, and we were watching the floor or the ceiling flex down across the entire venue every time the crowd was going up and down, I mean it was frightening.

I remember having the conversation that we need to stop the show and by the time we got back upstairs just getting from the back of the room to where the stairs were, back to the front of the stage was Mission Impossible.
It was a sardine can of humans pogoing and the show was over before we could stop it.
 I don't know if they ever put that many people back into that venue again and I'm sure that was not the only thing that went down that night but that was everything that I was concerned with.
Great band and a nice bunch of guys.

Kix,
The Empire Club 8-17-91
We get this 80s metal band and they have brought with them what I would consider the rock'n'roll version of "antique roadshow".
Not to be fair this was a band that was accustomed to carrying everything with them their sound their lights and their back lined much like my band did in the 80s and many bands on the East Coast club circuit did they were used to traveling self-contained.

At the empire club we had everything but their backline we had sound we had lights most of the time bands would just bringing their back line maybe occasional monitoring or but you know nobody ever brought in PA before because you know it was why and it was up two flights of stairs, so you know who wanted to do that.

But since this was a broadcast show for WMMS they wanted to bring in every single piece of crap out of their two 24-foot trucks and we did.
We dragged all that crap up there.
I would say the show was mediocre at best.

Kansas & The Steve Morse Band
Empire Club 8-23-91

Back in the 1970s somewhere in the mid 1970s I think maybe it was 76 I saw The Rolling Stones at Cleveland municipal stadium.
the stones had two opening acts that year Kansas and Peter Tosh.
I had no idea who Peter Tosh was, but I certainly knew who Kansas was and I was a fan.
"Carry on your wayward son", "Dust in the wind", hit after hit they were considered a great progressive American rock band that was certainly on the way up.
 Being a kid watching them opening for the Stones on the big stage it was just really a terrific experience, and I took away quite a bit from that.

Flash forward to 1991 and here I have Kansas coming into the club I'm working.
What I remember from the afternoon is that sound check was no big deal but the lead singer from Kansas, Steve something, he wasn't there.

We get the set change and get the Steve Morris band up there and I remember no big deal happening there.
I was a Steve Morris fan from the Dixie dregs days and I thought it was a great show.
We do the set change and now we're ready for Kansas.
Up to this point, I have not seen the lead singer for this band.
I was the monitor mixer for this show and the front of house mixer for the band, you know that guy that travels with them, and does their shows, he was the one that set the height of the downstage center vocal.
Since I had never seen this lead singer closer than 300 feet in the past 30 years ago, I would have no idea how tall this guy was.

We go into blackout, the intro music is playing and the bands all there noodling and getting their things together and here comes this guy who's got no shirt, on shorts like those 80s gym shirts that were a little too short for a man to be wearing in public, those kinds of shorts.

The crowd's going wild, and he goes to the downstate center vocal and immediately I noticed that the mic is too tall for him it's almost where his eyes are.
He attempts to loosen the clutch which is literally the only moving piece on the entire piece of equipment, a straight microphone stand and he just couldn't get it loose.
I saw him struggling with it and then he started violently slamming the stand into the stage.

Even for the people that were pressed up against the stage right in the front, you could see their facial expressions that we were all sharing the same facial expression which is what the fuck is this guy doing?
I notice that none of his technicians were running out there to help him and he was acting a little aggressive and it was just weird.
The monitor console was a probably I don't know 12 feet from the center of the stage it stage probably was 24 feet could have been much more than that and he comes over to the monitor council where I'm standing, he holds the mic stands sideways and the mic is still attached by the cable right and he hands me the stand and he spit all over me and right in my face as he screamed "FIX IT!!".

I don't know if it was him slamming that into the stage, I don't know what, but I grabbed it from him, I grabbed the clutch and I just easily turned it with my wrist with no effort whatsoever and handed it right back to him.
This action infuriated him, and he was immediately angrier than he was.

I don't know why this guy was so mad, I'm the one that got spit on.
By this point, the intro music has been playing and now the band starts.
The show starts, and the lights come on and he's over there on stage left dicking around with me cussing me out for something I didn't do.

Now he runs downstage carrying the microphone stand like his galloping off into battle and he's looking straightforward and he's not looking down and he trips over the downstage wedges, and he falls faced forward into the crowd with the mic.

The entire band started laughing and I just stood there with my arms folded.
There was no way in the world I was gonna run out there and help this guy after he just spit all over me for something I didn't even do. He had a couple other tantrums during the show he was doing these hand stands on the keyboard which was like wacky I really couldn't get what that was all about, but it was it was overtly trying to show the audience his amazing fitness which just didn't vibe with what the show was.
Watching the lead singer doing handstands during the guitar solo was just weird.
I've had other people tell me that he was a very nice guy to them and that he's terrific and this and that and he might be but all I know is that I had one chance to deal with them and that's how it turned out for me.

The Bullet Boys
The Empire Club 8-29-91
These guys had a hit called "Smooth up in you".
I believe it was a sexual connotation which is fair it's for the era.
The problem with these guys is they were five or six years too late to the party and if they were to come out a little sooner, they would have had something.

They played great and you could tell that they were a real band that had played together for some time and done some dates and we referred to them at the time as the best Van Halen tribute band that we had ever saw and I stand by that statement.
The Stage manager Mr. Burley kept referring to the lead singer as David Lee Rodriguez.
It was funny.
That said they put on a great show and the people that came to see them really loved it.

The Sun Rhythm Section.
Peabody's Down Under 8-30-91
This was a cool show because these guys were Elvis Presley's original band.
They were as old school as it gets, and they did a bunch of 50's songs and a bunch of Elvis stuff.
 I was thrilled to mix them, and it was just cool hanging out with these guys.

During the sound check you know guys that were a part of some real rock'n'roll history you know before anybody knew what any of this was about what it was going to be what it could be just tremendous to think the evolution of the industry that they saw in their lifetimes and on top of that they were nice guys.

Trixter, King of the Hill
The Empire Club 9-3-91

I don't remember anything about the load in or about the sound checks for these two acts.
I know I was the monitor mixer for both, and I remember that the bands had a lot of friends with them from a local motorcycle club that was in Cleveland.
What I do remember is when the show is over Jim Burley our stage manager asked a couple of the guys from the motorcycle club if they could move so we could start loading out and get these cases through and without saying a word the guy decked Jim in the face and knocked him right to the ground.
Instantly there is panic.

The first thing the security team did was leave the building. I think security was out faster than some of the patrons.
These guys were busting the place up and the security guys wanted no part of it.
My first wife was with me that night and the biggest stagehand we had was big Bob Prah.
I told Bob to grab my wife put her in the microphone closet and don't let anything happen to her and I went into the chaos.

The club had some Cleveland cop on the payroll and whenever we had problems or there were problems, I remember that they would text the cop instead of calling the Police Department and that's what happened.
Paying off police officers is one of the better values for your money in the northern Ohio area and within minutes the street was locked down and they had even sent a helicopter, a bunch of cops and this thing was over.

The one thing I remember about the loadout was that every single piece of equipment owned by those bands tumbled down to flights of stairs back to the sidewalk where they had maybe made a couple more flips there.

I don't know how much of that gear was damaged but I'm assuming all of it.
You know we are just guys at work trying to get a job done and it's a drag when you are dragged into somebody's aggressive nonsense that has no business in a concert environment.

Tribe Called Quest
Oberlin College 9-14-91
Me and the other Pete, Pete Felice get sent to Oberlin College so we could do this show with a group called Tribe called Quest.
The venue was the gymnasium of the college, and you know that right there is a bad sign because no matter what you're gonna do, it's gonna sound like a gym.
So, before we unload the truck before we do anything before one piece of equipment comes into the building, I go in first and I met with the people from the college.

I'm standing in the middle of the gym and I'm with these two women from the college, one of them 's holding a clipboard some guy in a suit and we're talking about where they're going to put the stage and where we want this and where we want that, and you know how it is in a gym.

When you're just speaking to each other, and your voice is reverberating around the room of all these nice hard reflections its easy for our conversation to carry.
As we're talking here comes my partner Pete and in a very loud voice walks in looks around and says for everyone to hear," Boy you could sure fuck allot of whores in here".

After a moment of silence, we all looked at each other and I said, "OK so about that stage where you want to put it?"

The Bobs
Peabody's Down Under 10-4-91
The Bobs were an acapella group and they did two shows that day. That's probably why I remember their songs.
My favorite was a song called "Spontaneous human combustion... watch out, poof and then you're gone".

Pere Ubu
Peabody's Down Under 10-2-91
What I remember from this show is that the fans of this group we're super excited that they were playing here.
the other thing that I remember is that their lighting guy after the support acts focused all the lights, what we call the "par cans" at everything but the artist.
During the show the lights made the stage look like a train wreck which I thought was awesome I've never seen anyone do it before or since but for using limited resources that the club had for lighting the guy made it look amazing by not doing what everyone else always did.

Murphey's Law, The Mighty Mighty Bosstones
Peabody's Down Under 10-6-91
With a lineup like this what could go wrong?
the truth was very little, this was my first time working with the Bosstones, they were fresh from Boston and Had to set up in front of Murphy's Law.
I will say from a crowded stage where these guys had no room to do anything they really put on a tremendous performance.
Six years later I would be doing them on the roof of Radio City for the opening of the MTV Video Music awards and I remember at the time thinking, wow me and these guys have sure come a long way.

Nirvana, Urge Overkill
Empire Club 10-10-91
I had no idea who these guys were, all they were to me was some band with a naked baby on the poster.
I don't remember anything special from the day you know I remember everything being super casual.
I was the monitor mixer that day we got that headliner together which was Nirvana, did the set change got Urge Overkill up and nothing really stands out from any of that.

Urge Overkill goes on that night, and they have a great performance, great energy, the crowd loved it.
I do the set change and now we're ready for the headliner.
The band comes out and they're noodling a bit and they played some they played around with some queen song and then when they stopped fucking around, they got into it and man they were great.

They were explosive and they were tight enough for the music they were playing.
Kurt Cobain was on the stage left side where the monitor console was and at some point, he jumped into the crowd with his guitar on.

I had never seen anyone stage dive with their guitar which was impressive.
Me and the tech ran out there and dragged him out of the crowd and got him back on stage and the rest of the show was uneventful, but it was a great show.

After the show myself the drummer and the bass player went into the mic closet, and we smoked some reefer together.
When I came out of the closet with the guys, it's obvious what we were just doing Kurt Cobain came up to me gave me a T-shirt and said, "Hey man thanks a lot".
The T-shirt on the back said" Fudge packing crack smoking Satan worshipping motherfucker".

Over the years I've seen Dave Grohl many times at different gigs and different events, I have even just stood there right next to him on a couple occasions.

As much as I stop myself from saying to him hey man you remember that one time that you came to Cleveland and we got high in that closet together, I am just as much tempted the next time I ever see him just say hey man you remember we got high in that closet together?

He was just a young drummer, I was just a young tech and every time I see him doing anything anywhere, it just always reminds me that he was just a young drummer, and we were getting high in the closet together.

The Exploited, Biohazard & Type O Negative
Peabody's Down Under 10-14-91

This show was unusual because I remember that the club had gotten a phone call from at least one of the previous clubs that this tour had been to that these guys were a real problem and to watch out. Well, that's a great way to start the day.

One of the things about the club is that there was no place to put any of the gear for all the bands there was just a small space on stage right and then there was a hallway that led up to the dressing rooms that you couldn't block so you really couldn't put anything out there either and our methodology was setting up the bands one in front of the other and then peeling them back as we go which is they call festival style and doing it in a tight nightclub that you know that's just how we did it.

I don't remember anything about the day during the sound checks.
I remember that Peter Steele being super tall, super deep voice and super nice he was all three of those at the same time.
What I remember about the day is that the headliner the exploited did not sound check that was fine as far as I was concerned.

We do the Type O Negative; I don't remember anything from it.
Then Biohazard I don't I don't remember anything about it and then we get the set change and I'm ready for the Exploited.

I want to say the band was bass, guitar and drums and they came out first and were noodling about and then just kind of the show just kind of kicked off and then here comes the lead singer.
Some punk with a big Mohawk and a bad attitude and the very first thing he did was he came on stage he grabbed the stage right vocal and he said, "Bruce I need more vocal" and then he took that vocal mic threw it on the floor and crushed it under his boot.
It made some God-awful sound through the system and immediately I muted it.
I had seen some shit in that nightclub up to that point, but I had never seen anything like that.

He then goes to the center vocal which was supposed to be his vocal and he did the exact same thing.
Grabbed it off the stand, he said "Bruce I need more vocal", he threw it on the floor, and he crushed it under his boot.

Now at this point I officially don't know what the fuck is going on and that's when he really surprised me, he jumped through the wedge.
Putting his boot right through the speaker.
Then he did the exact same thing to the stage right monitor.

Meanwhile the band is playing the song, whatever song they're playing, and the crowd is going wild in the mosh pit.
The guy crushes all three vocal mics down stage, and he jumps through all the wedges while the band is playing and now there's absolutely nothing for him to sing with.
So, what do you think he does?

He grabs the microphone from the drum kit that was on the first rack tom, and he tries to sing in that but the cables too short and it can't get away get away from the kit.
Frustrated at this point, he tries to throw that mic at me but because of the chord it only goes so far and drops to the stage.

Now he is looking for something else to throw at me.
He picked up a drumstick, threw that and missed me.
Then he picked up a beer bottle threw it, and it hit me.
I was completely pissed off.

I come around the monitor console come right by the guitar player, and I pushed him right into the drum set.
I Started hitting him with that microphone that he originally threw at me and that's when the crowd rushed the stage all the gear went down, and the show was over.

Tt took several security people and a Cleveland Police officer to restrain that asshole as the tour manager, the club owner, the promoter, and myself were on the phone with my boss trying to figure out what the damages were.

Ended up being a handful of microphones, handful of speakers a bunch of our time inconvenienced and I could almost see it if they were any good, but of all the punk bands I've ever done they were the worst.
I'm sure somebody loves them, it's just not me.

Seldom Scene
Peabody's Down Under 11-2-91
We had a promotor that was bringing in bluegrass music to the club and these guys were defiantly the cream of the crop.
Great old school bluegrass band.
All I remember is that they were great.
Oh..and they didn't throw any beer bottles at me.

Tito Puente & The Latino Jazz Allstars.
Peabody's Down Under 11-9-91

You know being a guy that grew up in northern Ohio and then being in a heavy metal band in the 80s I didn't know Jack Shit about Latin music; let alone Latin legends and I was going to learn a lot about both working with Tito Puente.

Tito Puente had his niece Millie P opening the show for him, she would just do a couple songs and as he said, "She was on her first album, and he just released his 100th.

Tito Puente was old school Latin salsa and when I asked him his advice on mixing him and his show he just said "Let it breathe"

We did two shows and in between the shows I went up to the dressing room to check on him and make sure that everything was good in the monitors, because one sound guy there was no one at the monitor console, we just kind of had to set it and make the changes in between the shows.

I couldn't get back and forth.

When I went upstairs to ask him how everything was on stage for him, he said to me "Hey Pete do you know why they call me TP?"

I said yeah because you're Tito Puente.

He said, "No it's because I'm the top Puerto Rican!"

He started laughing like he said that joke 1000 times and I laughed right along with him.

I don't know who the cats and his band were, but they were great. He announced them as the Latino jazz All Stars.

He was a terrific guy; I was thrilled to have met him and certainly thrilled to say that I've mixed Tito Puente.

Zaza
Empire Club 11-27-92
At the empire club it was very rare to have any local bands headline the club.
It was predominantly national acts that came through and the only headliners locally were usually like a reggae band or someone that could really pack the place.
It was rare for us to have a rock band that was local, and, on this night, we had a group that was named after the guitar player in the band and his last name was Zaza.

What I remember from that afternoon is that their road crew, sound people, local guys, that were not working the level of shows that I was doing felt that they had to act like big shots and tell us how it was all day long.

One of the things about the Empire Club is that next door to the club was a peanut factory.
Because we shared the same electrical transformer with that peanut factory there was a slight buzz in the audio system that we had since the day we installed the PA in there.
My boss did everything he could to try to get rid of that buzz and he couldn't figure it out and believe me he was a lot smarter than I was. Every national act that played there noticed the buzz and said something about the buzz and we all told them the same thing, "at 6:00 PM when the peanut factory closes, the buzz goes away".
And it did every day exactly at 6:00 PM.

Well, whoever this amateur hour sound guy was that they had with them refused to believe me.

He had a big tantrum trying to tell me who he was and who they were and they're not gonna stand for it and no national act would put up with this and this is bullshit and that they're going to the promoter and they're going to the club and they're not going to have it and they'll never play here again if we don't do something about it..

I mean this guy just went on and on and on and we stopped the sound check because now they refused to sound check until we get rid of the buzz and I'm just standing there telling the club owner and telling everybody else the exact same thing that we tell everybody that at 6:00 PM, it's going to disappear faster than me caring about this show.

So, what do you think happens?
After spending all day long listening to them stomp around, moan, cry and not do a sound check because They refused to do it with the buzz, 6:00 PM comes the buzz disappear and now we're hours behind schedule because they refused to proceed.
We did the show that night everybody lived and not once did anybody from their organization ever come up to me shake my hand and or apologize for their behavior during the afternoon.
Do you know how to prove to me that you are tough?
By doing the tough thing and apologize when you're wrong.

God knows I've been a dick about something and the moment I realized that I'm wrong I apologize immediately and get it out of the way because that's the right thing to do.
if you let it sit you let it fester then you're the one that really looks like a douchebag.

The guitar player from that band, Neil Zaza went on to do great things with his career and I wish him all the success in the world but when they came to the Empire Club on the 27th of November 1991 his group was completely unprofessional and proved to me then that they were not ready for prime time.

Helmet, Superchunk & Four Coyotes
Peabody's Down Under 1-24-92
I don't remember much or anything about the first two acts, but I remember helmet.
They weren't carrying a front of house mixer, so I mixed them which I was thrilled with because they were really tight.
One of the only bands of that level that came through where there were their own techs, their own roadies they carried in their own gear they didn't have no egos among them whatsoever just really a nice bunch of guys and a great band.
 You could tell that they were friends, they loved what they were doing, and it showed.

The Royal Crescent Mob
Peabody's Down Under 2-29-92
The RC mob was a original group out of Columbus OH that would eventually come through the club quite a bit.
They were what the Red-Hot Chili Peppers wanted to be.
Bass, guitar drums and a charismatic lead singer who was kind of David Lee Roth and Perry Farrell.
These guys should have been a national act by any standards their original music was great they had been together for a long time, and they were tight they had a great following and as with many good and great regional bands of that era that they were unable to get the attention the proper attention of the record companies from the coasts.

L7, Barbed Wire Dolls
Peabody's Down Under 3-25-92

From the moment this band and their crew showed up at Peabody's I knew we were in for something different.
I had never heard of them before but that was not much of a marker, I had usually never heard of anybody before they showed up at Peabody's.
This was the time before the Internet, the information dirt road just wasn't moving along. You had to hear it on college radio, see it in the local scene magazine but when new bands were coming in I didn't know who anybody was.
This show was about a month before their album Bricks are Heavy came out.
I don't remember anything from the sound check, that day and I don't remember the support act, but I remember L7.

It was like a nuclear crunch bomb went off on stage.
Heavy metal surf music and as much as they get classified as a punk band, I can't classify them. They are truly their own thing, hands down the best all female rock group I have ever seen since before or since.

After the show they gave me a T-shirt and on the front of the shirt it had a woman who had another woman's head by the hair and was shoved into her crotch and it said, "Smell the Magic".
Although I did not smell the magic, I certainly heard the magic I saw the magic for me two out of three that's pretty good.

I-Tal
Peabody's Down Under 3-26-92
This transition to have L7 on stage one night and then a reggae band like I-Tal the next, was always a little weird.
This concludes my memory of that show.

The Impotent Sea Snakes
Peabody's Down Under 3-29-92
This show had some freaky deaky for everybody.
We had a local group called the Floyd band that had opened the show and they were passive. I don't remember anything standing out one way or another.

Then we get to the Impotent Sea Snakes.
She stage was all television stacked up on top of each other with different porn playing and stuck to some of the TV's were dildos.

The lead singer, maybe all of them, I really don't remember but I remember for sure that the main person was on stilts and those rubber items hanging from the TV's were being inserted in all kinds of places during the performance.

I remember when the show was over being very careful about what I was touching because there was a lot of fluids on stage and not all of them were alcohol and to say that it was weird is putting it lightly.

Pearl Jam, Eleven
Peabody's Down Under 4-2-92
This show had been booked for some time.
It was supposed to happen some months earlier and for whatever reason the show cancelled and in between the initial show being booked them canceling the show that was booked, their hit came out on MTV and now they were a huge sensation.
The crew showed up and saw the size of the club they immediately bummed out and everyone was on trying to figure out a way to cancel the show.
They absolutely did not want to go forward with it.

To say that the Pearl Jam crew was not being cool about it was putting it mildly.
They knew that they were on the up track, and they had weight to throw around and they were throwing it.
The only person out of their camp that was cool at all was the guy that owned the sound company they were traveling with it and his name is Dave Ratt.

Dave from rat sound was a total professional through the entire thing unlike his crew but that's just how it was.
Since they brought in their own everything, my only function there was just to tie in their power and hang out and be the lighting guy at that point.
I think the capacity was 500 legal there had to be 700 people in this club for this performance.
It was jam packed wall to wall, people standing on the banisters down the ramp coming in.
I had never seen so many humans in there, I was at the front of house position where the lighting console was and there was 100% no way to get to the stage, it was that packed.

I remember the opening act Eleven being great and I think I got a CD from them that night.
I remember liking it and that's what I remember about that.

Now we have Pearl Jam, and the crowd goes wild.

Peabody's was too small a venue to put a barricade in because it would eat too much real estate on the floor, so the audience was just shoved up against the front of the stage.

During the performance there was a young woman that was or a couple young women that were being crushed down stage center by the crowd surging forward.

The lead singer for the group took a gallon of water and slammed it down on top of this guy's head.

Was it the guy pushing the girl's forward? Did he hit the wrong guy? I don't know but the girls got pulled out of the crowd onto the stage and there was a big commotion down stage center.

All this chaos was happening Eddie Vedder did his traditional thing climbing around the club and that's when the crowd surged forward and my buddy Larry went on stage to help security push some people back, and he accidentally stepped on the guitar pedal on stage right and broke the ¼" jack inside the pedal.

Instantly we lose the guitar rig, and the guitar player was pissed.
I don't remember how much longer after that the show went on or what they did to bypass that, but it was definitely an epic show for anyone that saw it.

It was truly the definition of 10 pounds of shit in a 5-pound bag.

Luka Bloom
Empire Club 4-9-92

We get this guy coming in and everyone tells me that its just one guy with an acoustic guitar and as the monitor guy I'm thrilled because what that means to me is it's not going to be a bunch of inputs on stage.
It's not going to be a bunch of musicians all yelling me yelling at me at the same time needing something, it's just going to be one guy acoustic guitar nice and easy low level and what could be so hard about that.

We get this acoustic guy, shows up with his technician and I asked the guy how many wedges he wants?
Speakers on the floor facing him, how many does he require for this event and I'm waiting for him to give the answer one or two and instead he asks me a question and he says, "How many do you have?"

I don't remember what that number was but whatever it was we used them all and I brought out every single wedge that we had including the side fills and we made that acoustic guitar hit rock concert volume.
Never in a million years BC did I ever think that I would be get an acoustic guitar that loud just crushing volume on stage on the verge of feeding back every second as the guy strolled around on stage barefoot strumming this this acoustic guitar turned up to 11.
Instead of it being a relaxing chilled out gig it was very stressful because I was waiting for that thing just to start feeding back at every any moment.

Funny part of that story is just a couple years ago I was doing a gig in New York City and there was an interesting acoustic guitar player on stage. I asked my buddy Simon who was mixing monitors, I said, "Have you ever hear of a guy named Luca Bloom?" and he said, "Yeah that's him right there."

Henry Rollins
Peabody's Down Under 5-6-92

Henry Rollins came back to Peabody's with his spoken word tour. This was completely different from the last time I saw him all greased up with two chicks rubbing him down before he came on stage to crush it with this band. This was going to be a totally different vibe.

Henry comes in and it's nice and simple and there's nothing on stage but one microphone stand, one microphone, the stool and that's all what it's about nice and easy straight up.
About two minutes before the show started one of the waiters from the club was standing on the other side of the mixing console and he kept saying to me "Boy you sure got an easy night tonight just one microphone"
And then he reaches behind the console and starts grabbing on different cables he goes "Which one is it is it this is it this that this?".

I'm like get the fuck out of here and at that moment Henry walks on stage picks up his microphone I turn it up, I turn it on and what do you think happened?
Not a goddam thing.
He had pulled it out of the jack just enough where it wasn't making the connection, it wasn't working, and the first 10 seconds of the fucking show is nobody hearing it because of that asshole.
I was completely pissed.

Next item on my learning curve agenda was that Henry was up there talking for a couple of hours.
At some point, the mic really started sounding different and started to feedback.
 Now I'm starting to dig into frequencies, and I just can't figure out what's going on with this microphone.
He's just been talking into it and that was the night that I discovered "diaphragm fatigue".
He was just talking in that microphone long enough and steady enough where the diaphragm was no longer doing its job.

I went up on stage and had him swap out to the spare and everything was groovy again.

As you can imagine when that show was over, I had a serious conversation with that waiter.

Integrity, Outface, Zero Tolerance
Peabody's Down Under 6-10-92
Hardcore bands were taking over the scene at that time and one of the hardest bands playing in our area was as hardcore as they got, and they were called "Integrity".
I don't remember anything about the first two acts and according to my book I mixed the front of house for all three bands.
Shockingly I found video on YouTube of this very show.
about 3 minutes into the show, you could see on the video that the singer stopped singing and is no longer holding his microphone to his face.
That's because it was no longer working.

The reason it was no longer working, is because somebody pulled a knife out in the crowd and cut the cable.
From the front of house mix position, I didn't know what was going on, all I knew is that the mic wasn't working anymore, and I had to go up there and get him a spare.
I go up there get the guy the new microphone and he points out to me the guy he thinks he's got the knife and then went back to my job and he went back to his.

For that genre for that era there were great, the lead singer had kind of a William Defoe from Platoon vibe going on which I kind of dig and I'll say this, he was authentic.
They were everything they said they were about, they were from Cleveland, they were hardcore and that's all they needed to be.

Gary Richrath
Shooters 9-19-92

For a couple of years there was a restaurant on the riverfront in the flats of Cleveland called Shooters.
It was one of those places where people would come and tie their boats up at and party like pirates.

It was definitely a place where people a few clicks above working class and working class would get together to party on the weekends.
Someone had the idea that the only way to make this place more crowded was to start bringing in national acts to perform there, and that's what we started doing.

The company I worked for put the sound system installation in there and we would go in and do the acts, mostly national acts that were coming into shooters.
It was tight.
They had like a gazebo that was the stage and for the monitor mix position, the guitar tech would set up around the backside of the gazebo.
There was not a lot of room and in front of the stage was a pool that occasionally accepted people and equipment.

Never once did a band show up there, look at where they were playing and was excited to be there.
Every band thought it sucked and immediately started thinking about a way to get out of it.

One of the first shows we had there was Cheap Trick.
When the drummer from Cheap Trick initially walked up to the stage, I remember him saying to his tech" Wow that is a bad ass drum riser".
Followed by the crushing disappointment all over his face when he realized that was not the drum riser that was the entire stage.
From that moment on he spent the rest of the sound check cussing at everything around him and announcing for all to hear" I can't believe I'm playing a fucking restaurant".

Gary and his crew were the first ones to come in and be nice to us and treat us like they got what was going on.
I was a fan of the early REO Speedwagon albums.
Those early albums of theirs had great hooks great rifts and certainly great guitar solos.
Gary Richrath was the poster child for a tasty guitar solo.
Not only was he a terrific guy and very easy to deal with, but the show was amazing.

The monitor console had to be like 3 feet away from Gary who was on the stage left side.
Watching that guy play all those classic songs from that close to him was just a really a big thrill for me and I'm certainly don't get a lot of thrills watching people play.

When he broke into "Riding the storm out", I thought every hair on my on my body was standing straight up, it was an electric moment for me.
When it was all over, he came over to the console and thanked me, it was the cherry on top for me.

Kings X
Empire Club 6-26-92

You know one of the reasons that you carry a sound person with you it's because number one, you believe that this person understands your material better than anybody else and secondly that you are confident that this person is more qualified to achieve your objectives consistently from night to night.

When Kings X came back to the Empire Club, they were had their own monitor mixer with them.

It's a fair statement to say that the guy was having a hard time. Several times Doug came over to the monitor console did his own EQing, looked at me and gave me the facial expression with the eye roll that you know" I wish you were doing this man, but we got this guy".

I remember sitting on the drum riser with Doug the bass player and just kind of have a moment talking about how we hear his things and how he needs a certain mid scooped out for him.

A really a great guy and he's still out there doing it and if you ever get a chance, please go see Kings X.

The Impotent Sea Snakes, Sissy
Peabody's Down Under 7-5-92

Back for another show of stacks of TVs with dildos and mystery fluids, the Snakes have returned.

Unfortunately, I don't remember anything about the opening act Sissy, but I remember this second time around with this group there was an incident with the stagehands and some of the TV dildos on the load out.

During the performance one of the performers inserted what could be described as an enormous dildo, into an unnamed body cavity of a volunteer from the audience.

Not the worst thing I ever saw in my career from a volunteer from the audience, but certainly noteworthy.

The Dead Milkmen
Peabody's Down Under 7-7-92
These guys were on tour promoting their album "If I had a Gun". What I do remember about these guys is that the show was fun. What made it funny for me, is when that show was over that night, I was actually driving a Bitchin Camaro.

Goober and The Peas
Peabody's Down Under 7-31-92
These guys dressed like they were out of a Cohen Brothers movie. Like a crooning cowboy of the Old West of the silent movie era that's exactly what these guys reminded me of.
I think they were from Detroit, and they had a song called "Funky cowboy", and they lived up to it the band was funky.

The lead singer looked like Gomer Pyle on acid, with a big cowboy hat and a big goofy smile but he delivered that act all night long and the crowd loved it.
One of the Performance elements of the Peas was that they would bring a couple bales of hay and throw into the mosh pit.
That always made for an interesting loadout.
They would become part of the rotation of bands coming through and they were always fun and the audience loved them.

Tori Amos
Peabody's Down Under 8-4-92

All this show was to me was a piano and a vocal mic on stage that's it.
I remember it was a later in the afternoon sound check because it wasn't much to it.
She had her own front of house mixer, and I was the in-house monitor mixer.
We're hanging out waiting for her to come downstairs from the dressing room so we could do a sound check, and she comes down and walks up on the stage and I'm standing by the piano and her people introduce me as Pete the monitor guy and she reaches out to shake my hand and says "Hi I'm Tori I'm sorry I'm late I had to take a shit".

As I'm shaking her hand, all I could come up with for a response was "Well that's fantastic", and we just proceeded on with the sound check, no big deal.

So, we had a support act," A man called E" and I don't remember anything about it.
Maybe if he was another letter, Id remembered it better.

We get her on stage, her show starts, and I don't think she was through the very first song when she stopped performing and announced that she wasn't going to play with all those glasses clinking behind the bar. They had to stop serving drinks at the bar for her to continue.

You could imagine, management was pissed, the promoter didn't know what to do, the tour manager is acting on behalf of their artist and the artist is just sitting there at the piano with her arms folded.

The show goes on with the bar not selling anything.

I don't know how much time went by, but not much time went by after that when a horrible smell started coming into the venue.

The sewer was backing up out of the bathrooms and now it was sewage a couple inches deep on the floor and now that was a problem.
I don't remember how long after that the show kept going but I don't think it was very long.
It was such a pause in the show, that the cleaning crew that use to work for in that same club, came down to try to wet vac up some of it.

I could understand the artist point of view that they don't want all this noise during their performance I get that.
I totally understand the point of view from the bar whose only purpose of life is to sell drinks, and without doing that you know what we are what are we there for.

And I could see the view from the promoter because at the end of the day the business is about personal relationships.
And from my point of view, the place smelled horrible I just wanted to go home.

The Zoo
Peabody's Down Under 8-25-92

Mick Fleetwood from Fleetwood Mac put together some band and it was called The Zoo.

It was one of those scenarios where even though the show was small and playing clubs, you had the sense that there was real money behind this.

All their stuff was very nice, and their people were very professional, and these were not the kind of people that you would usually see in nightclubs.

I was the monitor mixer for them and dealing with them, the band was nice and easy Mick was easy to deal with. He was just smiles all throughout the day and during the show and I have nothing negative to say at all, they played great, the audience loved them, and it was a fun show.

After the show when I had wrapped up all my cable Mick Fleetwood came down from the dressing room and asked me if I had a light and I did.

We smoked a joint together in that skinny hallway between the dressing room club entrance and the outside world and it was just me and Mick Fleetwood smoking a joint and hanging out.

After we got pretty high together, Mick said to me" You know the thing that always bothered me is that critics always talked about how much money Fleetwood Mac made but we never got credit for how good the music was, it still bothers me".

It was a combination of a really cool moment of, "Wow I can't believe that I'm hanging out with Mick Fleetwood and he's really opening up to me about his feelings", mixed with here is this multi-millionaire rock star who has everything in the world, and I'm just a broke sound guy from Cleveland making 50 bucks a night and all the fame success and money in the world and this guy is bothered by the fact that he feels like he didn't get enough credit for his achievements.

As the saying goes "everybody has their own problems".

All I know is that Mick Fleetwood is a nice guy, is a great drummer and gets very good weed.

The Byrds
<u>Shooters 8-28-92</u>
This might have been a cool show I wouldn't know because I don't remember it.
according to my book I was the monitor mixer and I have a notation that says," rain rain go away".
Being in Cleveland it's not a surprise that we would have a show washed out with the rain or half washed out or washed out through it maybe that's what happened, but truth is I don't remember, but I know that I like the Byrds.

Front Line Assembly
Peabody's Down Under 9-9-92
When electronic industrial music first started coming out and making the scene nobody knew what to do with it.
some of it sounded like everything was breaking for people in our industry that were mixers we were accustomed to making things sounding smooth and pleasant not crunchy distorted and unpleasant.

Front Line Assembly was touring on the album "Mindphaser" and it was sonically crushing.
For us guys working in nightclubs that had a certain amount of PA in the room all of a sudden we were faced with this problem of not having enough for what the artists were trying to accomplish.
it was not enough Subs, not enough highs, not enough mids, it was not enough.
This scenario of having of doing shows that were going to be turned up to 11 was it going to be a trend that was certainly going to continue.

Odd Girl Out
Front Row Theater 9-20-92

I started mixing a local band in Cleveland called" Odd Girl Out".
The group consisted of three women that were downstage the lead singer and two acoustic guitar players, and two men upstage the bass player and the drummer.
31 years later I could honestly say that this is one of the best bands I ever mixed that did not get the opportunity to go national.
They had great originals, great vocal harmonies and because they were a club band, they did a lot of shows and they understood rapport with the audience how to build a show and to keep the entertainment value through the entire set.

The fact that the three women in the band the odd girl out happened to be gay automatically brought out a certain crowd, but they were great regardless of any kind of affiliation to anything, they were just a great band.

They got a gig opening for somebody at the local theater in the round that was called " The Front Row Theater".

There was a time in the I think in the late 60s when the mob built all of these in the round theaters around the country all at the same time.
I don't know how many of them still exist but in my lifetime, I've done shows at the Front Row Theater in Cleveland and Westbury Music Fair in Westbury Long Island and both those venues are identical.
In the round the stage spins one way then it spins the other way everyone gets to see your face, and everyone gets to see your ass.

The band is a little nervous because this is a big gig and they wanted to sound good and other local bands that have gone into that venue before had a difficult time with the local crew.
Living up to the reputation the local crew at the front row were complete jerks from the moment we got there.
Being rude and hostile I could put up with that, but what made it worse is that they were incompetent.

By the time they got the headliner set whoever that was, there wasn't a lot of time to get us set and for me to get a sound check in before the show started.

By the time this gig came around in September of 1992 I had been writing down in my book of shows how many bands I had been working with since April of 91.

A total of 336 bands.

That means that I have miked up 336 bands in the last year and a half mostly by myself.

Now here I am on this professional stage with a union crew and between the five of them that were making the drum kit they got every input wrong.

Now there's no time to sound check and I have to do it all on headphones and every input is wrong.

Insult to injury, the mixing console they had there I think was a Yamaha PM 1000.

Super old school console that was 100% neglected and every move of the fader made a crunching sound that came through the audio system.

What saved that show was that my skill sets at that time to throw together a fast mix we're at an all-time high for mixing multiple bands per night with zero sound checks.

The show went fine, and I ended up mixing that band for some time after that.

Although that band never made the jump to lightspeed, it's my opinion that they certainly deserved it.

Screaming Trees, Luna
Peabody's Down Under 10-12-92

The thing about working at these clubs at this level and at that time was that you see all these great bands right when they were just breaking out.

A good example is the band Screaming Trees.

I think they're hit "Nearly lost you" had just come out a week before this show.

They could have absolutely sold out the Agora which is 5 times the capacity but already booked it was game on.

The opening act was called Luna and there was a lot of excitement about them they were one of those indie rock bands that people point to as being pioneers of something.

What I remember about them is that there were no problem, and they were very good.

Screaming Trees should have been a much bigger band than what they were. That night at their performance had a lot of energy they really connected with the audience and that's all you could ask for.

Ween
Peabody's Down Under 11-17-92

These guys were so young I remember security wanting to check their ID's it's always great dealing with a young fresh band that are excited about their craft excited about the show and everyone's attitude is positive.

They were great that night and I see that they're still out there touring they have certainly had some ride.

Longevity it's not easy in this business and for anybody to still be out there and selling 1 ticket like they did 30 plus years ago that's something to hold on to that's something to be proud of.

The Twist Offs
Peabodys
These guys were a college ska band from Kent.
In 1992 ska was all over the clubs and they were selling out.
We had the Mighty Mighty Bosstones as an opening act, then we had them as a headliner and then before you know it there were two big to play the venue.
We all thought that the Twist Offs we're going to be the next nig ska band that was going to get signed.
Their show was high energy from the moment the lights went on till it went down it was nonstop entertainment.
They were funny they were tight they were good they had terrific original music for ska you know I mean within its genre.

I'm thrilled to discover that that band is still together and if you ever get a chance even if you are not the number one school lover in the whole world you must go see the twist offs.

Warrior Soul
Peabody's Down Under 12-2-92
These guys had a lot of steam coming in, they had a hit called drugs God and the New Republic.
That's all I remember.

Odd Girl Out
Front Row Theater 12-4-92
According to my book we did another show there. I remember all that nonsense from the first show, but I don't remember one thing about the second one. if not for this being written down, I never would have known it happened.

The Toasters
Peabody's Down Under 12-7-92
One of the things about working in a venue consistently is you get to see the different crowds that come in and you get to see what we refer to as the usual suspects.

you know if it's going to be a metal show what kind of people are gonna come in for it you know if it's going to be a goth show what kind of people ******** industrial show and and so on.

when the toasters came every ska fan in Cleveland was there. New York City ska royalty bringing it right to the flats.

Compton's Most Wanted
Peabody's Down Under 12-21-92
This was my introduction to gangster rap.

As rap was evolving so many people didn't know what to do with it, the people making it didn't know how to describe what they wanted and there was a huge communications failure everywhere.

Once the vibe turned from party vibe to fuck you vibe, everything got a little ugly.

I don't remember anything from this show outside of that I felt it was an introduction for things to come.

Champion Bubblers
Peabody's Down Under 4-8-93
Local reggae band.

All I remember from this group is when I read their name, I had that sensation all over again of" Oh my God no, not the Champion Bubblers".

WTF is a Rave?
The Interbelt Nightclub. Akron Ohio 4-30-93

The sound company had me load up a rental truck full of gear and they said I was going to go down to a nightclub in Akron, set everything up and let DJ play through it all night long.
I was told I would get some labor there to help me Unload the truck and stack the PA.
I didn't know what a rave was, digital music was new all night dance parties like this were new. It was all new and I was just trying to make it happen.

I did have people that helped me unload the truck and then stacked the PA up in one big block on the dance floor and then when I asked about where was the electricity a guy took me downstairs and said they had a bit of a flood.

Where I was supposed to tie in the 220 Volt power, that electrical panel was on the wall in the basement there was about 10 inches of water on the floor.
With no other option available and no electrician provided to me to take care of this, *I had to stand on two upside down buckets* balancing myself with a flashlight in my armpit as I tied into this live power.

To say it was dangerous is a tremendous understatement.
I had a lot of experience with dangerous electric electrical distribution systems in the 80s and I and that was all that memory was just too fresh to me.
I didn't even have a hillbilly to hit me with a board.

I made it happen, any normal person would have said no but I just wasn't normal I was just trying to make it happen and for me getting these shows done was everything.
As promised the show went all night long and I remember not getting any help unstacking the PA.
7am is when all the enthusiastic people from 16 hours ago are now long gone.

I had to use a system like the pyramids sliding things down to another then down to another loading that whole truck by myself. The whole thing sucked.

Right Said Fred
Metropolis 5-22-93
I had been doing quite a few raves at this new club that opened in the flats called Metropolis.
It was 100% industrial with concrete floors, hard metal railings and everywhere it looked like the scene out of some post-apocalyptic movie.

My job was to bring in a ridiculous amount of PA.
We had a Renkus Heinz audio system that was much too large for the room.
I would build a wall of it across where a stage would have been, and that wall of PA is just what crushed the room all night long.
The guy who owned the club would come up to me during the night and say to me "I want you to save it I want you to save it and later on I want you to hurt everybody".

It was his agenda for everyone to leave that club with their ears ringing and their guts crushed from the low frequency in the room. Another interesting facet to the club and these all night long digital music parties a group of hippies that brought in a custom-made laser system.
One of the guys was a scientist that was in the army and was discharged for something heinous and he had burnt down his own house attempting to recreate ball lightning in his basement.
The guy in charge of all of them was really smart he was absolutely a very intelligent guy, and he was not like the minions that he had around him.
His name was Harry and I just referred to him as Laser Harry and the Hippies.

These lasers they had needed a tremendous amount of water and power and they spent their day loading in running hoses heavy electrical and putting mirrors all over the club.
They would also hang these mesh screens like a see-through scrim in the club for putting projections on it.

Nothing screams techno like giant green laser penises penetrating laser vaginas in full animation on the screens over the audience.
Sometimes the animation was just a woman walking in high heels but for the time, for the technology it looked amazing.
Besides the audio system raging at jet engine volumes for eight hours at a crack people were getting really loose there.

There were just parts of the club where it was just like an open sex club with people doing it everywhere and lots of drugs.
There's so much of what was happening there, wasn't legal and even at the time I had the feeling that something like this just couldn't last.

Anytime we had a national act perform there it was usually just for like 15 minutes or 30 minutes there was never like a full long show like concert style show like we did anywhere else this techno thing was completely different.
The DJ would just kind of play his thing and whoever the feature artist was would dip in and out then back to DJ and that was the show.

We had "Right Said Fred" come and bungee out of the ceiling. although he was too sexy for his hat, somebody had forgotten to figure out how we're going to get him out of the air when he was still bunging.
As with any new genre not everything was figured out just yet.
By the time this Dutch group LA style showed up we were kind of in a groove of it all.
It was interesting.

The Wallflowers, Greenhouse 27
Peabody's Down Under 6-3-93
The Wallflowers had just broken out and I don't even think they had a hit yet.
The opening group for that show was a local band that had just been signed with Bar None Records and they had a very promising future.
I don't remember much about The Wallflowers performance, but I remember bonding with the opening act and at some point, I would end up being their tour manager and doing up quite a bit a few shows with them.

The Tragically Hip, Crash Vegas
Peabody's Down Under 6-4-93
This was a show where everybody had the Maple fever.
two great Canadian bands in one show.
I had seen The Tragically Hip on Saturday Night Live being introduced by Dan Ackroyd as his favorite Canadian band and soon they were mine as well.
I had never heard a crash Vegas before but being Canadian they were very nice and polite, and they certainly put on a great show that night.

For anybody that's a fan of The Tragically Hip you know what kind of honest performance they deliver to their audience.
I didn't know all the songs they played that night, but I knew most of them and I was thrilled to mix monitors for The Tragically Hip.

Pat Benatar
Peabody's Down Under 6-10-93

I could remember exactly how excited I was that Pat Benatar was coming to the club.
I could remember all her MTV videos from the 80s even though I was not into chicks with short hair, she was unique, a rock star and I was definitely thrilled to get the chance to mix monitors for her.

One of the interesting things of their setup that was the first time I ever saw a guitar player play through a Leslie keyboard cabinet her husband Neil Geraldo played through that to get his sound and I thought that was pretty cool.
During the afternoon after sound check I was standing by the monitor console with Neil and his guitar tech and somebody else when he told us a funny story.
He said the reason that he doesn't tour with his favorite guitars anymore it's because he once had a guitar tech who happened to be Scottish.

Before a flight he reminded his guitar tech to detune all the guitars and what that means is to loosen up all the strings so that when they fly and there's pressure or no pressure however that works but if there's tension on the necks it could warp the necks dramatically.
He says they get to the next town and when they get to the gig, they unpack the guitars and every one of Neil's favorite guitars all the necks are warped.
Every one of the guitars have been destroyed.
When Neil asked the tech what happened "didn't you detune them?"
The tech replied to him" I tuned them up is tight as they would go". although he was very honest that happened to be the exact opposite of what he wanted him to do, and Neil Geraldo learned the lesson you never tour with your favorite guitars.
The highlight for me for that show was that during the afternoon after sound check Pat Benatar was doing an interview with somebody from the local TV station, and I was just sitting at the monitor console and those two were sitting up on the stage sitting

on stools and from where I was sitting, I could look right up Pat Benatar's skirt.

The moment I saw her black panties under that short skirt I knew that immediately I should look away and I don't think I did.
Just thinking back about it it's like the sensation of being a young teenager and seeing a live lady part.
It was exciting I was thrilled and I'm not sorry for looking.

The Average White Band
Peabody's Down Under 6-11-93
I mentioned quite a bit that I was excited about this show or excited about that show, but I was really excited about the Average White Band.
Getting to mix these guys was an absolute thrill for me.
I was familiar with all the material as a bass player III knew all the rifts, I knew all the runs and I knew where everything landed.
It was a perfect combination for me to be mixing them.
A night of hits, they were fun they were great.
The crowd loved them and it's just a great memory for me.

Toto
Peabody's Down Under 6-14-93

Toto was one of the few bands that came through that just carrying full production with them.

The club had two Turbosound TMS 4's per side that was the PA at that time.

When the technicians showed up for Toto, they walked in looked at the PA and had a big fit immediately that everything had to come down.

They insisted that I take this out, and I was just there by myself and I remember thinking like how is it even possible that I could take this out by myself?

it wasn't a motor system; it was a permanent installation and it was hanging by chains. This was not something that was going to come out easy at all.

Just before I was about to call my boss and see what he wanted to do about this, the mixer for Toto the row happened to be the owner of the sound company, a man named Dirk Schubert came in looked at the PA in good and said "Hey this is great I'll use this" and just like that this big issue was over.

They brought in their own mixing console which was a Gamble EX56, a big item and it took up a lot of real estate on the floor.

As far as the show, it sounded great and Toto had hits all night long.

What was important to me was the lesson that I learned from Dirk Schubert, you don't have to be an assshole to get your way, that you don't have to come in guns blazing all the time.

Walking on in and being the guy that's cool, that's the way to be.

Flipper, The Dwarves, Ed Hall
Peabody's Down Under 6-21-93

It wasn't unusual to have three to five bands a night at the club. There was no stage manager, it was just me I would get the bands on and off, I would mic everything up, I would get everybody the power, and then I would mix monitors for each group.

It was a non-stop agenda from the moment I got there to the moment it was all over plus the fact that there was not a lot of room in the club, and everything was always tight
We get these three groups, Flipper, The Dwarves and Ed Hall.
I think the only band that sound checked was the opening act, Ed Hall.
I know for sure that the middle act did not.
We get the first punk band up there Ed Hal, and I don't remember any problems with them.

Now we got the next group up called The Dwarfs.
The first thing that I noticed that was interesting was that the lead singer was wearing a pink Tutu.
The other band member that I thought was also interesting was on stage right, which was my side where the monitor console was at that time.
He was playing a Flying V guitar, he had converse tennis shoes on and that's all he was wearing.

As the band is tearing into their first song, I've got two Cleveland Police officers standing behind me they have raised the issue that you are not allowed to sell alcohol in Ohio if there is nudity in the club.
This was an old strip club law but here we were with naked guitar guy up on stage flashing his thing.
Very soon standing behind me on stage right is the Cleveland Police department, Club security, the club management, the promoter, and the band's tour manager.
Because it was so loud in there, it's not like these people were all having a quiet conversation.

It was yelling, finger pointing, lots of arm, hand gestures and frownie facial expressions.
As the adults were trying to resolve this issue, we had another issue that was brewing downstage right.

The stage of Peabody's was probably about three feet high.
I was on the stage right side and from my vantage point I could clearly see what was happening with the guitar player.
He was standing at the very edge of the stage and there was no barricade there, the crowd would just get right pressed right pressed against the stage.

The mosh pit was just swirling and there was one person, that would crowd surf up to the front of the stage, reach underneath that guitar and grab the guitar players genitals and yank on all of it.
The guitar player kicked him, and the guy surfed back into the crowd.

As the adults were behind me having this big argument, I'm laughing my ass off because I think this is really funny.
First off, who thinks it's a good idea to grab someone's cock while they're playing on stage?
2nd off, who gets their junk yanked and then it doesn't take one step back?

The same thing happens a second time.
The guy crowd surfs up he reaches up he grabs the guy's junk, he gets kicked in the face and he surfed back into the crowd.

At that point nobody else on the side of the stage but me and the guitar tech was watching this happen, everybody else was busy arguing.
The crowd surf guy comes in for the big reach and yank and the guitar player takes his guitar off and breaks that guy's head open with it.

Now everyone's attention on stage right is directed towards the stage.

The cops run up on stage to immediately arrest the guy while the band still playing, and the entire audience rushes the stage.
The gear goes down, the cops go down, the guitar guy goes, everything goes down and its total chaos.

One of the cops was pinned down on the stage and had his mace out and just held his finger down on the button.
There was some kid who is lying next to him also under the pile that just got soaked in mace.
It looked it looked like he could have been in the in the swimming pool full of Mace like he was swimming in Mace, he was all maced up.

We're pulling the people apart and getting everybody off of each other and I found this kid at the bottom of the pile with his two friends and I said, "Guys you gotta get him in the bathroom and you gotta wash this off him immediately".

They pull him away into the bathroom which was on that side of the stage, and I go back to the chaos on the deck.

As I'm trying to figure out what's still working, still salvageable on stage, the cops and security getting people off the stage when these two paramedics walked up.
I said to them" Hey some kid got maced pretty bad I sent him in the bathroom to wash it off".

One of the paramedics says to me" Oh man you don't want to get that wet, that's going to make it burn".
Like on cue, I could hear that kid screaming in the bathroom.
I felt terrible about it I really thought I was giving him good advice, turned out not so much.

The cops arrested the guitar player who goes by "hewhocannotbenamed", however it turns out that although he cannot be named, he can be arrested.

After the big bust and after the paramedics take away the kid with the broken skull some other people were ejected from the venue, we get Flipper on stage so we could just please Jesus get this show over with.

Flipper comes on stage, and I honestly don't remember how long it lasted but it wasn't very long.
The stage got rushed I went on stage and then I got tackled under the pile of humans that that had rushed the stage.
Some cop, I don't know if it was the same cop but emptied a can of mace on me and several other people that were laying there on the stage under all these humans and drum kit.

There was so much mace in my face that my hair was soaked (I had hair) and it was actually wet with mace.
I couldn't see anything, there was mucus coming out of every orifice above the chin.

As I was trying to stand up, I felt two people one on each side, picked me up and I heard one say to the other" We got to get him into the bathroom and wash this off him".
I hated that show.

Marc Cohen
Peabody's Down Under 7-6-93

Well well well look who is back, and playing a smaller venue at that, it's my least favorite piano player, Mark Cohen.

The last time I encountered this gentleman he was busy ruining my day with his nonsense.

The thing that really pissed me off, is that he didn't even remember me from the show a year earlier which almost cost me my job because it was such a debacle.

I was completely thrown under the bus, and I didn't dig it and this guy has zero understanding of the ripple from his actions.

You could tell that this was a guy who didn't give a shit about anybody under his class.

When he came to the Empire Club for the coffee break concert the very first thing, he said to me when he looked at the microphone that I put out for him was" don't you have anything more expensive?".

To this day 30 plus years later nobody has ever said that to me.

I don't know who he thought he was, but I knew who he was, and I wasn't going to kiss his ass.

It was July in Cleveland and God knows it was hot and the club wasn't known for running the AC when nobody was in there so during the day when we came in for a sound check, it was definitely warm in the club.

Mr. Cohen comes in sits down at the piano and says to me" Can't they make it livable in here?"

I stood there for a second and I just looked at him and I finally said" Maybe they don't know that you require something more expensive".

I could tell at that moment he remembered me, and that was the last thing I said to him.

X, Dillon Fence
Peabody's 7-12-93

We get these two bands, and I don't remember anything about the opening act.
I do remember that during the day we sound checked the headliner but one of the lead vocalists wasn't there.
How was sound check usually runs is that whoever is the front of house mixer that's traveling with the band they will come up on stage and they will call out to me how they want this microphone to sound because since they travel with the artist, they know what we're looking for so we can get it in the ballpark for where it needs to be.
the band sound checks without the vocalist there and as the band is playing their front of house sound mixer is testing the vocal mic and he's speaking in a very soft voice.
I noticed that the mic stand is set very low, and they tell me it's a female vocalist and he's speaking very softly so I'm turning it up to 11 to get it on top of this loud band that's playing.

Showtime comes I don't remember anything about the opening act. Now it's the top of the show we go into a blackout the crowd goes wild the band goes up on stage and starts playing.

Here comes the lead vocalist who walked right by me, give me a big smile, walked up on stage and I am 100% ready for a soft-spoken quiet vocal to come through the rig.
As the band was playing, she grabbed that mic and kind of ducked down almost in a squatting fetal position and produced what I could best describe as an air raid siren that came through that microphone.
Was so loud everything on the console lit up.
It scared the shit out of the band.
I immediately turned it down probably 60% from where it was.
It was a great lesson for me to never trust the front of house sound guy.
After the show the band thanked me and they gave me a copy of their CD "Hey Zeus", which I still listen to.

Southside Johnny & The Asbury Jukes
Nautica Stage 8-20-93

This is one of my first gigs working as a monitor mixer for a local company called Rock Capital.
The company had a lock on doing the mid-size shows in the area.

The big company in town that did all the major touring was Eighth Day Sound.
When I started working in the Eighth Day Sound shop in the late 80's they were in a rough part of downtown Cleveland right across the street from a police station.
One of the interesting aspects of this location was that the outdoor truck dock had probably an 8-foot gap over some type of death shaft, at a steep angle to get to the shop level.
That meant at the end of the night when you were coming back from a gig at 3:00 o'clock in the morning you had to lay a ramp out between the dock and the upper dock, and push everything uphill.
It sucked and it was dangerous.

One of the reasons the company moved out of that location besides the fact that they were running out of room, the other reason was because of the business that was operating downstairs.

In the basement of that building was a Chrome Plating shop.
Zero ventilation, some dirty windows, employees dying of mysterious lung illnesses and discount Chrome plating.
I had some knowledge of that industry because when I was a teenager I worked at a factory where we would acid bath aviation parts.
One time I brought in a motorcycle frame, and I thought I could just put the entire frame in a basket lower it into the acid and have it take off all the Bondo.
Instead, what happened is I lowered it into the vapors, and it melted the steel.
The employees that worked at that facility didn't wear any type of masks or respirators and they all seem to be dying at a fairly young age.

Now it's flash forward to working above this plating factory I knew this was bad news.

In the 80s you could not have a sound company if you did not have smart people.
There was no such thing as going to the store and buying what you needed, most items had to be fabricated.
It was a time when the manufacturers were behind the curve of what the sound companies were doing with their products.
Well, the smart guys that worked at 8th Day Sound figured out something very interesting.
They discovered that the vapors coming up through the floorboards from the vats of acid in the basement below we're dissolving the solder joints in all the electronic equipment.
Can you imagine?
$1,000,000 plus of electronic equipment all being dissolved from the acid vets below, freaking nightmare.

So, they moved out.
Who wouldn't?

And who moved in?
The new company I was working for, Rock Capital.
It seemed like I had no escape from pushing that gear up that death ramp into the death vapor shop.

The system for how we did every show is that at 5:00 o'clock in the morning I would pick up the rental truck and drive it to the shop.
Then I would meet the other person I'm working with, and we would pack all the cables that we needed for the show into the trunks and load the entire truck.
Once the truck was loaded, I drove straight to the venue.

Nautica stage was located in the Cleveland flats backed up against the Cuyahoga River.
Behind the stage was a wooden boardwalk wide enough for a couple people and then after that the river.

Huge barges would come up and down the river during the day or during the show and it would look like an apartment building was just cruising by.
At that time the venue did not have a roof, and the capacity was around 4000.

The local radio station WMMS had a disc jockey in the afternoon shift that was in love with everything from Jersey especially Southside Johnny.
Growing up in Cleveland the afternoon airways were crowded with the sounds of Jersey and especially the sounds of Southside Johnny and the Asbury Jukes.

June 5th, 1977, I'm at Cleveland stadium for the World Series of Rock and the headliner Aerosmith had cancelled.
The first band up was Nazareth and they were great.
Then came Southside Johnny and the Asbury jukes and I have never seen more items thrown at the stage then at that show.
I remember the guitar player little Steven looking out very nervous at all the projectiles that were coming at them.

Now it's the 90s and here I am at the Nautica stage working for a new company at the toxic shop and it's my turn to do monitors for Southside Johnny.

One of the first problems I had is that none of the monitors that the company owned were matching.
They all had different components in them.
The one that we used for the drummer instead of a 2-inch horn it had it had a foghorn and no high frequency above 1K.
I guess the thinking behind it was give it to the drummer he's the deafest guy he won't notice.
One of the wedges was blown and instead of the company sending me down a whole other monitor, they sent me down the raw speaker, so I had to change it there on the stage.
Nothing instills confidence in the client like getting out some tools and disassembling some equipment.

We survived the load in survived the sound check and now it was finally Showtime.
The band starts playing, the crowd loves it everything is great.
The lead singer of the band Southside Johnny kept asking me for more vocal in his monitors.
I kept turning it up.
Then he wanted more high frequency.
I kept turning it up
At one point I had frequencies feeding back on that stage that would have parted the hair of any normal human being, but due to the fact that South Side was so deaf from a lifetime in the concert business he couldn't hear anything above 500 Hertz.

Since he couldn't hear it, he never knew it fed back so nobody cared.

When the show was over, we tore it down put it in the truck drove back to the toxic shop, pushed all that heavy gear up the ramp over the death pit and then we would take the rental truck back.

At one point I figured out that if I was working at Burger King the exact same number of hours, I'd be making almost twice the money.

Mixing monitors at the Nautica stage was a big deal for me.
Although it was only across the river from Peabody's, for me it was a lot farther away than that.
As much grief as it was getting this show together, I knew that if I kept doing it, I could finally break out of doing shows in nightclubs.

Polka Festival
Slavic Village, Cleveland 8-21 to 8-22
One day I'm at Nautica doing Southside Johnny and the next thing I know I'm at a polka festival.
Brutal.

Besides the good kielbasa, the horrible music what I remember.
Non-stop polka bands doing every cheesy rendition of modern pop songs.
It was two days of the Achy Breaky polka.

They had cable ramps down so people wouldn't trip over the cables.
 I watched multiple women approach those ramps with their stroller, child in it and just ram the stroller into it instead of tipping it back and gently putting over.
They would just keep ramming it with the kid doing some 6G whiplash.
At least a half dozen women did that.

It was like I was living in a Polish joke at a Polish festival surrounded by polka music.
Although the perogies were amazing.

Chris Isaak
Nautica Stage 8-27-93
The one thing I remember from this show it was I was at the monitor console on stage left and when this guy did his hit, that sappy slow love song thingy I remember looking out over the audience and seeing almost every female faint.

It was like a mass hypnosis; I mean I don't even know how to describe Just so weird how all the women reacted the exact same way at the exact same time when that song kicked in.
it was weird.

Urge Overkill, The Vivians
Peabody's Down Under 9-3-93
The last time I did this band they were opening for Nirvana.
I don't remember what album they were touring on but man they were great.
Sorry Vivians, but I just don't remember you.

The Reunification Of the Hopi and Navajo Nations Festival.
Tuba City Arizona 9-15 to 9-21, 1993
I was told was that myself, my buddies Jebi and Mark Hall would be riding in a motorhome from Cleveland OH to the north wall of the Grand Canyon for a two-day festival for 50,000 people.
This was the reunification of the Hopi and the Navajo nations, after I don't know how long, but a very long time.
More than a week.

The people we were riding with were the people from the laser company that we did raves with.
Harry and the Hippies.

They were just hippies there were into the lasers, and how they got hooked up with this gig I have no idea.
One of the deals that we had made is that they didn't want to pay us to drive.
Jebi didn't want to drive, Mark Hall didn't drive trucks and I said if you're not paying me, I'm not driving, I'll sit in the motorhome and look out the window.

We meet them at their freaky deaky laser shop.
 The hippies, the lighting people and the three of us from the sound company got in the motorhome.
I think it was three different trucks and a bunch of cars that were following along which I found bizarre.
I couldn't wrap my head around who is going to drive across the continent like this.
It seemed very unprofessional at best.

As we're traveling on our way to Arizona, every time we would stop and get gas somewhere or pull over for food, one of the hippies would get out and start recruiting homeless people to come with us.
I gave him the nickname "Stivic" after the character from All in the Family.

We get this Meathead, "Dead from the neck up" wandering around every truck stop telling people" Hey man you know we're going to this thing, and you should come with us and it's gonna be awesome and everyone's gonna be there."

He was exactly the like the male version of that annoying chick from Cheech and Chong's up and smoke.
The only thing missing was him scoring weed at the police station.
He was annoying and inviting all these people to come onto this road trip, I was beyond annoyed.

Somewhere across the plains, it was nighttime and I remember caving and driving the sound truck just to keep the whole thing rolling and Mark Hall was driving the motorhome.
Before this day, my understanding was that the farthest Mark Hall ever drove was from W 65th to the Cleveland Agora and back.

I'm driving in front of the motor home and then look in my left rear-view mirror and I could see the motorhomes coming to pass me.
But instead of passing me, it just keeps on going to the left and into the median.
I watched it swing back while to the right back to the left back wall to the right and it pulled over, and I pulled over as well.

I casually walked back to the motorhome parked down the side of the road, and there was a bunch of people inside that were all panicking.
There was Mark Hall sitting in the driver's seat.
Looking like Jimmy Page covered in sweat he said "Pete, I pulled a Griswald".
Everybody lived so we pressed on.

After a couple days on the road, we finally made it to downtown Tuba City AZ on the Hopi Indian Reservation.
I remember we drove 100 miles without seeing a single telephone pole.
Downtown consisted of a gas station, a diner, and a high school with dorms.

Most people that lived there, lived so far away that if you went to school you had to live there. It was impractical to commute.
I don't remember sleeping there I remember taking showers there, I remember sleeping in the truck and being cold.

We finally get to the site.
This was up on some mesa overlooking the north wall of the Grand Canyon by the four corners where in New Mexico, Utah, Colorado, Arizona comes together.

There was a stage that was there brought in from Phoenix along with three generators one for sound, one for lights, one for lasers.
Driving in we drove past dozens and dozens of pallets of water.
The promoter was ready to make a killing selling water in the desert to his 50,000 attendees.
There was also an army of blue porta potties lined up.

I don't want to guess how many, but it was many.

The labor we had were just local Indians.

I backed up the sound truck to the side of the stage and kept the monitor rig in the truck, and out of the front of house we backed up one of the trucks and kept the front of house console in the truck with the back door open.
One of the caveats of being on the reservation was that there was no alcohol.

We gave the Indians some money for alcohol because they said they would be more than happy to drive off the reservation to get some if we bought something for them, we said sure no problem.
We never saw them again until the last day when they returned without alcohol or money.
They claimed something happened to the alcohol.
That I believed.

It was weird having such a giant site with nobody there yet, even though we got set up and the first day of the show was the following day it was just kind of bizarre to us how few people were there.
They set up catering right behind the stage which consisted of enough plywood to make three sides and a roof.
The only thing they fed us the entire time we were on site was Navajo tacos.

A Navajo Taco consisted of a flat piece of fried bread; some beans spread around it with some rotten lettuce on top.
Poof, you got yourself a Navajo Taco.

I think that my rectum was impacted until I got back to Ohio.
I don't remember much about the first day other than the fact that there was something missing, oh that's right people.
There were no people.
Instead of 50,000 people out there, had to be maybe 16 or 17 and they were all locals.
Every single person could have taken home a pallet of water and 10 porta potties, and we still would have been in great shape.

The next morning, they take us to the Navajo high school to take showers and we go have a decent breakfast over at the diner before going back to the site.
As we are sitting in the diner, I'm in a booth sipping my coffee and I see about a half dozen horses standing just standing in the road.
I said to one of the Indian guys sitting next to me I said," Hey man whose horses?"
Him and all the other guys all the other Indian guys just started laughing.
He looked at me and said, "Hey bro they're just horses' man".
Like how ignorant of me to assume that somebody owned them.
Just like a herd of deer standing in my yard, they're just deer.

We go back for the second day and there were more defiantly people there.
For the big Saturday show I think there was 30 people there.

I don't remember any of the acts that played; I only remember one duo that we had for both shows both days.
It was a father and son, and the father was playing acoustic guitar and the sun had to be I don't know 8-9 years old.
He was singing this song and the lyrics went" I love you just the way you are".
Then the kid would repeat the line" I love you just the way you are".
We all thought it resembled Jerry Lewis and Dean Martin doing a skit.

It was the highlight because out of 25 acts it's the only musical performance that I remember.

I also remember during the show losing all the power because one of those morons with the laser company who we called "Special Ed" shut our generator off during the show.
Usually, we frown on that kind of thing.
When I went back there to see what was going on of course I yelled at him "What the fuck are you doing?"
He responds "oh I'm just shutting off the laser generator"
Here is this guy that's supposed to be this genius and he doesn't even know what generator is running the lasers.

The one thing they did that was cool that completely spooked the locals, is on the Saturday night they aimed those lasers at the north wall of the Grand Canyon, and they made an image of an eagle in flight almost a mile across.

From where our perspective, I mean it was epic.
Definitely a once in a lifetime thing to see and the locals had a different opinion because this was a sacred place to them.
They were not cool with hippies on mushrooms putting green Eagles and mile wide penises on the north wall of their sacred monuments.

Finally, we tear this show down, put everything back in the trucks, we get this big hippie caravan ready to roll and we take everything and our impacted rectums back to Ohio.

There was some woman that was in charge, that was a category 5 moron, and I don't believe had ever been more than 50 miles away from home before, and if she had she'd certainly didn't act like it.

Now that this catastrophe is over, everyone just wants to go home and get out of here.
One of the conversations that we were having is that they wanted me to drive one of the trucks and I asked them point blank" Am I getting paid to drive?"
They said no but you're going so you should drive.
I said "Listen, I'm a professional driver I drive trucks all over the country. I've done it for years I've do it for a living and it's not something that I'm just going to you. It's not a service that I'm just going to give you for free when you hire me as a driver, you're also hiring my judgment that comes with it. It's a different item for me just sitting there and staring out the window".
Her response to me was "We don't need your experience or your anything we'll do it ourselves".

Apparently, this person who did not need my expertise didn't realize that when we drove there, we had come across Texas and then through New Mexico completely avoiding the Rocky Mountains.

I'm just sitting in the passenger seat of the motorhome, and I see a sign that we pass that said," Welcome to Colorado".
I turned to the expert, and asked her "Why are we in Colorado?"
She told me that we were going to go back her way that she looked at the map and that this would be shorter route and it wasn't my concern.
I must have had some facial expression.

I was looking at her like she was the stupidest person in the world.
I said to her "Do you know how much fuel you're going to burn going up and down the rocky fucking mountains? let alone the time. You might have added two days to this trip."

Next thing you know my predictions come true and we are crawling through Durango Co at 5 miles an hour.

it was 100% worst case scenario and on top of that now I had to drive because the person that was driving the sound truck was afraid to go through the mountains.
Rightfully So.
What kind of moron takes a Ryder rental truck over the rocky fucking mountains.

After many close calls and creeping over the mountains, I was right about everything.
I was right about the fuel consumption; I was right about the time, and I was right out of patience.
The only thing funny that happened on the trip home is that one of my buddies was having sex with one of the laser hippies' girlfriends. This guy was having to drive the motorhome while they were doing it and the overhead right above him.
Not everybody thought it was funny, but I thought it was funny.

Finally, like day three of this trip, we find ourselves on the outskirts of Indianapolis.
I'm driving the sound truck, there's two trucks behind me, I'm following the motorhome and I haven't seen the other vehicles in some time.
The motorhome gets off the highway at a random exit and pulls into a gas station.
I get out of the truck walk up to the motorhome and I asked the genius in charge what's the problem and why are we stopping here when we just fueled up not too long ago.

Now let me emphasize that this was before cell phones pagers this was back in a time where once you were lost once you were out there in America there was no way to find you there was no way to find other people you were just out there.

Captain Marvel explains to me that the person with the" coffee can" that had all the money in it, was in one of the cars following the caravan and now they can't find them.

So, it's like so you don't have any money at all?

127

She goes "No it was all in the coffee can, so we have to wait here until they find us".

I'm looking at this person and I said "How were they going to find us after we pulled off at some random exit off the highway? At least if we would have pulled over on the highway, we would still be a visible commodity, but you just picked a random exit you pulled us off and now where are they in front of us are they behind us who knows?"

This person was so stupid and unable to grasp what I was saying to them, that I got Mark, Jebi and all their luggage.
I put it in the truck, I put the two of them in the front seat of the truck with me and I drove nonstop from Indianapolis to Cleveland.

I don't know whatever happened to that laser company, but I heard that the guy that owned it ended up selling used Soviet MIG fighter jets.
I liked Harry, he was an interesting guy, I hope that worked out for him.

Robin Trower, Badfinger
Agora Theater 9-24-93

I was the monitor mixer for this show, and it was a great night of classic rock music.
First off Badfinger was great.
They played all their hits. I love a band that knows what the crowd wants.

I saw Robin Trower in the 70s so being on stage with him, I was really thrilled.
What made everything just a little bit better is that he was the nicest guy and working with him and getting his sounds together, you know just spending time with a guy that just had such a unique sound playing through the Leslie and his pedal assortment.
It was cool hanging out with him in his pocket getting him the sound that he needed to deliver his performance.

That night Robin Trower absolutely delivered to a packed house at the Agora, and it was one of those shows that he really knew how to pace it, he really understood dropping the tempo letting the show breathe and pick the energy back up.
Real old school stuff.

When the show was over, he came over to the monitor console and thanked me and I was unable to keep the smile off my face.

Penn & Teller
Music Hall 10-17-93

I'm moving up the ladder getting out of the nightclubs and now I'm here with the sound company and I'm mixing front of house for Penn and Teller.

Since only Penn speaks, his microphones are hidden in his glasses. From a mixers viewpoint the whole show was two inputs for the two microphones that were in his glasses the wireless and the playback that was it.

My buddy Jebi, who was much more experienced than I was supposed to mix the show, but I wanted to mix, and he wanted to go to the bar so we both did what we wanted to do.

After a sound check rehearsal in the afternoon, everything's cool and the one thing that they tell me that they're very adamant about, is that once the show starts never turn off Penn's microphone.
Their production manager said to me you never know when he's going to go behind the curtain or come back out or pop back in always leave the microphone on once the show starts.
OK no problem.

The show starts, I bring up his microphone, we got the playback at a certain level and this and that's it.
They are doing their gags and for me nothing's changing because the microphone levels not changing, the track levels not changing and when he disappears behind the curtain pops back out, he's back there, he's back out, what do I do?
I do not turn off his microphone.
Now this entire time since the show started, I'm just sitting by myself at the front of house mixing council and there isn't a lighting council behind me there isn't a stage manager there's nobody, I'm just sitting there by myself in the audience.
The show stops and we have an intermission.

Nobody said anything about an intermission.

Again, I'm just sitting there, and no one has said anything to me and I'm following those very specific instructions, I have not turned off that microphone.

The house lights are up and the music's playing, and you know how it is, people are milling about coming to the bathroom, coming back from the bathroom getting their drinks doing the things people do during the intermission and through the audio system we could hear Penn walking into a room with a lot of reverberation.
Next thing you know you could clearly hear him urinating and his vocalization of relief.
People in the audience are just looking around like what are we listening to?
Then we hear him wash his hands walk back to the stage have a conversation about the flight out in the morning and then they popped back on stage and the show continued.

Was it part of the show?
it was that night.
After the show I didn't want to bring it up nobody said anything to me and that was it.

White Zombie, Nudeswirl, Chemlab
Agora Theater 11-17-93

For this show I was a stagehand which meant that I had zero responsibilities with any of the equipment that the show brought in I was just labor there to assist and facilitate whatever the show needed and since I worked in that building quite a bit, you know it's just how it was.

They were on their "La Sexorcisto Devil Music Volume One" tour, the band was selling out everywhere and their show was on fire.
I don't remember the first two bands, but I remember being on stage left and we could tell there was a commotion in the crowd.
I looked out from the stage, and out by the front of house console was a situation.

Somebody had pulled the fire hose off the wall of the house right side of the building dragged it to where the mixing console was and then somebody turned it on.
By the time I saw what was happening it looked like a King Cobra dancing around the center of the venue, and it made its way to the White Zombie mixing console and as the band was tearing through" Black Sunshine" that fire hose blew all the knobs off the mixing console.

Instantly the audio system sounds like a dinosaur that's been shot with a cannon full of nails
It was an ugly, violent, sound that was happening.
The sensation of this raging show to the stage volume was abrupt.

All the chaos what do you think the lighting people did?
They put the entire venue in the stage and blackout so now nobody could see what's going on.
It was a full-blown disaster.
Meanwhile the Agora security had caught the guy and they threw him out the side door.
When the band found that out, they were furious.

They wanted to get the guy, make an announcement, and throw him off the stage into the crowd Roman style.
It was a thing between the local crew and the White Zombie people, none of us wanted the show to go down this way and it was very tense backstage.

There was an unsaid thing going on, that even though this guy did this, he was from Cleveland, and we were down with these freaks throwing down some BC justice.

That's it, the show was over, we loaded it out and I don't think they ever swept up all the knobs there were blown off that console.

Greenhouse 27
North East Tour, spring 94, 16 shows
These guys had come through Peabody's a couple of times and had just been signed by a label out of Hoboken NJ called Bar None. The drummer's father was wealthy and was backing everything up, they had hired me to be their tour manager and front of house mixer.

They were terrific guys and as far as bands go, they were tight with their own material.
I thought they deserved more attention than they got.
But those kinds of things aren't up to me.
The only thing I get a vote on, is where is the vocal in the mix, settling with the promoter and getting us to the next town.

Sheryl Crow
Cleveland Zoo 4-30-94

I'm with the sound company and we take a system into the zoo.
We were doing a series of shows there.
The city had a small amphitheater, and we had a new artist named Sheryl Crow.
She did not come to the sound check, but the rest of the band did.
Her front of house mixer worked with me to get her volume right so she could just walk in and be ready and do the show.
We get it loud, and I think that it's kind of loud for an acoustic guitar but it's not a matter of opinion, it's about doing what they want.
He said that's how they want it and that was it.

Showtime comes, it was in the afternoon, there was no lights it was still daytime.
She puts on her guitar, goes downstage, the bands is playing, she starts playing and immediately she snaps her head over at me and she yells at me to turn the guitar down.
That same guitar that I thought was too loud at sound check.
No problem so I turn it down.

She yells it to me again to turn it down, again no problem turn it down. All day long. Whatever you want to do, how her guy set it up with me, was 100% what she didn't want.

It was a great lesson for me that you just can't trust other people to always represent what their artist wants because sometimes they don't know.

Whenever possible it's always better to start from scratch, deal with the artist directly because at the end of the day you're the one getting the look, getting the stick thrown at you, getting the whatever you're the lightning rod up there when the front of house guy who set it up incorrectly is at the other end of the snake sipping a cocktail.

The Genitorturers
Agora Theater 5-17-94

One of the things about being a monitor mixer is that you're on stage with the action.
The bad news is that you are also on stage with all the action.
We get this freaky group, and they got a bunch of cages on stage and they've they're bringing up members of the audience and doing things to them while some kind of a band is playing.
One person came up from the audience, was put into a cage and had a baseball bat inserted in their rectum.
I guess that's getting some value out of your ticket purchase the original VIP package.

But not to be outdone, they brought a guy up out of the audience who I assume was a mental patient that escaped from the asylum. I'm giving him the benefit of the doubt because I just don't want to assume or assert that we have people walking amongst us that are not in in asylums that would volunteer to do something like this.
So, there I am at the monitor console on stage left with stagehands and we watch as they nail this man's penis to the stage.

Like many magic tricks this one didn't work out so well.
Turns out it was much easier to nail his penis to the stage than it was to remove the nail.

At some point the show ended, the audience left, and we loaded that show out as the Cleveland fire department worked in the center of the stage attempting to remove that man's penis from the deck.
Really puts the P in the VIP package.

B Stage
Great American Rib Cook Off 5-27,28,29,30-94
What was funny about this gig was that everybody was fighting to work on the "A" stage, and I knew better.
We had three stages, The "A stage" with the national acts, the "B stage" with the local bands and the best rib contest and the kids' stage with the whatevers.

Over at the main stage the guys were panicked with all the gear that wasn't working and the national acts yelling at them.
Meanwhile, me and my buddy Billy were over at the B Stage stuffing our faces with ribs.
You see, the thing about the rib cook off is that nobody had any intentions of feeding the peasants any ribs, we had the crappy catering from the lowest bidder, and they dished that out to us like we were orphans.
We had a five-drawer work box on stage that was about 5 feet high, and every drawer was filled with ribs that were left over from all the contests.
Add to the mix that we had a week of local bands not complaining about anything, we had a good week.

Stuttering John
Agora Ballroom 6-3-94
The Agora Ballroom was across the hall from the Agora Theater, and I want to say it had probably like a 500-seat capacity.
If you couldn't sell the theater, they put you in the ballroom.
We're loading in this band from New York and the artist is Stuttering John from the Howard Stern show.
Turns out he's got some band he's put together and that's what it's all about.

The tour manager pulls me aside and says "Listen I really need you to make this guy happy."
Which I responded, "listen I really need you to understand that happiness comes from the inside and I have nothing to do with this man's happiness. I can only make things louder, if he wants it louder, that I could do. Happiness not my department".

Back then, most Agora Ballroom shows consisted of Chris from the lighting company, Mark Hall was the Stage Manager, and I was with the sound company.
We did hundreds of shows together.

The star of the show doesn't come in for sound check and we just muddle along without him.
We do the support act no big deal and now it's showtime and His Highness graces our presence.
Before the show started, I go out like I do every show and I check the mics to make sure it's not going to feedback to make sure it's loud to make sure it's present and make sure it's ready to go.

This guy comes out, the band starts playing, he grabs the microphone says one thing and then immediately starts yelling at me and quite frankly I just couldn't understand what he was trying to say and it's not because he was stuttering it's just because he was just kind of spit yelling.

It's been my observation that the more uncomfortable somebody is on stage in front of a live audience the more they are apt two outbursts on stage over small issues.
He had no talent; he had no connection to the audience his only move was some kind of Pogo thing it really looked like he was having a seizure.

I could tell that he was getting irritated that I wasn't engaging with him. I wasn't getting angry, I wasn't getting flustered, I just didn't care you. Want it louder, have it louder, you want it softer, have it softer.
I turned it up and then he told me to turn it down, then I turned it down then he had me turn it back up and this went on and on and finally I turned it up so loud that he couldn't even walk downstage to the edge of the stage, that's how loud it was, and I went over to the bar and got some drinks.

He spent the rest of the show wondering where I was, and I spent the rest of the show not caring about him.
What's important is that the drinks were fabulous.

Chuck Mangione, Sha Na Na
Cleveland's Public Square 6-5-94

I don't remember if all the Canadians in Cleveland faced north when Chuck played the equivalent of the Canadian National anthem, "Feels So Good".

I do remember what didn't feel good and that was my interactions with the promoter for the event, some chubby pushy guy named Mark Chimpledick.

Mr. Chimpledick had a very high opinion of himself, and you could tell that he was one of these people that just looked down on everybody follow his class.

Cleveland had quite the caste system, and there was a mentality and culture amongst some of the white-collar class of Cleveland that really felt that us working class peasant folks should just not look them in the eye, shut up and be happy for any scraps that were being thrown our way.

This was one of my early encounters with Mr. Chimpledick and he didn't disappoint.

After the show he came on stage and I was standing with a couple of the guys from Sha Na Na.

they were thanking me and we were shaking hands and Mr. Chimpledick Walks up to the circle and starts shaking the hands of the guys in the group.

When he got to me standing there, he started to shake my hand and the moment he realized that I wasn't in the band He said to me" I'm not shaking your hand you're just some nobody technician".

This is exactly the honest opinion that this guy had for everybody that came to work did a job and made his show happen.

I guess every industry has them, sociopaths that view every human being as just another line item to be paid.

One of my favorite quotes, Genesis song from the album the Lamb Lies Down on Broadway.

"I'd rather trust a man who works with his hands he looks at you once you know he understands if I choose this side, he won't take me for a ride"

I have always remembered that, and it always stayed with me. Generally, as a rule I will say that the most decent and honest people that I have ever encountered, people that worked with their hands not people that worked with their hands on their hips.

The Neville Brothers
The Plain Dealer 6-12-94
This was a private function for the local newspaper, they throw these parties for themselves so they could remind each other how awesome they are and give out awards to each other.
You know just like every other show.

I'm there with the sound company and I'm the monitor mixer and I was on the stage right side, and it was a big tent and some field or some parking lot those details I mean I just don't remember.
But what I do remember is that the editor of the newspaper president CEO whoever the big kahuna is was standing up at the podium trying to speak to the room of I guess couple maybe 1000 people and his mic wasn't on.

We have a little phone system that we call the com, and I'm calling the front of house guy Mr. Jones, and Mr. Jones isn't answering the phone.
Now I could physically see him from where I'm at, and what I see is him sitting in a chair with a newspaper opened with zero view of the stage.
If there was one thing you could count on for Mr. Jones, is that he would be reading every moment he got, that's why he's such an intelligent fellow because he reads quite a bit.
Mr. Jones is trapped in this reading coma, and we got to get this show going and my boss, our boss is standing right next to me freaking out.
My boss, Mr. jurist, took off one of his shoes and threw it almost 100 feet.

Even more remarkable the distance of that throw was the accuracy, which went right through the front of that newspaper that Mister Jones was holding.
The mic got turned down the guy got to speak everybody lived my boss got to live the experience of walking up to front of house with one shoe on and I don't remember anything about the Neville Brothers.

Doug Stone, Martina McBride, Tim McGraw, Daron Norwood, Joe Diffie, Sammy Kershaw, Rick Trevino, Colin Raye, Pattie Loveless, John & Audrey Wiggins and Pony Express.

Pepsi Country Music Festival 6-17,18,19-94
According to my collection of backstage passes I did this show three years in a row.
The venue for this show was the Berea fairgrounds just West of southwest of Cleveland.
 it was a featureless landscape outside of a horse track.

The staging company local staging when lighting company electric stage put up the stage and the lighting rig and I was with rock capital with the audio system of course I drove the truck.
today when I go to work for a show like this with this many elements, we would have a dozen people working a show like this.

We would have a front of house mixer, a front of house technician, wireless microphone coordinator, somebody to deal with intercom, minimum two audio "A2" to mic up the bands, A monitor technician just to move wedges on stage, somebody to AC wherever it's needed and a Monitor mixer.
For the Pepsi country music festival, we did it with two guys.
By any standards it was brutal.
the first day I drove the truck out there of course from the sound shop and somebody had to take me back to my car which was downtown Cleveland and then me go back home to Cleveland Heights on the east side.

This was just a little over an hour commute for me to get to the gig in the morning so that's the first part of the suck of the day.
The thing about doing multiple acts like this is that everybody thinks they're the special headliner.
Back when we were advancing this show and getting the needs of all the different acts it was a lot of conference calls.

One of the groups on this bill demanding that they bring their own thrust that would go on the front of the stage and thrust out into the audience.

The only reason I'm on the phone call is to chime in about audio questions and answers.

Many people wanted to bring in their own sound systems and like you know you know we're not doing that; I'm not taking out my PA or making room for your system so you could play an hour, that's not how it's going to go down.

Finally, the production manager for this group said to this our stage manager Larry Dolan "We're going to get our thrust because we just sold-out Texas stadium".
As dry as a hot Texas day, Larry calmly replied "Well, we are just a little north of there and you're not getting a thrust".

Day one was very hectic.
The company didn't have anything that we refer to has breakaway or quick anything.
Everything had to be hard patched to the split, we had nothing that is considered "quick disconnect".

We needed to be doing multiple acts in the same day with the same microphone package.
What that means is that I didn't have each individually band pre miked up just to roll into place on risers and plug it in no no no no.

I had to move all the microphones from the last band onto the new band as we go peeling it off as we went
Moving all the electrical, making sure everyone had power and moving all the wedges and then going through the mixes with everybody.
It was beyond hectic and then moving the patch.

The front of house mixer that was working with me was such a douche that he would ask me to move inputs on the patch because he was too lazy to walk around the back of his console and make a move.

Just imagine the guy holding the coffee cup from the movie Office Space
I would be in the middle of doing five things at once and he would call me up on the com and say something like" yeah, I'm gonna need you to move that acoustic guitar two channels over because I've got a compressor on that that I would like to use".
Like I didn't have enough to do, it was non-stop from the moment I got there till the moment I left.

The show itself was Friday night, all day Saturday and Saturday night and then all-day Sunday and I think maybe even into Sunday night followed by a brutal loadout.

On that Saturday I was on the stage for 14 consecutive hours.
I didn't leave the stage to pee to eat to cry to reconsider my life choices nothing nada not a nothing.
I didn't have to worry about peeing because there was no time to drink and anything I would have drank, I would have sweated it back out because I was running like a madman trying to do Mission Impossible with these set changes.
At some point somebody had mercy and brought, I don't even know where they found it, brought a couch up on stage and put it behind the monitor console so every moment I had I could sit down on that couch.

You know during the day the lighting guys are hanging out doing nothing and the back line guy who was there to provide backline for any bands that needed it was sitting on the couch behind me playing one of the rental guitars.
I got a DI box, I plugged him into the mixing console, I turned him up into the cue wedge and we were listening to Tommy jam along with the band.
It was great.

At some point I moved the patch from my monitor console to the main split and I called up the front of house mixer on the com and I told him we had a new input.

There we are a nice Saturday afternoon, 20,000 plus people out there in the field, band on stage just jamming along and that's when the front of house mixer turned up Tommy's solo.
The band was looking around, they couldn't figure out where they were was coming from and that guitar solo was just wailing along, it was so funny.
Tommy played the rest of the set with them, and they never knew it.

As far as nutritional value to keep a crew of hard-working people going, I may not know what the best way is. Is it fruit? is it light pasta? I'm not really sure but I know what is not the best way and that was the literal garbage that they were feeding us.
The local Cleveland promoter fed the crew imitation Turkey meatloaf for three days.

Probably assisted and me not using the restroom for 14 hours on stage my body was too impacted with Turkey meatloaf.
What else do you want on a hot summer day?
We were culinary hostages, no other place to go no other options.

For me the highlight was the very last act on the Sunday night, and it was Joe Diffie.

I was so happy that he had his own monitor mixer, and I could have some quality time on the couch before having to go right into a loadout.
The guy was a little twitchy, a little nervous and he didn't seem like he was OK.

I'm sitting on the couch, the band is on stage, packed crowd people as far as you could see.
The announcer says" Ladies and gentlemen please welcome Joe Diffie" and at that moment the monitor mixer took off his headphones, threw them on the floor and announced "I can't do this" and he left the stage.
Damn it.

I really can't explain how disappointed I was.

I was so ready just to sit there with my eyes closed for 30 minutes 40 minutes however long that guy was going to play and just have a moment but no not even a moment.
So, I get up and I step up to the console and I'm looking around at what this guy did.
I've been mixing 5 bands a day on the same console for the past three days; this wasn't a magic trick to me and I certainly wasn't nervous about it.
Joe Diffie walks on stage waving to the crowd says a couple things in the mic looks over to the monitor guy to ask for an adjustment and it was just me waving at him "Hey man".

I got him what he needed and at some point, he came over to the console in between songs and asked him what asked me what happened to his guy.
I said, "Man I just don't know; I don't think he could take it".

We did the show, and everyone survived.

I know I did another one there at the same location, but I don't remember anything from it I'll chalk that up as a good thing.

One thing I remember from the second time I did country fest at the Berea fairgrounds was my buddy Blaine and I got in trouble for racing 24-foot trucks on the horse track.

Truck racing was very popular in Cleveland, and it was the standard for us to race trucks from the shop back to the truck rental place at 3:00 o'clock in the morning after shows.
Many a night we would be airborne over the railroad tracks in a 24-foot truck so you could imagine us having a actual racetrack how could we resist.

John Mellencamp's Birthday Party
Bloomington Indiana 7-3-94
This was a weird gig, they set me and one other person and a 24 truck out to Indiana.
The gig was John Mellencamp's family wanted to have a drive-in movie style experience on their front yard.

We show up at this location there's no stage because there's no performance there was just a screen company that had a screen up. There and they had some scaffold left and right that we put the sound on it and that was it and some guy who I assume was him showed up with this family and they sat on blankets and had a picnic and watched a couple of movies.
 I don't remember what movies, but I remembered the second one was black and white.

I remember thinking you know this was a big pain in the ass to go all this way just for this but at the same time thinking if I could, this would be a nice thing to do with my family, so I had a great appreciation for what they were doing.

It was a long drive back to Cleveland.

Margaritaville
Buckeye Lake, 7-16-94

We get sent out to do this Margaritaville which is the party before a Jimmy Buffett show.

Usually, this kind of thing happens in the parking lot or in the surrounding area but for this venue they had a specific area to do the Margarita Margaritaville which consisted of different vendors and of course lots of alcohol and a little stage with some local bands and that's what we were there for.

The only thing that I was really excited about was that this was over the moment the Jimmy Buffett show started, so that meant we can go load out get out of there because we had to travel directly out of state with the same gear to the very next show.

The only thing that stands out from my memory of that event was there is this one really annoying chubby guy that had on a grass skirt and nothing else and nothing under this skirt.

He was circling the stage, a drink in each hand yelling every party slogan he had ever read on a hat.

By the time our show is over, and we were loading out I remember putting the last piece on the truck, I could hear the Jimmy Buffett show happening down the hill and right in front of the stage that we had just loaded out that now had nothing at it and nobody there and nothing happening and nothing going on there was Mr. I've got nothing under my grass skirt face down in the mud passed out.

My memory will forever be scarred from the site of his flabby ass with that Hawaiian skirt over his face down in the mud he didn't even look like a human form he looked more like a beach drift.

Ronnie Milsap
Indiana Pensylvania 7-17-94
This was some County Fair funnel cake gig in the middle of nowhere. No hotel or anything civilized, we had driven right from the previous gig right to this load in.

For those of you that don't know Ronnie Milsap was blind.
He was a piano player and had a great show for what it was, and I was the monitor mixer and Ray was at front of house for this run. There was a part of the show when Ronnie would get up from his piano and walk 4 paces downstage say something to the audience and walk the four paces back to his piano.

His crew would nail down a small strip of wood exactly 4 paces away from him so when he walked his four paces, he could touch it with his toe, and he knew where he was on stage.
Ray the front of house guy comes up, stands around stage with his hands in his pockets he says "what's this? We got to get rid of this". He starts kicking it and their guy freaked out.
Ray didn't come back to the stage after that.

George H. Bush, George Voinovich
Landerhaven 7-18-94
So, after almost three days of no sleep, we come straight to this corporate gig with the ex-president at some swanky place and all my clothes still smell like Pennsylvania funnel cake.

Best part, the guy I've been working with there had been the front of house mixer of every show we went to now this one he doesn't want to mix it and you know why?
Because we do not have enough PA to cover this area.
They had added like another thousand seats to the right and they added a video screen, but they didn't add audio.
What I had on my truck is what I had and that was it and it wasn't enough, it wasn't cool, and we suffered through it.

Moonwalk 94
Wapakoneta Ohio 7-20-94
This was the opening of the John Glenn Museum in Wapakoneta OH for the 25th anniversary of the Apollo 11 moon landing.
I don't remember about what band played or any of that, but I remember two things.

I remember everyone being disappointed that John Glenn didn't show up and I remember the fireworks.
I wasn't mixing for that show, so I was just hanging out and I saw this area where the guys had all the fireworks for the lunch, and I went over there just to hang out and talk to them.

They had all the fireworks laid out on the ground with all the electrical wires coming into one car battery, that went to a board that had all these nails attached to the board.
Each nail had a little wire wrapped around it and that went to the car battery, there had to be 60 some nails on this board.

When it came time to launch everything, they just grabbed the other wire from the positive side of the battery terminal and started touching all the nails sending the voltage and launching the fireworks.

it was one of the most hillbilly things I had ever seen in my life, and I thought it was so cool.

Dion
Shooters 7-21-94
"Run around Sue, The Wonderer", these were all the songs that he wished he was performing at a better venue.

Sarah McLachlan, Big Sugar, Odd Girl Out
Nautica Stage 7-22-94
This was my first of three days at the same venue with the same system.
it was really very rare, and I was excited because that meant to me is that I was avoiding two load ins and two loadouts.
This show must have gone great because I don't remember anything about it.

Green Day, Collective Soul, Junkhouse, Fury in the Slaughterhouse, God's Child, Moist, Pansy Division and The Pinheads.
Nautica Stage 7-23-94
This was one of those radio station festival things with a bunch of bands just thrown at us.
That day I had my ex-wife's nephew with me, he was a big fan of these bands, and I told him that he just sat on a stool behind the monitor console and didn't act like a fool he could hang out.

Nautica stage was backed right up against the Cuyahoga River and on that day, there was no backdrop on the stage.
You could see right through the stage with the Cleveland downtown skyline as the backdrop.
The show started early that day it was predominantly a day/afternoon show that was going to go into the night.
Some of the acts that were on this bill had gotten big over the summer, especially Green Day.

That venue I think held around 4000 people and it was before they put a roof over the place.
I was on stage the entire time and the view from the stage was that the venue looked a little overcrowded.
I had been on that stage many times, looked out over a lot of audiences and this one was swelling.
From the stage we could see people that were pulling boards off the fence to climb through the fence and over the fence.
It got to a point where people were pouring through and over the walls.

Since I had been on stage since 8:00 o'clock in the morning, I had no idea what was going on out there but apparently there was thousands of people trying to get into the venue and it was total chaos outside.

I could ascertain that there was a lot of chaos happening inside.
I don't remember what band was on stage, but it was late afternoon when the Cleveland Police department came back full force backstage, came up to me on stage the monitor console and they told me to shut everything off.
I asked the police officer in charge if he wanted to make an announcement to the crowd before I shut off the audio system and his response was," No".

I was definitely surprised, and I asked him a second time and he snapped back me, he was pretty pissed that I asked him a second time, but I couldn't believe what he was asking me.
I am not an expert in crowd control but you know, to shut down the rig with thousands of people there, thousands of people climbing in and not even making any kind of announcement "Hey people get back or we got to pause the show" or we got to do this or that but it was just zero communication and now the crowd is just out there murmuring, the band is still on stage and they don't know what the fuck is going on.

In perfect synchronization, two things then simultaneously happened.
There were two big wooden gates that were backstage on what would be considered the stage right house left side where we would bring in the trucks to the stage.

The gates opened and the entire width was lined up with police with Shields and not just night sticks, but the really long ones.
In between the cops dressed up like the Roman legion, motorcycle cops and cops on horseback.
That's when the big police boat pulled up right behind the stage.

153

Now at this moment, I'm standing off stage left with my nephew, the stage manager, the promoter rep, 5 cops and the bass player from Green Day.
My nephew is standing there talking to the bass player from Green Day telling him how he's been a major influence on his life, how their music really touches his soul, how he really never understood who he was until he heard their music and the entire time he is droning on with this teenage dribble the guy he's talking to was holding one of those big flashlights and he was drooling on the light and watching the spit sizzle.
Hands down the deepest conversation I ever witnessed in my life.

As Rain Man and Spitty Drizzle casually continued their conversation, the cops started beating everybody in their pathway.

Up on stage the band just set their instruments down, the drummer put down his sticks and they got off the stage.

When the cops told him to get off, we were all under the impression, that well we wouldn't really know what there was no reason to believe that we weren't going to continue the show.
Everything was still set up ready to go.

As the cops we're beating everybody in front of the stage off to the house left side, the police boat fired up its water cannon and aimed it at the crowd and started firing it over the stage and into the crowd.
The problem with this is that in between that the boat and the crowd was all the gear that was on stage.
The guitars, amps, drum kit, all the wedges, everything got blasted out into the audience.

I can't imagine the people that got hit with drum hardware coming at the speed of water cannon.

That cannon was so powerful it was hitting the front of house console where my buddy John Conde was out there with the lighting guy Dean trying to hold the tent down as the riot surged with the water cannon from behind the stage wreaking havoc on everything.

At one point, my boss said to me, "You got to go up there and rescue the gear".
After watching a 90-pound speaker get flung into the audience from that water cannon like somebody flicking a cigarette butt, I politely declined.

Green Day never did get to play, and the place got destroyed.

It was beyond unprofessional for the Cleveland Police department to march in there like a Viking horde without making an announcement and forcing the crowd into the corner with no escape.
The police had blocked all the exits and the crowd had torn away boards of the fence to escape from the approaching Police Department.

It was supposed to be just straight up festival show without a loadout now turned into a big cleanup and salvage because we had a show coming in the next day and now, we had to go through everything, figure out what was working, it was a huge mess.

Tony Bennett
Nautica Stage 7-24-94

This was textbook gig culture shock.
It was just a week earlier that I was in some Pennsylvania funnel cake festival with Ronnie Milsap, the previous day we had a riot and now I'm here with Tony Bennett.

Tony's crew were great when they came in that day, and they had heard about what happened the previous day, so everybody was thankful to have a nice easy day.
The guy mixing Tony was Vance, and he had just spent a decade doing shows in South America specifically in Brazil.

His experience in Brazil was that they only used one microphone for everything which was the Shure SM58 the industry standard vocal microphone, it was just unusual that we used it on everything.
Another part of the setup that was unusual is because Tony was such an old school guy, he didn't want to hear his vocal directly like most people do he wanted an ambient feel like he was singing in an old concert hall.

For Tony's monitor on stage, we hung side fills at the four corners of the stage all pointing straight in adding his vocal and the overheads from the drum kit in the side fills.
it was the only time in my career I ever put the overheads from the drum kit in the side fills for the singer it's never happened again.

Tony didn't come for sound check, no big deal.
Showtime comes and I'm standing at the monitor console, and I was tapping my sharpie on the board.
I was wearing my pass from the night before I hung my sharpie and my little flashlight from it.
When Tony walked up on stage he came and stood next to me at the monitor console.
He saw me tapping my sharpie and he's turned and said to me," Hey do you want an autograph?" and he picked up the sharpie out of my hand and signed my pass from the previous day.

To this day that is the only autograph that I have from an artist.
I never ask for autographs, and I never get my picture taken with an artist because I never want them to think for a second that I want anything from them.

Over the next decade I would end up doing over 50 shows with Tony Bennett.

Kansas
Shooters 7-26-94
Thankfully I don't remember anything about this show.
It says in my calendar that I did monitors, and they had an opening act
I'm sure at the time I was still pretty pissed about the last show I did with them.

Hal Ketcham, Donnie Iris
Canton Rib Cook Off 7-27,28-94

I was the monitor mixer for this festival for two days and I don't remember anything about the shows.
What I do remember is that during the loadout the labor had left and it was raining and we had already loaded the sound truck.

My buddy Chris was with the company "Electrostage" that had provided the lighting and the stage for the event.
He was by himself having the land towers trust towers in the rain after the hands had walked and the guy, I was with insisted that we split, and we had to leave him there.
I always thought that sucked for multiple reasons.

There was so much expected of us working roadies around Cleveland. We were worked to death up until the moment they didn't need us and that we were discarded like yesterday's newspaper.
I don't know what time Chris got home that night, but the sun was up.

30 years later he is a leader in the event industry and is the poster child for "You never know who started off getting the job done in the mud".

I always say in this business "you never know who you're talking to" and it's always foolish to assume what somebody else's experience is.

7 rap groups for African Family Day
Luke Easter Park, East Cleveland 7-30-94
This was a show outdoors on a city stage, daytime, supposed to be over before it's dark.
From the audio company it's just me and Mr. Jones.
Not a big PA, it's a 24 ft truck, what we call flat packed.
We had the truck still up to the stage to make it easier for the loadout and I had the monitor rig in the truck.
Audience of several thousand.

At some point a fight broke out in the crowd.
The guys were still on stage rapping and the fight got bigger, and the circle got bigger and now it's not 100 people fighting, now it's like 150 people fighting and it's getting bigger and bigger.
Mr. Jones left the front house, comes to the stage, I'm standing next to two cops, and I asked the cops, "What do you think?".
The cop says to me "I'll tell you what I think, I think we're leaving in 10 minutes".
Mr. Jones and I broke a record of loading a show into a 24ft truck in 9 minutes.

As we were driving away the fight was hundreds of people deep and the cops passed us on the way out of there.

Violent Femmes, Candlebox, L7, Judy Bats, Material Issue, Seed, Cause and Effect, The Clarks, The Gigolo Aunts.
Endfest 94, Geauga Fairgrounds 8-4-94
This was one of those outdoor radio festivals with the side-by-side stages.
One band plays and the other band sound checks and annoys the band that's playing and back and forth it goes.

We weren't very far into the show when a black sky just rolled in. You clearly see the lightning through the black clouds, and it was a hazard having 20,000 plus people out in this open field.
For whatever reason the owner of the lighting company Bob Stegmiller was the stage manager for this event.
Bob was a real combo pack of personality all wrapped up into one Hawaiian shirt with a food stain.
Bob was a bit Java the Hut from Star Wars, Dom DeLuise from Blazing Saddles and Herbert the Pervert from Family Guy.
As the storm is approaching, Bob goes out, stops the band from playing it announces to the crowd, "There is a severe lightning storm approaching everyone needs to seek shelter at the barns at the back of the field".

And just like that 20,000 people started running.
Bob started screeching into the microphone "Stop running", but it was too late the crowd was in full panic mode.
it was unreal from the stage watching that many people run in panic in the same direction.

Typical Ohio style it rained hard for an hour or so, and then it stopped, and the show continued.
Well now we've got something new to contend with and that is lots and lots of mud.
The audience thought it would be funny to start throwing mud at the stage.
I was up on stage when L7 was getting hit with big patches of mud and grass and the band was throwing them back into the crowd.
The stage was 100% mud water and grass.

Bob Stegmiller went out in between one of the L7 songs and tried to appeal to the crowd.
As he's out there saying to the crowd" if you don't stop throwing mud, we will stop the show" and in perfect timing with perfect aim someone hit him right in his big fat belly with a big glob of mud and exploded all over him.
Back and to the left, he stumbled back, fell on his fat ass as everyone was laughing.

At that point the band started laughing, kicked into the next song and the mud fest was on.
The next thing that I remember about that gig of any particular importance was being under the stage after the show was over, during the loadout, the electrical feeder cable was just buried in the mud.
All the heavy cable had sunk.
It completely sucked; I had big concerns about losing a shoe.
The last thing I remember about that show is driving the truck back to the sound shop that night completely wet covered in mud, totally miserable and still laughing about the mud that hit Stegmiller.

Bad Company, Leslie West
Agora Theater 8-6-94

Leslie West had come through the Cleveland Agora Ballroom quite a few times, and him and I were on a first name basis.

(God dammit dog you're gonna kill yourself stop it stop it stop it No more)

When he came in as the opening act for Bad Company I knew what was up, what it was all about.
The main difference this time for this show was that since we were in the theater, I had a much bigger stage monitor system than what we have in the ballroom.
At that time Leslie was playing through a "Zoom" pedal.
It was direct out of the guitar, into the Zoom and out of there into the audio system.
Unlike a microphone in front of a cabinet there was zero chance of feedback there was nothing stopping me from turning it up into Infinity.
and that's exactly what he wanted.
His guitar on stage through all the wedges, and the side fills was so loud it was like walking through water on stage.

The drummer was hitting the cymbals and I couldn't hear them.
At one point the bass player came up to me and asked," Do you think there's any chance I could hear myself tonight?".
With all honesty I looked right at him and gave him my honest assessment, "It's not looking good".

Bad Company was great.

America
Shooters 8-16-94

I loved this show.
The guys were super nice, and it was classic hits all night long.

Overkill, Pro-Pain, Concussion
Agora Theater 8-25-94

This was one of these shows that absolutely felt like audio combat.
The only thing better than a heavy metal hardcore show Is one that hands out mini baseball bats to the audience.
That's exactly what Pro-Pain did.

Had the bands logo stamped right in everyone.
genius marketing really.
And have no doubt, it went exactly how you thought it would.

Nine Inch Nails, Hole
Nautica Stage 8-30-94

Trent Reznor came home to Cleveland with an epic show that we stuffed into the Nautica stage.
It was a full-blown arena show and the production brought all of it in.
I was a stagehand for the gig and I was thrilled not to have any responsibility for a change.

It was the only time at Nautica that we ever brought in so much audio that it was stacked on the ground on the outsides of the stage.
Big piles of carpeted Electrotech fuzzy speaker cabinets.
Back then there was two kinds of sound companies, the kind that painted their cabinets and the kind that vacuumed there's speaker cabinets.
These were the vacuuming kind.
The show looked amazing, sounded amazing and certainly stands out as one of the best shows I ever saw.

Oh yeah, and Hole played.
Legend has it that when Courtney Love flashed her vagina to the audience everyone that looked turned to stone.
I can't confirm this, but I could see it happening.

Blue Oyster Cult, Uriah Heep
Cory Pennsylvania 9-2-94
The thing I remember about this gig is that I was thrilled to do a show with these two bands.
Two bands that I saw in the 70s in their heyday.

The venue was weird, it was like some barn, they had no lights in there and when I mean no lights, I don't mean just concert lighting I mean there was no lights at all no light bulbs hanging no fixtures no fluorescence nothing.
They had some clip lights and some other kind of hillbilly lighting but certainly nothing permanent.

I'm sure there was two things that this promoter was unable to provide, a certificate of occupancy and a liquor license.
I remember that the bands were great there was no issues with the set change and the only thing that was that the guitar tech for Blue Öyster Cult, Chris Fenn was a complete dick.

He fit right in with the band, heavy Brooklyn accent and had the I don't give a fuck attitude.
Just five years later him and I would be working together, and we became great friends.

That loadout sucked so bad, I remember we had to open the loading doors and use the headlights from the truck as our light to load that damn show out.

Green Day, Moist, Beatnik Termites
Blossom Music Center 9-10-94

Growing up in Cleveland I saw a lot of shows at Blossom Music Center, so it was a big deal for me when to go in there and do my first show there.

This was the makeup concert for Green Day after the debacle at the Nautica stage in their show that never happened.
What I remember from that day is that the local crew were total dicks to us and during the show the audience started small fires out on the lawn.
The other development was that the audience was filling these clear plastic cups from their beverages, filling them with dirt and grass and throwing them at the stage.
we had projectiles coming in from all angles, fires burning out there it was crazy.

Of course, Cleveland style I was the only person working on stage from the sound company.
During that loadout I packed everything up from the monitor rig and then I helped the front of house guy land the PA.
Now this guy didn't help me do one thing on stage before during or after the show.
I go get the truck, bring it to the loading dock, we're ready to load the truck.

When I come back to the stage, I walk on stage and the front of house tech has emptied all of the cable trunks that I filled, and he spread the cable all over the floor.
I was so pissed.
"What the Fuck are you doing??" I screamed at him.
He started immediately mumbling about oh I'm just trying to count it in oh I'm just trying to see what we have all I'm just trying to make sure what's here.
I'm yelling at him you idiot this isn't a tour we're all going back to the shop just look around if there isn't any cable on the floor that means we have it.

He had done this to me before and apparently, I was not clear with my displeasure.
I made sure that I humiliated him in front of everybody and he never did that to me ever again.

Joe Cocker
Agora Theater 9-12-94
I will say that being on stage with this guy was a complete thrill for me.
his performance was from the center of the earth.
He was great.

I just don't remember anything else from this show, other that it was a little intimidating.

Plant Merger Announcement
Walton Hills Ford Plant 9-22-94

Northern Ohio was all about industry.
When I was growing up Cleveland was one of the manufacturing capitals of the world.
Steel, tool and die, engines, military parts, you name it we made it.
When NAFTA came online, we started doing events at different factories and the common theme that ran through all of them was," We are shutting this place down and sending your jobs to Mexico".
Most of these gigs we were there over 24 hours because We had to do the same show for all three shifts.
This was still the time when you couldn't bring a Mitsubishi truck onto a union site, it was forbidden.
You could not drive up to an American factory with a foreign vehicle, it's just not how it was done.

We did a bunch of these style of gigs, but I will never forget this one.
The factory that we were at made van panels, the sides for vans.
So, when I say the show starts, I mean we we're doing this show in the factory they clear out a space where they could put a small stage a video screen put some speakers around as many as we can and that's how we do it.
It was challenging because since we're in a factory and it never 100% shuts down the noise floor just idling was loud.
By today's standards the equipment we were using was garbage.
we did the best of what we could with what we had and just at the end of the day always made it happen.

The vice president of the Ford Motor Company approaches the podium, and the entire shift is all sitting out there in their seats.
He says to the group, "I've got one thing to say to you".
and on the screen behind him, in giant black letters, it said two words.
YOU SUCK.
He said it out loud, "you suck".

He went on to explain that the product that came out of this factory was so poor that they had to ship all these panels to an identical factory in Mexico and have all the panels redrilled and then sent back up to the states to Flint or wherever that factory was to part up with the rest of the vehicle it was costing them millions of dollars and because of that they were shutting the place down or cutting it in half or doing something with it that nobody was happy about.

We did a lot of these shows and a lot of different factories, and it was always the same thing watching the employees walk in just kind of talking to each other and just another day at work but after the presentation was over it was always quiet and solemn when these people walked out of the room realizing that they were about to lose their job forever.

Los Lobos
Oberlin College 9-23-94

Almost a year earlier I had done a show with these guys working as a stagehand.

I was sitting by myself in catering having a cup of coffee and a piece of pie when a couple of the members of the band came in and sat down at the table I was at.

At that time the band had two semis of production that they were carrying with them.

They were talking about the tour, talking about how long it had been going on and talking about how they wished they had more money to go home with when this thing was all over.

Not trying to eavesdrop into their conversation, but I was just sitting there, and I said to the two of them "At the end of a tour you have a choice of either having a memory of all your production or a new condo in Florida".

They both paused for a second then the one guy asked me what I meant.

I said "you're carrying two semis of production for what? you guys aren't some big elaborate show, you're just a bunch of musicians jamming. Next time you go out don't rent all this crap, use the local production and with the money you save you could each buy a condo at the end of the run".

At that point they had to go get ready for the show and I had to go outside and get high, we all had things to do.

Now here it is, a year later and Los Lobos is using local production. I don't know for a fact that I was responsible for that, But I'd like to think that I started that fire.

State of the Division Meeting
GM Lordstown 10-5,6-94

This is a GM factory that's off the Ohio Turnpike and you drive by it for several minutes at 65 miles an hour.
The factory is so massive it would be almost impossible to walk through it.
At one end of the factory a roll of steel is dropped off and at the other end it spits out a car.
Many automobile factories have the chassis delivered, have the engines delivered have big piece of it put together at Lordstown they build the entire damn thing.
I could be wrong, but my understanding was that the only thing they delivered was the windshields and the tires.

It was impressive from the one side where all The Dirty Work is really happening with the heavy rolls of steel to this one amazing part of the factory where the chassis with the engine and the tires rolling come out of the basement and meets the conveyor line where the body meets and that's where it becomes the car and they've bolted altogether it's really something to see.

Much more impressive than watching 3 shifts of employees learn that they're losing their jobs.

Drew Carey, Ellen Cleghorn
Kent State University 10-8-94

This is another one of those scenarios where it was a one-man operation.

I drove the truck, had some local crew of dippy college kids and I was going to mix the show consisting of three comedians.

The venue is the gymnasium of the college, and anybody that knows anything or once in their life bounced a basketball inside of a gymnasium comprehends that there is a lot of reverberation, because there is a lot of hard surfaces.

A gym is a great place to do gym stuff and a horrible place to do show stuff.

Why they didn't do this in some theater I have no idea, we did it in the gym.

As I say, I don't order the pizza I deliver the pizza.

So, I get everything all set up all tested and the microphone is clearly intelligible throughout the listening environment and that is the objective.

We get the first comedian up there who I don't remember, what their name was, and I don't remember anything about them outside the fact that there was no big deal.

Then we get Ellen Cleghorn from Saturday Night Live up on the stage.

She comes out, says a couple things to the audience and then starts talking about the echo.

She keeps saying "You know I'm from New York and we have professionals in New York, and I'm not used to this kind of thing because in New York we have real professionals that know how to get rid of echo and I know that that there are no professionals here and that's why there are echoes because we don't have that New York".

She's just rambling on about this echo which the first comedian didn't bring up, didn't say a word about it because you know, we're in a gym.

She keeps going off on this, she's not doing her act, she's not saying anything funny, and the audience is just sitting there.
Finally, I had enough of being berated by her that I wasn't an expert like the people in New York.

I had my own microphone at the mixing console with me that I used to test the PA with earlier and I picked it up, turned it up and said for the entire audience to hear, "HEY LADY, YOUR IN A GYM".

The entire audience busted out laughing.
She left the stage.
I put on some music and go backstage to see what's going on.
At this point this was before Drew Carey had his TV show, he was an up-and-coming comedian and I think he was on HBO or something like that, but he was popular before he really exploded.
 I see the promoter Rep and they tell me that Drew Carey and his manager want to see me in the dressing room.
Immediately I think Oh my God, I'm in trouble.

I knock on the door; the door opens and its Drew Carry and he's laughing his ass off.
I go in there and it's him and his tour manager and they can't stop laughing over what I said to her.
It was a great feeling going from Oh my God I'm in trouble too how awesome it is that I made these guys laugh.
Next thing I knew we were all smoking a joint together and still laughing about me cracking on Ellen Cleghorn.
After the joint was over it was time for the show and went back out front of house and I remember thinking that I might have been a little too high.

The backstage announcement, ladies and gentlemen will you please welcome and Drew Carey comes out and he's already laughing.
He was so high he was laughing before telling each joke. Busting himself up it made it the whole thing that much funnier.

At the end of the day Drew Carey is a funny guy, he's a nice guy and he gets great weed.

Entombed, Sodimized
Agora Theater 9-25-94
Thankfully, I remember nothing from this show.

The Smithereens, Iodine
Agora Ballroom 10-16-94
The lead singer from The Smithereens put so much spit into the microphone that I'd had to change it out four times during their set. I remember after the show having the sensation that I really felt I should throw those mics out.

311, Sons of Elvis
Agora Theater 10-19-94
For this show I was the monitor mixer for 311 and I mixed front of house for a new group called the Sons of Elvis.
The Sons of Elvis were one of the most exciting and explosive bands that I ever seen, and they were a lot of fun to mix they were a lot of fun to be around, and I would eventually become their tour manager and spend quite a bit of time with these guys.

State of the Division Meetings
GM Lansing Michigan 10-25,26,27,28-94

This was challenging because we did it in two locations right after the other.

The first was in this giant factory and the speakers we had were junk and we had to fly them very high in the air much there were so far away from the audience that every noise in the factory was louder than the speakers could ever get.

We needed digital delays to properly time align all the speakers but the company didn't own any so we used Yamaha SPX 90's, And it was difficult but we've made it work.

Second series of presentations for the 3 shifts was in the building where they did all the designing of the cars.

In a time before the key card swipe, we were left to wander the building in the middle of the night after we had set up.

We saw Toyotas up on lifts that were being taken apart, different German cars in different conditions of being stripped and reverse engineered.

The coolest thing we saw was the 1999 Corvette, this was 1994 so seeing the future stuff was cool for us.

Sitting through so many automobile factory meetings I learned quite a bit about the manufacturing process and about the thought process of upper management and has they saw things.

Up until the early 80s American automobile companies would retool the factory once a year for the next year's model car and they had to be shut down X amount of time to accommodate that.

That was up until some bean counter figured out that if you don't change the shape of the car every year, you don't have to shut the factory down ever, and you can keep making the same car that nobody wants and that's exactly what happened.

It's easy to look at automobiles from the 80s that were made in America and clearly see that instead of changing the body style every year they now going to do it every three years and the only thing that would change annually with the nonsense things like the trim.

It was another classic example of upper management trying to save money by cheapening their product and blaming the cost overruns on the working man who made it.

Bone Thugs & Harmony, Menajatwa, Low Nappy Fros
Agora Theater 10-30-94
Bone Thugs and Harmony were from the east side of Cleveland, just had a hit and were making it big.
At that time at the Cleveland Agora we were having a lot of hardcore gangster rap groups come through and we had lots of problems. Before this show we had a Snoop show where my buddy Jon Conde was doing monitors and he did the whole show with a loaded 357 magnum sitting on the console.
That's how crazy it was getting back then.

We had an act come through called" Scarface" With probably 100 people on stage and everything got out of hand and the artist announced to the crowd "Whitey is coming down here and we make a stand".

The entire bar staff locked themselves into a walk-in cooler and me and the stagehands went up into the grid as the audience and artist destroyed the place.

So now here we are with this show and the one thing that we all agree on is that nobody wants to be there.

The headliner was on Ruthless Records so there were some other acts traveling with them that were also on the same label.
One of the guys that was just hanging with the tour was a West Coast rapper named Easy E.
He had come through a few times before and me and him kind of hit it off and we would smoke weed together.

You know how it is with rap groups, nobody sound checks, they just show up and go which is fine by me.

The first group up were called low nappy fros, and they were a local group.
when I asked the guy why he named his group that he said to me" You will always remember it" and he was right.
But I don't remember them so let's move on.

We do a couple more groups I think I have it written down that there were seven in total.
think about a crowd at a gangster rap show is that everyone is trying to out tough the next guy.
it's an audience full of testosterone and FU attitude.

We get to the point where we only have one more group before the headliner.
I'm at the monitor console and I'm passing a joint with Eazy E and here comes our next act.
it's a group called "Menajatwa" and they are straight out of Compton direct to Cleveland.
These two women that made-up the rap group were dressed in black leather dark sunglasses and they each had a giant muscle dude who was almost naked on a chain leash and they both had collars.

Easy E informed me that we were about to see some "Hardcore Shit" and he was right.
The women went out on stage and somebody from the audience said something to one of them and I don't I didn't hear what the guy said to her, but I heard what she said to him.
She picked up the mic and said, "Shut the fuck up you little dick motherfucker" And the other one said "I'm gonna get my man to bust your cheeks".
I didn't know what that meant, and Easy E explained it to me.

For the next 30 minutes those two women ripped into every man in the room.
It got uncomfortable in there.

They had a song called "Give the ass to no one' about being in prison.
My favorite lyrics from the show was when the chick bent down, looked into the crowd and said, "Life is too short, and so is your dick, there wont be any fucking, so nigga just lick".

Words to live by.
After the set they gave me a copy of their CD which I still have to this day.

And you better believe that whenever I had the opportunity when anybody ever asked me at a show" Do you have any rap music?" you know what I was playing... some Menajatwa.

De La Soul
Oberlin Ohio 11-5-94
What I remember about this show is that it was some night club near Oberlin College.
My buddy Blaine was with me, and we both remember a different third person being with us.
But what we all agree on is that at some point a riot broke out and the police tear gassed the whole club, we had to go out and wait in the truck for some time while the tear gas filled out.

Olga Tanon
Aragon Ballroom 11-18-94
I knew this show was a bad idea, I didn't want to take it but I needed the money.
Some Latin show at a venue I had never been to before that was partially out of business and from the moment, we got there it had the vibe that the liquor license and certificate of occupancy might have been in question.
The show was completely oversold, and it was just a sea of humanity in there with no room to move.
When it was all over, we discovered that all our road cases have been flipped upside down and used as a garbage cans.
With every case filled with broken beer bottles it was a rough loadout.

Nine Inch Nails
Odeon 12-15-94

This band was in the middle of an arena tour and needed to work in a new drummer.
They chose this venue to do a hometown show and get one gig in under their belt before they went back on the arena tour.
I was the house sound guy, and the band's lighting director was ordering lights from the local company right up till doors.

It was the most lights I've ever seen in a nightclub, literally blinding. During the show the guy who owned the audio system was standing next to me in the sound booth with a tear coming down his cheek as the Nine Inch Nails sound mixer was tearing every component in the rig.
I will never forget the data flash strobe lights from Mr. from the song "Mr. Self Destruct", It was nothing short of epic.

As interesting as that was that was not the biggest drama of the gig. As you can imagine, it was impossible to get a ticket for this show.

There was a line outside all the way down the block to get in and people were milling about people were across the street and there were people that were trying to buy tickets.

That year there was one woman that was at almost every show trying to get backstage to meet the band.
She was a brunette, that wore the same denim jacket, black thigh high leather boots and we gave her the nickname "Bootsy".
I could not count how many times that year I saw Bootsy go on and off a random tour bus.

One of the stagehands offered Bootsy a backstage pass if she would go to his car and have sex with him.
Since his car was parked right across the street from the club and there were hundreds of people all over the street, it wasn't very discreet what was going on here.

After they were "done", when she got out of the car the entire line of people waiting to get into the club all started cheering.
I was smoking a joint with two other guys when this went down, and I remember thinking that the whole thing wasn't as funny as it was kind of shitty.
I have never traded a backstage pass for any sexual anything, I always felt that it just wasn't sexy.
Well, it turns out that this woman was humiliated and was not happy about this at all.
It also turns out that she wasn't a woman, she was a girl, and that's a big difference.
After the show with her backstage pass in hand she met Trent Reznor.
And the first thing she did was tell him what she had to do to get that pass, how she was humiliated, and she will never get over it for as long as she lives.

And that was the night that he banned everyone in his crew from getting backstage passes.

Really none of it was fair.
I don't know what's worse, the women that volunteered to do anything to have sex with a celebrity or the guy that takes advantage of her to help her facilitate what she's trying to get.

At that point is he taking advantage of her or are they just bartering? Each wants a different commodity, and each has set a price.

Sons of Elvis
National Tour, January to June 1995, 52 shows

I first met these guys when they were a support act for 311 at the Cleveland Agora.
They had just been signed to Priority Records and they had one video on rotation on MTV for their song "Formaldehyde".
John Borland on Vocals, Tim Parnin on guitar, Dave Hill on bass and Pat Casa on Drums, The Sons of Elvis.
Hands down one of the most exciting live bands that I had ever seen or worked with in my life.
These guys were explosive on stage.
Their material was great, and it was 100 percent 1995, it fit in with everything that was going on, yet they were still distinct and unique.

I'm hired in to be their tour manager in front of house mixer.
I bring in my buddy Mark Hall to be the back line guy for the band and we're ready to go.
Our first show together is in Tempe AZ at a place called the Electric Ballroom.
We're there opening for a band that just came over from the UK, and they were called Bush.
I want to say this is right about when their hit was breaking.
We had partied with the guys the night before at the hotel and we confirmed the reason for naming the band Bush.
Should have been Burning Bush.

The next day we do this show.
No doubt about it, I deliberately mixed the band loud.
They were so exciting on stage that I didn't want anybody in the building to be able to ignore what was happening up there.
Another thing I did with this group, was I made the lighting plot "all white, all on".
My attitude was that if you are a patron of the same venue and you go back again and again seeing different acts, sure you're seeing different bands but you're seeing the same lights the same light show.
All white all on, something that nobody had ever seen before.
It was stunning and it looked great.

The best part was all the lighting guys pouting like adolescents every gig because I made them do that.
If they had flashing moving lights would let him use it for the last song.

And one of the things I was not ready for at this first gig with these guys, Is the last song of the set, the bass player stepped on this distortion boost pedal.
Instantly it blew all the subs in the sound system.
Now Bush had to play without Subs.
Their sound guy who was pissed, and I don't blame him.
And that was not the last time we were scheduled to open for Bush, yet it was the last time we ever opened for Bush.

After we got back east the band bought a big pimping conversion van with thick red shag carpet and a trailer to put the gear in.
That's how we rolled.
We crisscrossed the country performing at clubs and festivals.

Typical day was getting to the new city from the last one, getting the rooms checked in, go to the club load in sound check then go to a radio station or an in-store record appearance then back to the club to do the show.

Touring with these guys was like living inside of the movie "A hard day's night".
They were funny, they were completely uninhibited, and they were unpredictable.
It was a total kindergarten field trip.
We get down to a club called "Jimmy's" in New Orleans.
The previous show was in Birmingham, so we got to New Orleans a day early which in retrospect was a mistake on my part.
Those four guys loose in New Orleans was worst case scenario for me.
First night there I got a call in my hotel room at 3:00 o'clock in the morning that the singer had thrown up in a cab and got into a fight out in front of my favorite bar in the quarter, Lafitte's.

Now I'm out of bed and down in the French Quarter with some cash to solve some problems.

The next night after the show the local promoter and some people from the radio station took us out to dinner.
We were in some restaurant right on Saint Charles that was all glass on the corner.
We're at a big round table, because there's probably 15 of us and my back is to the windows.
As I'm looking at the menu, I noticed that there are people in the restaurant that are laughing and looking my way.
That's when I noticed, oh my God Dave is missing.
I turn around and there is Dave our base player 100% naked with his genitals and belly shmushed up against the window behind me.
I was horrified.
I immediately stand-up, blocking him from the eyes behind me, mouthing everything in the world to him to please stop doing that and put on his clothes.
After turning around and heading out the restaurant to stop him Tim the guitar player has never removed all of his clothes inside the restaurant, and I had to drag those two naked guys out of there.

Our next show was the 616 Club in Memphis TN.
We had gotten there a day early because I was in a big hurry to get those guys out of New Orleans as fast as possible.
With a day off in Memphis with a band called the Sons of Elvis there was only one field trip destination that the guys were interested in and that was Graceland.

I take the guys to Graceland, and we take the tour.
if you have never been it's weird that by today's standards the house really isn't very big at all it's just like a standard house with a super cool jungle room.

We get through the whole tour without incident and when we finally make it to Elvis's grave Pat the drummer steps over that little security chain and he literally threw himself on Elvis Presley's grave.

Yes, we were escorted out by security, and we're asked to never come back.

We were on our way to a gig at Club Dewalsh in Madison WI. Somewhere on the way in in the middle of dairy land nowhere we pulled over to get gas.
We always did a head count before we pulled away because you never wanted to leave anybody behind. The drummer was still in the convenient Mart and we thought it would be funny if we pulled around back and let him believe that we left him
just like a bunch of kids snickering we're back there sitting in the van laughing a few minutes goes by OK that's enough and we drive around front.
He's not there.
I was the only one with a cell phone, because in 1995 a cell phone was $0.60 a minute and I had the Motorola Gray flip.
Now we're all panicked, what happened to Pat?
It was February, cold outside and pat left the van only wearing a thin denim jacket.
Finally, we drive back to the highway and there he is walking up the Interstate with his hands in his pockets.

We played Chicago then went to Pontiac MI where we opened for an act called" Kid Rock".
During the show there was something going on in the mosh pit between the crowd and our lead singer John.
I couldn't see from my vantage point but before the last song was over, I left the front of house mixing console to the tech and went up to the stage.
Turns out that the guy in the crowd was starting a fight with John with all his buddies and the thing was getting ugly fast.
We got out of there in a big hurry.

Next stop was opening for KMFDM in Grand Rapids MI at the Reptile House.
The crowd for this show was out of hand and the energy in the room was electric.

Since the budget was tight, I opened an account with Red Roof Inns. In most places we stayed at a Red Roof Inn, always close to the highway and convenient in and out that's all I care about, and on budget.
It had come to my attention, that Dave the bass player felt that Red Roof was missing a key component, a mascot.
I get a knock on my door one night at about 10:00 PM, I opened the door and it's Dave.
Dave has an ice bucket on his head with his skull cap over it.
He introduces himself to me as "Roofie, the Red Roof Mascot. Would you like some complimentary water?".
He then unzipped his pants; he had a water bottle shoved down his pants.
Unscrewing the cap, he squeezed the water thru the zipper into a small plastic cup, yes you are imagining this correctly, just like he was peeing in a cup.
After he handed me my "complimentary water" I had the realization that in mind was not the first room he came to, it was the last.
He had already visited every room and offered every occupant some complimentary water from his zipper.
Just then, the phone in my room rang, it was the front desk.
Guess what it was concerning?

Since we were tight on rooms, I put two band members in a room. It was always amusing when I would check in before the guys showed up, I would go into one room and turn the AC all the way up. I would go into the other room and turn the heat all the way up. I let those rooms sit there for the next 6-7 hours while we do the show, about the time we got back to the rooms it was always the furnace and the ice box.
It was always funny.

Three months on the road, the guys came back to sell out a hometown gig at the Odeon, the place was packed, and the band was on fire.

After the show in Cleveland, we played Kent and then went to Nashville.

Down in Nashville our backline guy Mark Hall bought a pair of "Hee Haw" overalls and would wear them every show for the rest of the tour.
After Nashville it was back to The Nick in Birmingham and then back to New Orleans.
This time back in New Orleans we were playing the big club in town, headlining Tipitinas.
This was the premier Roadhouse in town, and we had a great turnout.
Thankfully I don't remember anything crazy happening this time around.

Our next show was in Tampa at a punk rock club called the Stone Lounge.
It was hands down one of the saddest clubs I've ever been to, and I've been to a club that had a hitching post for your horse.
the lighting for the stage was a single bulb hanging from a wire like you would see in some black and white prison movie.
The only thing worse than the lighting was the audio system.

It was a home stereo system with some crappy mixer, I was horrified. Shockingly the place was filled with people
and the band played great like they always did.

I had several hobbies to entertain myself when I was on the road. One of those hobbies was every night that we went out for dinner, I would tell the waiter or waitress that it was one of the guy's birthdays so they would come out and sing the song and bring the cake and make a big deal out of it, it was funny every time.

One of the arguments I kept having with the record company was that I needed road cases for the band's gear.
I was spending more money replacing stuff than it would have cost to put it in proper cases, but they wouldn't allocate the funds.
We had ordered cases before the tour and the record company said they were handling it.
They had no problem paying to replace something but didn't see the urgency in spending money to protect what we already had.

So, you can imagine how irritated I was when the record company flew themselves out to our show in Atlanta, just to take us out to dinner.

Nobody else could see the irony that here I am begging for money to protect your artist stuff and instead you blow thousands flying yourself out here for nothing.

After the show, I don't remember why we didn't have the van now, but the record company people wanted to take us out for dinner and there wasn't enough room in the three cars for all of us.

Dave the bass player says, "I'll ride in the trunk".

All these LA types don't know what to say, they're shocked and finally they give in, and he gets in the trunk.

We pull into the parking lot of some fancy Mexican restaurant admission #1 is to get Dave out of the trunk.

The woman from the label opens the trunk and there is Dave completely naked.

As usual, he has removed all his clothes.

We get his clothes back on him and go into the restaurant.

Inside the restaurant you know the first thing I do; I tell the waiter that it's Dave's birthday tonight and make it real special.

The big moment comes when the entire staff bring in a cake full of sparklers, and they're all singing Happy Birthday for Dave.

The best part was the giant sombrero on his head.

Dave proudly stood up, raised his glass, and in perfect Spanish announced to the room, "Me follo a mi madre!" and repeated it several times.

The Spanish staff started busted out laughing.

All the record company people had these stupid smirks on their faces, and they were all clapping.

Apparently, none of them spoke Spanish, and none of them were aware that what he was really saying was "I fuck my mother".

One of the women from the record company sitting next to me leaned over and said to me "I didn't even know it was his birthday I'm going to have to make a note."

After playing a bunch of gigs in the South, on our way back North we stopped to do a gig in Washington DC.
Our hotel was in Chinatown and when we got there, I backed the van up against the building so the rear doors of the trailer was up against the building, inaccessible.
By the time I had gone in and checked everybody in and come back to the van, it had been broken into.
Now I've got a broken window, some crap missing from the inside and I send Mark Hall to get the window fixed wile I take the band to some interview thing.

The story that Mark Hall told, was that when he pulled up to the auto glass repair place, there was no place to pull over with the van and the trailer.
He says some guy walks out and tells him "I'll pull this around back for you" and Mark Hall gets out of the van and this guy gets in the driver's seat.
The van goes around the block comes back to where Mark Hall was still standing, and the guy gets out of the van and he's got an arm full of VHS tapes and some other stuff.
Mark Hall says, "Hey man what are you doing?"
And the guy calmly replied, "Oh I don't work here I'm robbing you".
That night after the show we came outside to find out that somebody had put a brick through one of the windows and scraped out the rest of the valuables.
I always hated playing DC.

We're heading out to a club in Long Island New York.
The gig was super inconvenient for us because the previous gig was in Port Chester NY and the next gig was at Club Babyhead in Providence RI.
We had some radio station thing to do in the afternoon and then to the club.
When I advanced the show and asked the sound company what kind of audio system would be in the room, the response they gave me was that it would be "8 EAW KFC 850s", 4 per side.

For that size capacity I thought that would be fine I said no problem. After the radio station interview, it went a little long because there was a fire in the building.
Thankfully none of my guys started that fire.

We show up at this venue and the stage is on one side of the room and on the other side of the room is a dance floor that has 8 EAW KF 850s, but they are all pointed at the dance floor hung in clusters of two.

I was completely fucking pissed.
This was 100% bullshit.

What was going on here, was that they had a dance night that was going to happen after we played and the club thought that they would double dip, and since the promoter was paying for "a sound system" they had the sound company come in and install it for their dance night leaving my band with nothing pointed at their audience. It was ridiculous.

I tried to cancel the show, I tried to get a new system in, there was no time for anything we just had to go and go through with it.
What irritated me the most through the whole thing was this smug bully attitude that these guys had the entire time we were there.
I told the guy from the sound company "since the PA isn't pointed at the audience, I would hate to blow something up because I can't hear it".
He said to me, "you can't blow anything up I've got limiters on everything" and he gave me the finger.

5 minutes before the show started, I reached over and hit the bypass switch on all the limiters.

The show starts and it's everything I thought it would be, it sounds horrible because nothing is pointed at the audience and the sound is just bouncing off the dance floor with nobody on it.
The last song comes, Dave hits that distortion bass pedal and the entire PA exploded.
I knew this was coming and I had Raul start packing the show before it was over.
We set the world record for loading that van in minutes, those guys were up on the ladders trying to figure out what was wrong with all the speakers, and when they peeled the grills back it was nothing but paper.
All the speakers exploded.
I never did find out how dance night went.

We were at the Mercury Lounge in NYC.
My father lived in the neighborhood and came out to the show.
After the show my father and I, a couple guys from the band we're standing on the sidewalk on Houston St. right in front of the club, it was about 3:00 AM.
We were all just standing there talking and there was a huge explosion on the street behind us.
A Lincoln town car had T boned a garbage truck that was making a turn.
The engine from the Lincoln was in the front seat of the car.
The car from the steering wheel forward was gone.
It was gruesome.
I walked over to the garbage truck, and you couldn't even tell anything happened to it except for the glass that was in the tire well.

Six years later a garbage truck would hit me on that very same street and spun me through the intersection.
I couldn't tell if there was any damage to the garbage truck because it never stopped.

Just a week later we would return to New York City and headline Irving Plaza much bigger venue.
The place was packed, and the guys put on a fantastic show.

After that we went to Philadelphia then did a show at the Odeon, Cleveland again and then it was back to New York City for the Jon Stewart show.

One of the features of the band's live performance was that at the end of the last song the drummer pat would always kick over the drum kit and knock everything down.
I paid for allot of microphones and broken mic stands on that tour I always gave the audio people a heads up on what was going to go down.

To try to alleviate some of the damage to the microphones, I would always ask that they leave a little coil of cable at each mic position on the drum kit in case they had to travel.
The guys would always say to me" what do you mean travel?".
Fair question.
Usually the drum mics don't travel, but with the Sons of Elvis, we made an exception.
John the singer was also very hard on mic stands and I knew he was gonna break at least one per night.

When we went into the Jon Stewart show I just couldn't guarantee that these guys weren't going to trash the place with the show was over.
I remember asking the television a twos who are responsible for making the drug the stage, "Hey guys could you leave me a little coil at the bottom of each mic?" and they thought it was a very bizarre request.

Another idiosyncrasy that they couldn't wrap their heads around, is they didn't understand why we couldn't use a rental drum kit.
Pat's drum kit was covered in fur and on his drumhead was a picture of Barry White.
They had named their album "Glodean" After Barry White's wife.
Nothing about these guys was average.

Since this was a fly date, we capitulated and used the rental drum kits and thank God, the guys didn't wreck the place.

Our next gig after this was back in Ohio at Kent State University, Then Toledo, Cincinnati and then we headlined a festival at John Carroll university called "Carrolpalooza".
One of my functions is tour manager was dealing with the merchandise.
Every show I would have the venue provide someone to sell T-shirts for and it was a matter of counting in counting back out and the difference was self-evident.
Every venue gets a cut some more than others, it's just how it is.
One of the irritants that I was having at some of these festivals, is that they would print a T-shirt with all the band's names on it, including the Sons of Elvis.

My question was "Who authorized you to use the band's name printed on something that you're selling for a profit?"
I asked, "Are you steering people to buy this shirt when they come to the booth to buy one of the shirts from my band because the name is on it"?
The band's attorneys were crystal clear on the matter, that nobody had the right to use the band's name to sell merchandise without permission.

Another thing about this gig is that it was only two miles from my house, and it happened to be "Bring your daughter to work day".
I have my 10-year-old daughter with me and when I walk in the venue the first thing, I see it's a booth set up that has a T-shirt for sale and at the top of the T-shirt is "The Sons of Elvis".
I got the person in charge and ask them my favorite question, "Who exactly gave you permission to put this band's name on a T-shirt and sell it for a profit?".

Not only did I stop them from selling those shirts, but I also made everybody that was wearing them take them off.
I admit I was a total dick about it.
We had played other festivals that had used the band's name with permission from management and we got a cut of the sale.
This time I just wasn't having it.

My daughter got to mix some of the show, and we got to hang out and that was what was important.
For a 10-year-old hanging out with dad at the show, she had a good time.

Exactly one year later my buddy Pete called me up and asked me if I would come do a show with him at John Carroll university.
I said sure I'll meet you there.
It turns out, it's Carrolpalooza time again.
So, we load this thing in and after we get all set up, I asked him, "how did you get the gig?".
He says to me, "The college said that some guy came through here last year with one of the headliners, and was such a jerk to everybody, that they vowed never again to deal with the artist and hired us to come in and take care of everything".

I looked right at Pete and said, "You're welcome".

We had been playing festivals throughout the South and now we were at Athens fairgrounds in Athens GA.
Ever it was a tough gig to advance because I couldn't get any straight answers out of the promoter.
A real red flag for me.

The only thing that got sorted out was the hotels were prepaid by the promoter.
When we show up at the gig my first question to the promoter, "When do we get paid?".
I remember not liking his answer.
The situation was clear to me, this guy was in over his head, there was not enough people there to cover the cost of this whole thing and he was in trouble and giving me the runaround.
He was a total hippie type and all the people working for him were also hippies.
At the time I had a crew cut and the last thing in the world I looked like was a hippie.

This guy thought he could just keep stalling me until it was time for us to go on.
I saw the Sheriff's Department standing by the front gates and I approached them.

I introduced myself to the sheriff and I showed him a copy of the contract that we had, and I said to him "That guy contracted us to be here, payment due on arrival, and here we are and he's refusing to pay us".

There must have been some words between them before I got there, because immediately this guy was on my side.
The sheriff, several deputies and I walked up to the box office and the sheriff demanded that they pay me.
They didn't have enough money to pay what they owed us, so the sheriff made them give us everything they had.
I cleaned out every dollar out of the box office, even took the change.
I thanked the sheriff, and I went back to the stage.

I wasn't the only tour manager there that was walking around with a concerned look on my face, I was just the only one that did anything about it.
I knew this thing was going to get uglier the moment everybody else realized that I had confiscated all the money.

By the time I got back to the stage it started raining and I told Raul let's pack it up and we split without the band ever playing.
Knowing full well that we would never see the rest of that money, I told everybody to rent as many movies as possible your hotel room.

After six months on the road, every time we came to New Orleans, we played a bigger venue.
This time we were playing the biggest of them all there the annual "Zephyr Fest".
12 bands performing outside in the hot sun for 20,000 plus people and the scheduled headliner that night was Bush.

Because of the incident in Arizona six months earlier, they refused to go on after us, so they switched the bill and the Sons of Elvis ended up headlining.

After six months on the road and over 50 live shows under their belt, they were ready to headline.
the band came out and opened with their song "Reggie makes the scene".
The crowd went wild.
I had watched the reactions of the crowd of the other bands that day, and it was wild watching 20,000 plus people jumping up and down with the beat.
These guys were no longer the kids that I put in the van six months ago, now they were a seasoned touring rock band and it showed.

Six days later we would play at the Akron rib cook off and that was my last show with the guys.
The record company foolishly refused to release their second video and the budget for the second record disappeared.

The problem with the band's label, Priority Records is that they were predominantly a rap label.
They had an attitude that the band should be successful because of word of mouth, you know just like with rap.
Almost every single time that we showed up at a club, the promotional posters for the band would arrive the same day.
I kept asking the record people, "How is anybody seeing these advertisements if they're showing up day of show?".
Another example of a great band being driven into the ground by mediocre management that felt that the best use of their money was flying themselves around to have dinners and pat themselves on the back.

The band's manager dropped the ball and one of the greatest bands of the 90s were sidelined just when they were getting started.
I was honestly disgusted with how I saw the record company waste money on nonsense instead of putting it where it was needed.

As with everything, it's all about the budget.
These guys should have been one of the biggest bands of the 90's, not just a footnote.

As the saying goes, "Mercenary Roadies, once the money is gone so are we", and Raul and I went on to our next gigs.

Watch the performance at the Jon Stewart show on YouTube.
These guys were as good as they get.

Ned's Atomic Dustbin, Orange 9MM
Phantasy Theater 5-10-95
I was home in between shows with the Sons of Elvis and I got asked to come down and do monitors for the show.
Nothing was out of the ordinary it was some band from the UK here doing their thing and I don't really remember much about either the acts, but I remember the front of house mixer for Ned's Atomic Dustbin.

The guy mixing them, Simon, looked more like a rock star than anybody in the band.
What made him stand out to me was that he was very friendly very knowledgeable had a long ponytail and he kept jumping up and down off the stage instead of using the stairs.

Almost 20 years later I get the epiphany that my buddy that I've been working with in New York City for years was that same young guy from that night at the Phantasy Theater.
It's not till a bunch of us are sitting around in catering and talking about old shows, that's when we make these connections.

Stanley Clark, Al Damilola, Jean Luc Ponte
Nautica Stage, I didn't write down the date
I must have been the front of house tech for this because I wasn't on stage, and I wasn't mixing.
If there is one thing that a mixer hates, it's being told how to mix.

That's why they're there, somebody hired them because they felt this was the best option, having this person mix the show and yet somehow people that are not hired to mix shows feel that they should weigh in with their unprofessional opinions.
Usually it's the manager, some tone-deaf record executive who's trying to impress the girl from the strip club that he brought with him.
For this show it was worse than all of that.
The front of house mixer had all three wives from each principal player out at the front of the house console telling him what to do.

It was brutal.
Unable to watch this man get berated by these three women, I did the only thing I could do.
I went to catering and had some burnt coffee.

Helmet, Prick, Catherine Wheel, Girls vrs Boys, Verve, Soul Coughing.
Nautica stage 7-29-95
I was there for two reasons, babysit the PA and mix Helmet.
The last time I mixed this band was across the river in a 500-seat nightclub, tonight was going to have a little more energy.

After spending the last six months mixing a heavy band in multiple outdoor festival settings, this was just like going through the motions for me.

The band was great, the crowd had a great time, and I didn't have to make anybody put their clothes back on.

Thrill Kill Cult, Lords of Acid
The Metro, Pittsburg Pennsylvania 7-30-95
This show was out of control.
The entire audience was freaks, not one normal looking person in the entire crowd.
And all I got to say is thank God for that, because I hooked up with these two wild women and we did the everything behind the PA stack during the show.

I remember the loadout being rough, not because I was low on bodily fluids but because whatever was in that pipe being passing around was a little bit more than reefer.
That is truly thrill kill cult roulette

Engelbart Humperdinck
IC Light Amphitheater, Pittsburg Pennsylvania 7-25-95

This was my second and final time to this venue, I don't remember what the first one was, apparently, I didn't write it down.
But what I do remember about the first time I was there was that they weren't hanging the lights from the roof, they were building a ground support trust system.

During the afternoon before sound check, there was a guy up in the trust focusing the lights and a gust of wind came down and the entire structure fell forward onto the stage and this guy's collarbone popped right out of his skin.
It was gruesome.

Imagine my surprise to come back to this venue and see that same guy Working on stage.
This man was clearly permanently injured but I know damn well he was lucky if they gave him a ride to the hospital.

The one thing that Cleveland and Pittsburgh both had in common was the treatment of the non-union stagehands.

This venue was what we call a "Mountain Stage" and it looked like an erector set that wasn't complete.
Another special feature of the venue was that it was alongside the river.
And subsequently along the railroad tracks.
The venue didn't have a roof over the main audience and there was a tent area in the back.
We finally get to showtime, and Engelbart walks out on stage and the first thing he says to the audience was "Look what they've done with this place, nothing!".

He spent the first 10 minutes of the show ripping on the venue.
He was saying "Who booked me in this dump?" and during the show he was continually apologizing to the audience that they had to come to a parking lot like this to see him perform.

This was all happening of course before he realized that there were train tracks by the stage.
The first train that came through, he stopped the show and said "You gotta be kidding me" and he sat down on the drum riser with his legs crossed and waited for the train to leave before continuing the song.

Next interruption happened when the Pittsburgh Pirates hit a home run.
From across the river, fireworks started going off and again he sat down on the drum riser, stopping the show.

This went on the entire time he did his set, and it ended a little early.
I was just doing my thing and taking down the PA and putting it in the truck so I can get out of here.
I had all the stagehands because the promoter was super pissed that they had been trashed all night by the artist.

Right before I got in the truck to drive back to Cleveland, I was stopped by the tour manager from the group who asked me if I had gotten paid because they were not getting paid.
I don't remember what I said to him, but I don't think it was very encouraging.

Worst Show Ever
BumFuck Ohio August 1995

I always remembered my boss Bob Bock telling us about his adventures in China when he was the tour manager for Richard Marx.

They were at some gig, some monsoon weather came in destroyed the site and Bob ended up with a gun in his mouth with a local gangster yelling "We want concert!".

The irony that he would send me into that exact same situation.

Bob had taken cash money from a motorcycle club that was throwing a party for themselves on some farm out the middle of nowhere.

Immediately I thought this was a bad idea.

He wanted me and John Conde to take a truck full of audio gear out to their party and then take that truck straight to the Rocking Reggae show that was happening Sunday morning.

John and I were both Harley riders, and we both grew up around Ohio bikers and him and I had zero misunderstandings of what this thing was going to be.

Not professional and not cool.

When I protested about doing this show Bob said to me" You're just a big pussy".

So, with my new job title of Big Pussy, John and I split and went out to go do that show.

We drove through cornfield Ohio for quite some time before finding the turnoff road that took us to the back of the field.

They had taken two 40-foot flatbed trailers and parked them together for the stage and they were assembling a boat tarp with pieces of two by fours for the roof system.

The trailers weren't even that close together and there was a bit of a gap in the middle of the stage.

The bikers were dicks from the moment we got there.

There was a lot of attitudes coming off them and they kept talking about how much the cost and there's too much money and they're paying this and they're paying that, and I'm just trying to unload this truck and set up this thing for their show.

They had set the stage area up on the low corner of the field and people were showing up and setting up tents and camps everywhere.
There were three bands to perform, Molly Hatchet, Leslie West and Jefferson Starship.
Only Molly Hatchet had a tour bus, the other groups came in vans.

The back line for Leslie West and Jefferson Starship were provided by our buddy Tommy and the local lighting company sent out Frank with a small stand-up lighting rig that we brought in our truck.

During the day the heat was triple digit.
It had to be one of the hottest days that I ever remember living in Ohio and the humidity was crushing.
Just walking from the stage to the front of house mixing tent was laborious.
Outside of a couple of bottles of water in the truck, that was all the provisions we had.
There was no food, there were no restrooms, there was no beverage there was no nothing.

Molly Hatchet, had their tour bus awkwardly parked in front of the house left stage right side of the stage.
The schedule for the show was that Molly Hatchet was going to play first, then Leslie West with his band and then Jefferson Starship would close it out and then we would all run as fast as possible out of there.

The show started right around dusk, and at this point there were hundreds of tents and little campsites spread throughout this giant field.
As Molly Hatchet started their first song, a black sky was rolling up behind the stage and the temperature was dropping fast.

Now let me emphasize this, I've been in the jungle in the South Pacific, I've been in the Central American rainforest, and I've lived in South Florida and never in my life have I ever seen rain come out the sky like this.

The temperature had to drop 40 degrees and the rain was coming down in drops the size of golf balls.
At that time, Leslie West and I were on a first name basis because of how many times he had come through the Cleveland Agora in the past couple of years.

John Conde had totally wrapped up the monitor council and amp racks with multiple tarps, and now him, me, and Leslie West were all at front of house together each one of us holding down one of the tent legs.

Leslie West kept saying the same thing repeatedly to me, "Pete, were in a bad spot".
And he was right.
That heavy rain poured out of the sky for the next several hours.

Up to this point, the Molly Hatchet band gear was still on stage and the blue boat tarp that the bikers had strung up for a for a roof, now looked
like a swimming pool suspended over the stage.
That was when the entire tarp system collapsed, and God knows how many gallons of water dumped into every item on stage.

The other development that was happening, was that this site that they chose was a marshland that had dried up over the past drought of the summer.
The low side of the site that was the stage, was now almost knee-deep water.
Every single tent, campsite was underwater with people's property and beer cans just floating everywhere.
After the collapse on stage, the bulk of the storm had passed and now it was just drizzling, and the Molly Hatchet band and crew were in a fast panic to get all their stuff and get out of there.

Because of how deep the water was on site, they were unable to open the Bay doors underneath the bus.
They were taking cymbal stands with the cymbals still on them and dragged everything they could and marching them right up the stairs of the bus.

When the bikers realized that these guys were trying to make an escape, they surrounded the bus and got everybody off the bus at gunpoint.
The tires of the bus were just spinning in the mud they were stuck and weren't going anywhere.
I was up on stage just stunned what I was looking at.
Finally, one of the bikers came up to me and John Condi and he pointed a handgun right in my face and said, "We want concert".
I remember telling the guy "Everything's been underwater, I don't even know what I can or cannot get to work".
He physically pushed the gun against my face and said, "Well you better figure out something".

John Condi and I got enough of it working again where we can get this show back on.
We get Molly Hatchett back on stage and they start playing but the singers missing.
The bikers went on the tour bus, dragged him and his ostrich skin boots back to the stage.
The guy was trashed and who could blame him.
He would sing a little bit, then go throw up behind the drum kit.
several times he tried to run into monitor world, but John Condi spun him back around and pushed him back on the stage, he had no friends there.
He was successful of throwing up on our buddies rented back line gear.

After they're set, the bikers had a tractor without a trailer on site that they had used to bring in the stage, and with a super long chain they pulled the bus out and those guys split.

Next up was Leslie, and he was no must no fuss and he was super excited to get out of there.

By the time we got Jefferson Starship up on stage it was 3:00 o'clock in the morning.

John Candy and I had switched positions and I went up on stage to do monitors and he went to front of house.

Another caveat of the gig was that they had put the generator right behind the stage and the diesel fumes were smoking everybody out.

The next thing I remember was John Condi kicking me saying "Pete get up".

I was sleeping in a puddle on stage.

I guess the stage was feeding back and I had no idea, I was busy sleeping in a puddle.

Low blood sugar, dehydrated, wet cold and miserable was the order of the day.

The only thing we had going for us was that I had left the truck all the way butted up against the stage so we could just put everything right in and split.

I was on stage wrapping up some cable and the lead singer from Jefferson Starship Marty was carrying two keyboard cases to the van.

Everybody in the band had something, it was all hands-on deck to get out of there.

Because Marty isn't very tall, and the water was so deep he was unable to physically pull the keyboard cases all the way out of the water, he was like walking and treading water with them.

The last time I saw him, he had tripped, and because the water was so deep, he completely face planted forward but he was still holding on to the keyboard cases.

All I saw was his elbow sticking out of the water.

As amusing it is that was, I had my own problems.

I had great concerns about getting the truck out of there, and unfortunately my concerns were validated by the axles of the truck sinking all the way down into the mud.

There was no way to get this truck out, and there was no way we were going to make it to the rocking reggae show in a couple hours. John Condi had parked his car on what was now the high ground that was dry at the end of the property.
We left the truck and split to go find some cell service so we can call Bob Bock with the good news that there was no way possible that we were going to get that truck out and make it to the next gig.

What John Condi and I should have done at that point was call the Sheriff's Department and have them go out there and arrest those assholes for holding us at gunpoint.
But that's exactly what we did not do.
Instead, we both went home and got guns and went back out there with one of those giant tow trucks that we hired to pull us out.
Of course, we didn't explain to the tow company that we were going out there to deal with a bunch of psychopaths with guns.

When we got back out to the site, the light of day was exposing the real disaster that this thing was.
All the campers were gone, the water had receded, and the entire field was nothing but garbage and mud.

The bikers had brought a backhoe to the site to pull out the trailers. It turned out they had "borrowed them" for the weekend and needed to get them back in place before Monday morning.
The backhoe was listing at a 40-degree angle completely stuck in the mud and they were surrounding it with shovels and just doing what they could to try to dig it out.
Every one of their personal vehicles was also stuck in the mud.
John Condi had left his car back on the main road and we road in with the tow truck.
The only other vehicle besides the tow truck that we arrived in that was not in the mud, was a cab over tractor that was parked on the only dry spot.

The bikers were not happy to see us and told us that after we pulled our truck out, we would be helping to pull their backhoe out.
That was absolutely not going to happen.

We get out of the truck and the driver made a wide swing to turn around so he could back up and tow our truck out.
As he did this, he got stuck in the mud.
Now the rescue vehicle that we had hired to come out here and rescue us, needed to be rescued.

As the bikers were dealing with the backhoe, and our tow truck guy was sinking deeper and deeper, we started talking to the guy that had the tractor on the dry spot and John Condi and I ran a chain from that truck to our truck.
Nobody was really paying attention to us, as we slowly started pulling our truck out.

I get the truck rolling at its own power, and I yelled out to John to disconnect the tow chain.
It was almost like we had rehearsed it 100 times, he got the chain off the truck as I was still rolling.

Now the truck that had just pulled us out, turned as I was still going forward, and he got stuck in the mud.
At this moment, the only vehicle on the site that was not stuck in the mud was our truck rolling at 5 miles an hour.
The bikers started yelling at us to come help them and I yelled to John, "Jump in the truck".

In my rearview mirror was a dozen angry men chasing us and it was tense as I just kept rolling trying to keep my forward momentum. There was a sharp left turn out of there and that was the moment that I was the most stressed, if there was one place, I could have gotten stuck it was there, but we didn't.

I felt bad about leaving our tow truck driver that we had hired, but he probably had a CB in his truck and could at least call somebody for help.

I was always looking forward to seeing Leslie West again so we could talk about that gig, but I never saw him again.

It was hands down the worst concert ever, it really slapped me in the face about how shitty my job was, and I was completely ready for a career change after that.

Concert for the Rock & Roll Hall of Fame
Cleveland Stadium, 9-2-95

It was a big deal when the Rock and Roll Hall of Fame came to Cleveland.
I was brought in with the usual suspects to work on the site, I had nothing to do with what was happening on stage.
The reason for that was because the local promoter that refused to use union labor all year long, brought in union labor for this show.

For reasons that I will never understand, when I was a non-union stagehand working in Cleveland, the union seemed to have zero interest in recruiting and because of that it created an environment where the local promoter got away with having the benefit of hiring stagehands without paying them benefits.

I had season tickets for the Cleveland Browns from 1989 to 1995, I worked at the stadium in the 70s, it's not a stretch to say that I knew my way around the building.

At that time, I smoked cigarettes and I had just walked back into the stadium from smoking outside.

As I'm walking by the men's room some guy in a southern accent asked me "Hey buddy do you have a light?"
There was a little concrete wall that blocked the visual entrance to the men's room, I walked over and the guy who asked me for a light, was Greg Allman.
Standing next to him was Clarence Clemons from the E St. band and the Godfather of Soul James Brown.

I was stunned, I didn't know what to say I just handed him my lighter.
These guys were just ripping on each other and after Greg lit the joint, instead of handing me back my lighter, he handed me the joint.
I didn't want to be rude, so I took a drag off it and handed it to Clarence Clemons.

I was incapable of speech, standing in the best marijuana circle of my life.
I had my back to the Causeway when I heard a guy say, "You boys should stay off that reefer" and I turned around and it was Johnny Cash.

Clarence Clemons got down on his knees and with both arms raised he bowed to the ground and said, "we're not worthy".
This whole thing happens so fast I couldn't even process what was going on.
After the Johnny Cash drive by, the joint was about done, James Brown and Clarence Clemens walked away.
Greg Allman hands me the burning roach and says, "Hold this for me" and he went in the restroom.

Two Cleveland Police officers walk around the corner and there I am holding that burning Roach.
before they could say anything to me, Greg Allman popped out of the bathroom, said "thanks man", grabbed the roach from me and kept on walking.

I did the same thing I kept on walking.

Over the next couple decades, I would do many shows with Greg Allman, and now that he's gone I'm left with the final conclusion that I don't think I'm ever gonna get my lighter back.

Alanis Morrissette, Prick, Jewel, Goo Goo Dolls, Dance Hall Crashers, Green Apple Quick Step, The Tea Party and Universal Honey.

Blossom Music Center 9-9-95

This was one of those WMMS Buzzardfests that we would do at Blossom Music Center.
I was the monitor mixer for that day, and I really don't remember anything about any of the bands that day until we get to the last one, Alanis Morrissette.

She had just broken out and I happened to know the tour manager, he used to come through Peabody's quite a bit.
For a reason I don't remember, her vocal channel ended up in an input strip that I had not previously used during the day.
You know these shows were what we call throw and go, there was no real sound checks we would just get you out there get you what you needed and get this thing going.

The band starts, I get everybody what they need, she comes out on the deck skipping out there with this like shillelagh cane she had and start singing her thing.
Immediately the drummer needed more of her vocal.
I go to spin more vocal up for him and very quickly I run out of knob, it's turned up to 10, but because the vocal gained on that channel had been gained down. No way to turn it up again without changing it for her and she was cool.

The only way I could mix my way out of this problem, was to slowly turn down all of the individual sends to him while simultaneously pushing up the master to get her vocal on top of everything for him.

I immediately understood what the problem was and as I was looking down dialing it up, a drunk stick came skipping off the monitor console.
I looked up, and another one binged me in the shoulder.

I immediately came around the monitor console, the drummer stopped playing jumped off his riser, and came at me on stage and his people intervened and grabbed him, and we both just went back to doing our jobs.

Years later I would end up doing a bunch of shows with that same guy when he was the drummer for another group, and we always got along great because him and I had both completely forgotten about it.

It wasn't until the guy passed away that I the epiphany that he was the same guy I had a fight with on stage with Alanis Morrissette.

Truck Driving 101
Im outta this business, Fall 1995

I was 100% sick of constantly working, constantly being broke and it sucked.

Being at all these cool shows was meaningless to me when I was struggling to pay my bills.

I answered an ad for a trucking company call Schneider, that promised they would train me to pass the exam for a Class A license. At no cost.

I was busting my ass in the concert business, and I couldn't even afford to put myself through truck driving school.

The thing about living in Cleveland and working concerts is that we didn't work in the winter, and I couldn't save money if I wasn't scraping by when I was working.

I took the leap, and I went up to Green Bay WI for a month of driving school living at a local motel.

We had vouchers for Denny's, I secretly felt that there are training our intestinal system for what was about to come with the life of eating at truck stops.

Growing up I always heard, that when you're driving down the highway you could always tell where the good food is because that's where all the truckers go.

But the truth is, the truckers go to where the truck parking is.

I had already been all over the country driving straight trucks and I've done it drunk and high, these people that I'm with have never been out of their county before.

The worst part was sitting in a truck with a couple other people, fearing for my life is some moron that's never been and anything bigger than a Volkswagen learns how to maneuver a 53-foot trailer. The cool thing that they had, was a 10-acre Teflon skid pad and they had trucks that were set where somebody could lock up different sets of tires with remote.

The trick was to maneuver the truck while staying in your lane as somebody was locking up different tires and making the truck go out of control.
You had to recover it from the spin.
Spinning in a 53-foot trailer when you're sitting nine feet high in the air it's an unnerving feeling, but I could say 100% that the skills that I learned on that skid pad absolutely saved my life six months later.

They were right about the fact that I did get my Class A license, but they were wrong about me sticking around and working for them.
I did some runs for them taking windshields to Dallas from Chicago, Bunch of other stuff that I don't remember but I remember that I thought the pay sucked because we were paid on the household movers guide.
That is the industry standard for paying over the road drivers, it's not the miles on your odometer, it's the calculated miles by the mover's guide.
This is the same guide that will tell you that it's only 8 miles from Gary IN to Chicago.
Yeah, if you draw a line right across lake MI that's true.
I was in and out of Chicago a lot and it always sucked, because of the traffic, because every bridge overpass was improperly labeled because it didn't account for how many times the road had been resurfaced.

Another deal breaker for me with this company was having a Co-driver.
Who thinks that living with another man inside of a metal box is a good idea, even two prisoners in a cell get some yard time.
The guy I was driving with was irritated that I wanted to go to a truck stop once a day and take a shower.
That was the end of co driving for me.

I discovered quickly that the way to make money and over the road trucking was to haul something dangerous, so I chose steel.
I hooked up with a company out of Eagle Grove IA that specialized in transporting steel on flatbed trucks.
I spent two weeks with them learning about strapping down steel.

It's definitely a skill set, and there is no room for error.

I've butted heads with the "safety director" who claimed that by the company not paying for us to be on a toll road we were saving money.
anybody who has ever driven between Chicago and Pittsburgh understands that there's only one way to do it and that's on I-80 a toll road.
I said to the guy "How are we being safe and saving money driving through Amish country through every back road, through nowhere Ohio stopping and starting at every light I mean are you kidding me? How much fuel do you think we're burning going through the gears every time I'm going through some small towns instead of staying on the highway humming along at 55 miles an hour?"

You know those people that are so stuck to their position that no matter how much logic and facts you try to pour into their brain it's just impenetrable.
I paid for my own tolls.

My first assignment was picking up a single 55,000-pound roll of steel in Chicago, taking it to a tool company in Nebraska.
The procedure at a steel mill was to get in line behind 75 trucks, and when it was your turn, it was the driver's responsibility to make the call where the machine was gonna set it down on your trailer.
The equation was 500 pounds per inch in either direction, that's how the weight would distribute.
Two inches is in the wrong direction I could be 1000 pounds off.

On the way out after chaining it, tarping it, you would go over the scales and make sure that your weight is right.
If it wasn't, you had to get back at the end of the line and go through it all over again so that giant machine can come and move it an inch.

It was January, it was cold, and I was out somewhere in Iowa by the side of some train tracks.

The factory I was sitting outside was closed, my delivery was scheduled for 8:00 AM but it was midnight and I just wanted to park, get the tarp off the steel, go to sleep.
The steel tarp weighed 300 pounds; add to that that it was frozen it was difficult to manage for one person.
I had to unroll it from the load, so in the morning they could just start right away unloading it.
It was starting to snow heavily, and I was standing on top of the load trying to roll the tarp and I lost my balance and landed on my back.
It had to be an 8-foot drop and I was completely unable to breathe.
I was just laying on my back, watching the snow come down around me and just thinking in the moment that I hope they find my body underneath the snow.

After that I picked up a load going to Akron OH, and I got a call from the local lighting company in Cleveland Electrostage, and they said that they had heard that I got my Class A license and wanted to know if I would drive a stage for Alanis Morrissette.
I told them I'd be there tomorrow.

Alanis Morrisette
Somewhere Pennsylvania, Jacksonville Florida February 1996
Of course, Cleveland style my job was not just to drive the truck but to build the stage as well.
I got a 60 by 40-foot stage in the truck and I'm heading to some small college somewhere in Pennsylvania and it was snowing hard.
I was at the top of a steep hill that had a fresh foot of snow on it.
As I made my descent down the hill, the truck tires were sliding on the ice faster than they were rolling.
Thankfully there was nobody else on the road as I slid down it sideways.

The gig went fine no big deal about it, the thing about building a stage is that you're the first one in, last one out.
The other thing that was kind of nice too is that nothing about the stage is going to buzz, it's not like audio.
I took that same stage, that same truck down to Florida right after that gig, to do something in the local arena but this time their people there were setting the stage, up I just had to get the truck there.

With two days with nothing to do but hang out in the hotel that's what I did.
The best entertainment I had was that the couple in the room next to me word loudly procreating for the entire time I was there.
At one point I thought that their headboard was going to come right through my wall.

When I checked out of the hotel, I used the phone in the lobby to give them a call and thank them for all the entertainment for the past couple days.
Since I knew they were upstairs in their room having boom boom, I had been down in the hotel bar charging all my meals and drinks to their room.
It worked out for everybody.

Morris Day and The Time
Agora Theater, 2-8-96

In the 80s it was impossible to turn on Showtime or Cinemax and not see the movie, "Purple Rain".
I was out of the truck, and back in my spot as the monitor mixer at the Cleveland Agora.
Of course, I had driven the straight truck there.

The guys came in for sound check that afternoon and hanging out with those guys is exactly how you think it would be.
They were fun, they were funny, and we spent more time laughing than we did doing any audio.

Showtime comes, and the band was on stage playing the intro.
Morris Day walks up to me and looking straight out onto the stage without turning his head to me he says, "What you got in my monitors Pete?".
I said, "Nothing but you Morris".
He replied, "That's good that's good that's real good" and then he made what could best be described as a "squawk sound", and he ran out on stage.

It was everything you wanted a Morris Day and the Time show to be. Jerome holding the mirror, doing the bird, it was awesome.

At some point, they slowed the show down and Jerome brought a small round table on stage, that had a white tablecloth, a single rose in a vase, and two chairs.
Morris, sitting there as the band was playing a soft number said to Jerome, "I need a special lady to share a special moment with".

So, Jerome goes out in the crowd, and brings up a young lady to sit next to Morris.
This woman was thrilled, she was so excited to be up there with him. Morris looked at her, looked at the crowd, looked back at her, then looked up to Jerome and said, "She's good, but she's not good enough for me", and he waved her off.

The audience busted out laughing and the girl was crushed.
The next one they brought up on stage looked like a hamster in a snake cage.

After the show Morris came over and thanked me, gave me a CD and doing a show with those guys was bucket list.

Little Richard
<u>CSU 5-4-96</u>
This was some bunch of band Fiesta at the local college arena.
what I remember is not having lunch and having to work every minute right up to doors.
whoever was putting this show on had hired their own front of house mixer to mix all the groups and he was 100% incompetent and inexperienced and unprepared to execute an event like this.

Mixing on an arena audio system is a skill that he didn't have.

We finally got to get away and get some dinner at catering, and the moment I sat down with my plate of food, my first plate of food of the day some guy came over to me and said they had to check something right away.
Man, I just fucking snapped.
I said to the guy "Really? I don't get to eat. You had me out there all day long with your fucked up plan and that idiot mixing who can't get anything together and now I'm supposed to not have dinner over it?"
I was really pissed.

So, we finally start the show, and every song from every group, the PA is feeding back.
It was embarrassing.
We had no feedback on stage because, I was the monitor mixer and I'm a professional.

We finally get Little Richard out on stage, and the moment he says his first words in his microphone, it starts feeding back through the PA.
Not even Little Richard can believe that it's the PA feeding back, so he walks over to stage left, and my monitor console was off the stage on the floor.
He comes over to me in the spotlight follows him.
Little Richard then spends the next 5 minutes ripping into me because, he thinks the stage is feeding back.

He says to me over the microphone, "All these people came to see me tonight and you're ruining my show. why are you ruining my show? you shouldn't be here if you're going to ruin my show".

I shut every fader off right in front of him, showing it wasn't the stage that was feeding back, and he still didn't get it.
I just stood there with my arms folded until he ran out of steam like any other toddler throwing a tantrum.

Bob Dylan, Oroboros
Nautica Stage 5-17-96

If I wasn't at Nautica Stage as the monitor mixer I was there as a stagehand.
This show was carrying full production and a local band was going to open the show.

We had a young rigger named Brad that was an amazing climber, but he had a reputation for showing up at the last minute, with last night's stripper still in the back of his motorcycle.
Brad looked just like Brad Pitt, so he was not having a hard time finding a new volunteer to occupy the rear seat of his motorcycle every evening.
I don't know how he trained them, but sometimes he would do the whole call without them leaving the back of the bike.

We got the first truck unloaded and our handsome rigger shows up and immediately starts talking to the production manager.
The production manager was an older British guy, that was stirring a cup of tea.
The production manager kept saying to Brad, "I need my point to hang right here" as he was slowly stirring his tea.
Brad kept responding with, "Well you know if I put it over here it would be easier" and this went back and forth with them for a couple of rounds.
At some point the production manager turned to me, handed me his tea, and said "Would you be so kind and hold this for me while I suck his cock".
I busted out laughing so hard I almost dropped the guy's tea.

We survived all that and got the show up and running.

The crew chief for the stagehands would occasionally introduce the bands.
Larry walks out and says to the crowd "ladies and gentlemen please welcome Oroboros! closing the show tonight for Oroboros tonight will be Bob Dylan".

Dylan's production staff was so angry that the promoter didn't let him announce a band for quite some time.

Candlebox, 311, No Doubt, The Tragically Hip, Berlin, Goldfinger, The Nixons, Dash Riprock
WMMS Buzzard Fest, Blossom Music Center 5-18-96
Here I was back in my element.
Mixing monitors for the big gig the only difference this time is that I was the one that drove the semi.

I don't remember much about the early bands, but I remember how great The Tragically Hip were.
I was surprised that the lead singer had remembered me from when they came to Peabody's.
They were on tour for their album "Trouble at the henhouse" which I consider one of the greatest rock albums of all time.

No Doubt was a new band that I didn't know anything about.
The band was out on stage, and I was dialing in all their sounds while Drew Barrymore and some other blonde was hanging out with me smoking a joint.
miss Barrymore remembered me from the last time she was in Ohio getting high backstage, so we were just chilling and passing the joint as I was dialing up the band.
I didn't know who the other woman was, but at some point, she turned to me and said "Thanks" and then she ran on stage.
Turns out she was the lead singer for the group.

One of the side dramas we had going all day long, was that we really frowned on people bringing in any extra crap that was going to make the set changes longer.
Number one in that department is floor lighting.
That crap could tangle up the floor and really hinder what we got to do with getting the band off and getting the next one on.

The lighting guy from 311 running cable around the place all day long one at a time acting like nobody was noticing, but I was noticing.
So of course, the last minute he rolls up these lights that he's already got the electric and signal cable ran to these locations and he throws them down and they have their little show.

The last group up had their own monitor rig and their own monitor guy so I had nothing to do with them.
I was hanging out at front of house for the last group, which is something I never do.
The front of house tech Marty and I we're just standing there when suddenly, it sounded like somebody was unplugging and plugging a guitar in, only at jet engine volume through the PA system.
It happened again and it was only happening on the House left side. As him and I were heading to the stage, a big plume of white smoke drifted across the stage from the stage right house left side.

At this point, the audio system on the right-hand side of the stage sounded like a dinosaur screaming.
What had happened, was when that lighting guy was picking up his cable, he snagged the cross-stage signal to the amp racks, it shorted out and started the fire.

After putting the fire out with a fire extinguisher, we got signal back over to that side of the stage and used whatever amps hadn't burnt.

It's just evidence, that the moment you think you could relax and just take a second to chill out, no something always happens.

Chuck Berry
GARCO 5-24-96

Here we are at America's favorite overpriced hoedown, the Great American Rib Cook Off.
One day we would have hippie band another day it would be a country band that would be a rock band and one of the nights we had Chuck Berry.

Chuck Berry did not travel with a band, he traveled with a guitar and a bag of clothes.
The deal with hiring Chuck Berry for a gig at that time was that you had to provide a band for him that knew the songs and his setlist, you had to give him a Cadillac at the airport, and he would drive himself around and it was cash up front.

I had sound checked the band in the afternoon, and at some point, when this thing was ready to go Chuck would just walk out there plug in and do his thing.

I was hanging out behind the stage a few minutes before the show and Chuck Berry walked up to me and asked me if I had any reefer, I could sell him.
I told him no, but I'll smoke some with you.

We walked back to this parking lot area that was behind the stage and behind the generators, and we got into Chuck's Cadillac.
I had one of those old-style "brass bowls" that was made from multiple pieces.
The kind that burnt your lips when it got too hot, the kind that you couldn't put back in your pocket after you used it because it would be too hot.

I guess I had a little more than two joints worth in a baggie.
Somehow, I had it in my mind, I would just hand Chuck the baggie, the lighter and the bowl, he would just take a couple puffs, get high and be all set.
That's not what happened.

Chuck used his giant thumb to stuff that bowl with half the bag, and he completely stoked the bowl out to 1000 degrees Fahrenheit.
We were like Cheech and Chong sitting in that car it was completely filled with marijuana smoke.
He smoked all my weed which quite honestly, I wasn't prepared for that, but I was hanging out with Chuck Berry.
He gives me back the bowl and the lighter and we get out of the car. Walking back to the stage, Chuck had his arm around me, and we were both laughing.

Who wasn't laughing, was the stage manager and the promoter Rep. The band was up on stage, the audience was sitting out there and nobody knew where we were.
The promoter started ripping into me and Chuck immediately started defending me telling them "He was with me".

It was obvious that we both smelled like weed, both of us were just a little bit too high and giggling.
We both went up on stage together, I unmuted the mixing console and he picked up his guitar and went on stage.
He played a great show that night, and at one point came over to the monitor console and said to me "Pete I'm having a great time".

When the show is over, he thanked me for my hospitality, he tried to fuck my ex-wife and then he left with some other woman from the crowd.
it worked out for everybody, and to be fair, she did rock those thigh high leather boots.

Southern Comfort Blues Festival
Starlake Amphitheater Pittsburg Pennsylvania 6-22-96
Mr. Jones and I take a semi down to Pittsburgh to do a show with George Clinton and the P Funk All Stars.
Over the years, we had done a lot of shows with these guys, and it was usually one song that went on for three hours.

When we get there in the morning, we were walking across stage together and there was a huge banner hanging up over the stage and it said, "Southern Comfort Blues Festival", and me and Mr. Jones said to each other something to the effect of, "Wow I wonder when that was?".

Well, it was today it was the show we were doing.
We thought we we're doing one band and now it's a full day festival.

The only other act I remember, was that the show opened with Taj Mahal.
Fast forward to the last band of the night, George Clinton and the P Funk All Stars.
There were so many people on stage with this group, that we had 26 vocals.

As a monitor mixer, the way I reference what's happening on stage is that I have the exact same speaker that the artist has on stage next to me so I could listen to what they're listening to.
We call that a "Cue Wedge".

I had two "cue wedges" on road cases next to me and a sub on the floor behind me.
My little pocket was crushing.

One of the reasons I always had an epic Q system, is that if there was a bunch of posers that started hanging around me, I would queue up the most obnoxious things like a high hat and turn it up to 11 forcing everyone to leave my area.

Another thing most monitors mixers do, is that we make our own mix for us to listen to separate from what the band is hearing.

The P Funk All Stars had been on stage for like 15 minutes without George and I had them all dialed in.
I was just hanging at the console listening to my own mix of the show, when the smell of skunk weed just overpowered me.
It was George Clinton, holding the biggest joint I ever saw in my life.

He was standing right next to me, and he handed me the joint.
as I was taken a drag from it, he started grooving listening to the mix I had coming through my cue wedges.
He asked me to bring up the keyboards in my mix, and George Clinton and I spent the next 30 minutes on the side of the stage smoking that joint and rocking out together.

It was so funny that his band was out there for like 45 minutes without him as we were puffing a cloud across the stage.

I remember being so high, that I had to stick my head in a cooler full of ice to snap out of it so I could drive that semi back to Cleveland.

Loverboy, Zapp, Joe Diffie, Foghat, Blackhawk
Akron Rib Cook Off 7-3,4,5,6,7-96

We were gonna be here for a week, and we had three stages at the site.
Jon Conde and I were at the mainstage, he was going to be at front of house I was going to stay on stage and do monitors.

The day we showed up to load in it had been rainy and windy off and, on all day, long.
I was having an argument with the owner of the staging lighting company Over the inadequacies of the tent that he provided where I needed to set up the monitor world.
I was insisting I wasn't going to unload anything until the tent was properly strapped down and as he was saying to me "This tent isn't going anywhere" on cue a gust of wind came through, picked up that tent and took it down the street.

With two of his minions running after it, I just stood there in silence staring at him.
That was the last thing he said to me for the rest of the week.

He called my boss and demand that I get removed from the show.
When my boss called me about it, I found it interesting that I had to explain to him that my actions were all about saving his gear.

One of the nights we had the group Loverboy.
The lead singer was wearing his traditional red shirt with matching red headband, and he was just kind of hanging out with me at the monitor console before he went on.

There was a box of donuts from breakfast on a road case next to the console, and the only ones left in the box were powdered sugar jelly donuts.
I said to the singer, "Hey man you want a donut?
He said, "Yeah that'd be great".
So, I extend the box to him, and he grabs one of those powdered sugar donuts and as he's eating it, he's getting it all over himself.
He's got powdered sugar and Jelly drips down the front of his shirt.

As soon as he finished it, I said, "Here man have another one".
He ate the other one, same effect.
By the time he went on stage he was covered in powdered sugar and Jelly.
John called me on the com, he was dying, he looked like he was covered in cocaine.

After the show John came up on stage and according to him, the singer was trying to thank me, and I was telling the guy "You should get together with Meatloaf and do a meat lovers tour".
I don't remember that, but it sounds like something I would say.

The next day was R&B Day, and the highlight was the group" Zapp". Before their shows started, one of their guys went to the edge of the stage, and said to the audience, "OK before we get this party started, we gotta get all the good-looking people to the front and all the ugly people to the back".
he looked down at this one guy and said, "come on man you know you belong back there".
It was funny and we spent the rest of the afternoon with more bounce to the ounce.

One of the things about doing shows in the 90s before the Internet, is that if the client wanted you to play a certain kind of music, you had to bring her with you.
The third day of this hoedown was Country Day, and neither John nor I carried any country music.

The only thing I had, was a Johnny Cash solo acoustic CD that was produced by Rick Rubin.
The temperature that day was in the 90s, and the audience was sitting in folded chairs on the street.
This CD sounded like Appalachian funeral music.

Johnny was singing "I've got the number 13 tattooed on my neck" and the audience was so bummed out listening to it, but nobody could complain because it was Johnny Cash.

They sent somebody to the record store that day to buy some country music for us to play.

Foghat was no problem, Roger the drummer, was thrilled that I gave him one of the PA cabinets for a drum fill.
I don't remember anything about the country band we had on the last day at our stage.

The last day I get called on the walkie-talkie to come over to the B stage.
When I get there, I see a couple of idiots from the radio station that are trying to put a banner and on our speaker towers.
This scaffold towers were probably 12 feet high, with four speaker cabinets on the tower, each cabinet weighing around 400 pounds.
The tower was also secured to the ground with 4 water ballast tanks, 55-gallon drum and eight pounds per gallon.

I explained to the guys, that you can't do this because your banner is not" blow through" allowing for the wind and the sound to pass through it".
Immediately the guy goes into "don't you know who we are and we're sponsoring this thing and you don't tell us what to do and I'll take responsibility for this, and you don't get to say so".
All the usual nonsense.
And I still said no.
Under the right conditions, a banner can become a sail.

Just a few years earlier, I was working as a stagehand in downtown Cleveland at what we called" the floating stage"
The floating stage was in the harbor near the old stadium, and we had concerts there.
We were there for one reason, and that was to install a banner and some show is coming in the next day.
The stage had to be, maybe 60 feet by 60 feet, it was huge with a roof system floating on a barge.
There was an aluminum ramp between the dock and the stage, that was the only way to get gear on or off.

The banner that we were hanging just so happened to not be a blow through.

When we got it on the position, a gust of wind came through, It popped open like a sail and we left the dock.
The ramp went into the drink, and we were on the move out to Lake Erie.
One of the stagehands, pulled out a knife and cut the ropes of one of the corners, but because it had been so taught, now it was an out-of-control whip, and nobody can get near it.
Total disaster, and it gave me a whole new respect for the power of wind.

I told the people that worked for us on that stage, under no circumstances allow them to put that up.
A few hours later, I was back at the mainstage when a call came over the walkie-talkie "Hey Pete you gotta get over to the B stage".
I get over there and what do you think I see?

The house left PA tower fell over into the crowd and landed on a picnic table where there was a family sitting there enjoying the show.
Guess what was attached to the front of the tower?

THAT MOTHERFUCKING BANNER THAT I TOLD THOSE ASSHOLES NOT TO PUT UP THERE!

I was really pissed.
These people were injured, now there is a big mess to contend with and the people from the radio station nowhere to be seen.

Second time in the same week, on the same site that I was correct in predicting the potentiality and consequences of high winds.

My favorite part of this fiasco was the headline in the local paper the next day.
Do you think it said, "Radio people with an overinflated opinion of themselves, refused to listen to experienced professional?"

That's not what it said.

The headline read, "Local sound company injuries family at Rib Cook Off"

I would spend the rest of my career being a total jerk about safety issues.
I have pissed off many a promoter and client over safety issues and I don't care.
In my lifetime I have left work three times in an ambulance, and there is nothing barer minimum to me then the basic principle that everybody should get home safely.
If there isn't enough time to do it safe, then we're not doing it.

The Monkees
Starlake Amphitheater/ Nautica Stage 7-12,13-96
I was excited to be doing a couple shows with The Monkees.
The first of two shows were in Pittsburgh, and I was driving the semi. My passenger was my boss Bob Bock, he spent his trip with his head rattling against the window, passed out from partying too hard the previous night.

One of the mechanical features of a semi-truck is that there are two springs that control the resistance of the gas pedal and its relationship to the carburetor of the vehicle.
The springs are what keeps the gas pedal from collapsing to the floor.

Some of the hardcore drivers Did not like driving with the two springs, because it made for more resistance on the pedal, and if you spend 16 hours a day with your foot on a pedal that it might make a difference to you, and you would remove 1 spring.
but the truth is, the reason there are two springs is because if one breaks you have still had one.

We were going down a fairly steep hill in Pennsylvania, and my gas pedal just collapsed to the floor.
I had heard of this scenario from other drivers in the past.
I couldn't clutch out of the gear I was in because I was incapable of revving the motor back up.
We were picking up a lot of speed, the moment that Bob woke up we're going around a curve at about 90 miles an hour.

Waking up inside of a runaway semi after sleeping against the window for an hour was fairly abrupt.
Adding to his look of surprise, his toupee was sideways.

When I finally got the vehicle to a stop on the side of the road, I flipped the hood up, found the spring and reattached it.
it was just a little much to start the day like that.

We get down to the venue, meet the rest of our crew, I'm the monitor guy, the guys were terrific, and we had a great show.

The next night was at the Nautica stage in Cleveland.
My wife and daughter came to the show that night and we're backstage hanging out and catering.
Davy Jones saw us together, came over and introduced himself.
Anything that you ever heard about Davy Jones being an incredibly nice guy was all true.

All the guys were terrific.
Davy Jones, Peter Tork, Mickey Dolenz, and a couple of other musicians.
I could never say enough about how great this group was.
Every song was great, and the crowd went wild for them.

That night we had a heavy rainstorm that came in, and in the past we had stopped shows with less rain than this.
But they wanted to keep playing if the audience wanted to stay and we pushed all the gear all the way upstage and the Monkees performed the rest of the show huddled together in a in a small little space upstage center.

It really said a lot for who these guys were and how they really felt about their fans.
the rock and roll Hall of Fame says that they're ineligible because they didn't play the instruments on their albums.
They played when I was with them, and they were great.

Busted
I-77 Cleveland Ohio, 7-15-96
I had picked up this semi from the rental place on Thursday, did the Monkees in Pittsburgh on Friday, then in Cleveland on Saturday, then on Sunday I did another show and now it's Monday.
We had unloaded this truck the previous night and I had to drop the trailer off at one location and then take the tractor to another location.
it was a tremendous quantity of time doing this and always the issue of who was going to get pick me up from dropping the truck off?

I'm in the left lane and a state trooper jumped out from behind one of those pillars under a bridge over pass and motion for me to pull over.
The guy approaches my truck, and he is just super aggressive and claims I was doing 60 in a 55.
I give the guy my license, paperwork and he goes back to his car.
He returns to my truck and asks me to step out.

When I ascended down out of the truck, he spun me around pushed my face into the side of the vehicle and handcuffed me.
Next thing I know I'm in the back of this police car.
I'm asking this guy a very simple question, "Why am I being arrested?", and he won't say anything to me.
We get to this garage, takes me out of the car, sits me down on a bench, chained my hands to my ankles and then chained my ankles to the floor.
According to the clock on the wall, I was left there in that position for 14 hours.

Finally, a different sadist shows up, unchains me from the floor and puts me in the back of a different car.
I'm asking this guy, "why have I been arrested? why can't I make a phone call? why can't I use the restroom?" and the only thing he told me was "Shut the fuck up".
We spent the next couple hours driving around picking up other prisoners from other municipalities.

By the time we were done there was four of us in the back seat of that car and I had been wearing these handcuffs for 16 hours.

We finally get to our destination; the Shaker Heights police station.
They bring us in, process us, take away my belt and my shoelaces my wedding ring and they put each of us in a cell.

Bonus to all of it, they had already done the meals for the day, there was nothing to eat, and I was starving.
Finally at some point, then let me call my wife.
Of course, everyone was panicked because at this point, I had been missing for almost a full day.
The semi was still on the side of the road somewhere.

I told her to come down, arrange to get pay my bail and Get Me Out of here, at this point I still didn't know why I was arrested.
They took me back to my cell, and I don't know how it turned out, but I had the remote to the TV that was bolted to the wall underneath a cage.

All the other inmates were yelling at me to give them the remote.
I was so irritated about this shitty day that I flipped the channels until I found The Golden Girls.
I turned the volume all the way up, took the two batteries out of the remote and I winged them across the floor.

Right after I did this one of the dungeon masters came in and took me out of my cage.
They take me out through a series of doors and there's my wife standing there at the other side of the counter.

They hand me a bag with my belt my shoelaces and my wedding ring.
I asked my wife "how much was my bond?"
She said there wasn't any bond, she had just paid the fine.
Fine?

It turned out, that I had an outstanding ticket with the city of Shaker Heights OH, and for "Not wearing a seatbelt".
For that they had put out a warrant for my arrest.
The total cost of my ticket, including fines and court cost was $27.00.

I was kidnapped off the streets of the country I was born in over a dispute with my government that had a value of less than $30.00.

Maple Fever
Hamilton Ontario, 7-20-96
We did a bunch of these Amway shows but they weren't called Amway they were called something else that I don't remember.
Only people I ever knew that were embarrassed to mention the names of their own product.
Some people call it a pyramid scheme, other people call it a scam I have no idea if it works or not, but it was just very cult like.

It was always the same old thing, some guy up on-stage flashing all of his gaudy wealth, a fancy motorhome parked by the side of the stage, him getting the cameraman to get a close up on his diamond ring.
He would weep like a cheap TV preacher and would use this classic line" People I wish I could just do it for you".

Whatever nobody cares what I think about anything I'm here to put up the sound system and drive the truck.

They're sending me and Mr. Jones to Canada with a semi full of gear and we've been instructed that all we must do is installed the system, make it operational and they have their own people to run it.
I had never driven a semi into Canada before, so I had questions.
We get all the paperwork together, me and Mr. Jones head for the peace bridge.
As we're going across the bridge, there was eight lanes in each direction, and the sign clearly read, "all trucks stay to the right".
We pull up into this wide pull off area, and nice fellow in an official uniform approached the truck, and I handed him all my paperwork.
He looked at this, he looked at that, he stamped something with a fancy looking stamp and he told me to have a nice day, Welcome to Canada.

And we proceeded on our journey
We get to downtown Hamilton and there was a glass pedestrian bridge that spanned across the road.
There was a sign indicating the height of the bridge, it was 4.7.

Of course, I had no idea what 4.7 was I knew what 13 feet 6 inches was.
Mr. Jones was nice enough to jump out of the truck as I slowly crept under that glass bridge.

Next, we found the venue, and as with most arenas in the north the loading dock was underground.
The problem here, was that the underground dark space was designed for trucks with a 45-foot trailer.
I was pulling a 53-foot trailer.
This was a serious problem.

If you had ever seen the Austin Powers movie where he is trapped in a tight space with a golf cart that's exactly what this was.
There was one point I had the truck so jackknifed stuffing that trailer in there, I thought for sure they'd have to disassemble the vehicle to get it out of there.
It was stressful, and it took a long time.

This was a midnight load in, so the plan was to get everything up and running so when the crew came in at 8:00 o'clock in the morning they were ready to start this show which was one of these things that went on all day and into the night.

We get everything working 100%, all the audio mixer had to do was push the fader up and he was all set.
No feedback, everyone in the venue can clearly hear it, it couldn't get any easier.
Video playback, walk in music and people speaking at the podium that's it.

8:00 o'clock in the morning came around, the crew showed up and we gave them the tour of everything.
After demonstrating everything in the system, we gave them the keys to the car and Mr. Jones, and I split to the hotel for some much-needed rest.
We did not have to be back until the loadout, and I had zero intention of seeing one minute of that show.

I wasn't in my bed for 40 minutes before the phone rang.
We have a situation in the arena we need you guys back here.

I walked back into the arena to hear the audio system feeding back. As I stepped up onto the front of house mix platform, I walked right by the client, pushed the sound mixer out of the way and immediately started to assess the mixing console.
This idiot had found a way to touch every single knob on the console and that is some accomplishment.
By making a small change on everything, he ended up making a huge change on everything.
Some people can't grasp the concept of accumulation.
He was one of them.

After I got everything sorted out the client asked if I would stay and mix the show, my response was something to the effect of "well then who's going to drive the truck back to Ohio? Who's going to unload this thing out who's going to sleep for me?

I didn't answer the phone again it didn't go back into the arena until the loadout.
Mr. Jones and I were so happy to be leaving there.

We get back down to the peace bridge, same thing, some nice Canadian officer came over, looked at our paperwork, put some fancy stamp on it and told us to have a nice day.

We pull up to this booth on the American side and the guy asked for me for my paperwork.
I handed him everything I had, and he asked me where my" whatever whatever was?".

I honestly didn't know what he was talking about, and the guy just went off on me.
As he was screaming at me about the differences between Canada and the United States, Mr. Jones was sitting next to me humming the "Battle hymn of the Republic".

As annoying as that was, it was very funny

We pull over into an area that's got a bunch of other trucks lined up and head into this little office area.
Inside the office was about a half dozen drivers all sitting in uncomfortable plastic chairs with the collective facial expressions of people that are making serious considerations about their careers.

We find out that what we need is a bond to enter the country.
When they asked us the value of what was in the truck I just off the top of my head estimated about $1,000,000 and the guy freaked out.
Turns out the average value of what was coming across the border was in the $50,000 neighborhood.

They insisted that we unload the truck so they could see what was in it.
I insisted that required a forklift, minimum of four professional stagehands.

It was early Sunday morning and waking up people in Cleveland and getting a bondsman at the border was our mission #1.

Mr. Jones was on the phone to the people in Cleveland and I was hanging out in the driver's lounge waiting for an answer about this unloading of the truck unpleasantness that was being discussed.

One of the drivers told me that he had been there for three days, and he had a truck full of peanuts.
He said every day they would unload more boxes out of that truck, take a sample of peanuts and then have him put the stuff back in the truck.

Another driver that was sitting there told me that he had a truck full of rugs from India.
He was not being allowed into the country because he was being told by US customs that there was a trade embargo against India.

The driver kept trying to explain that it's not India, it's Iran that has the trade embargo.
He had been there for two weeks.

These stories were not filling me with hope.
Finally, a nice young man in a US customs uniform came out of the office and approached Mr. Jones and I with good news.
We were free to leave, but they were confiscating the truck and everything inside of it.

Since we found these terms unacceptable, we eventually got a bond and eventually got out of there.
That was the last time I ever drove a semi to Canada.

The Plumbers
Agora Theater, July 1996

For about a year when we were working at the Cleveland Agora, we would see the plumbers working on the sprinkler system.
Every load in, we would see these two guys walking around, carrying tools, carrying pipes, and we saw them every time we went to work.

They even had a little area set up down the basement that was their work spot.
At one point they actually finished the job.
We were loading in a show, and Mark Hall the stage manager and I saw the Cleveland fire department walking through inspecting the sprinkler system.
After watching these guys install this for a year, we were curious, what the professionals thought of the job they did.

Mark Hall approached the Fire Chief with the fancy hat and asked him, "What do you think of the sprinkler installation?".
The guy stopped, thought for a second, looked at both of us and said, "If there is ever a fire in here, nobody will survive".
Mark and I looked at each other like what is this guy talking about?

The Fire Chief goes on to explain, "The code for the diameter of pipe for a fire suppression sprinkler system is half inch pipe. These guys used 6-inch pipe.
If there is ever a fire in here and this system is activated, everyone in the building is going to drown".

Turns out the guys did a pretty good job after all.

The Experts from New York
Cleveland Flats, July 1996

This was the kind of show that none of us wanted to do.
Outdoors, portable stage, we had to be there early in the morning, they wanted to get all the sound checks done before noon because the show started at 1:00 o'clock in the afternoon.

The lineup for the day consisted of several bands and several track acts.
we have another name for track acts in the business, it's called karaoke.
From a production standpoint there was nothing easier to execute than a track act.
Give them a microphone, and after that the only question is "How loud do you want the track?".
It's just that simple.
With a full band there's a bunch of variables, with the track act its two, the vocal and the track.

We sound check two bands one track act, and we're ready for the next track act a sound check.
Their management people come up to us and inform me that we can't sound check them until the "Experts from New York" get here.
I must have had some facial expression because they said it twice.

Don't matter to me, I just walked away from them, went back to the monitor console and we sound checked the next band.

After some time, a cab pulled up and the Experts from New York jumped out of the cab.
Walking up on stage came two sharp dressed gentlemen and one of them was carrying a fancy Anvil briefcase.
This was the official purse of the audio person from the 80s and 90s.
You just weren't legitimate unless you had an Anvil briefcase to carry your little bits in.
One of the things that you would carry in an Anvil case was anything fragile, like microphones for example.

The expert with the fancy briefcase comes up to me and says "Oh I see we're ready for sound check well OK do you have that what you call it fancy microphone that nobody ever heard of?"

I said to the guy "I have no idea what you're talking about, nobody advanced anything with us, and if this microphone is so important to you why didn't you bring it with you? What's in that briefcase of yours? Did your mom pack you a sandwich and an apple?" and I walked away from him.

We did the show successfully with that that stupid microphone he was asking for and everybody lived.

Years later I would move to New York City, and I worked for an audio company there
The first time they sent me out of state to do a show, when I arrived at the venue I was introduced to the client,' This is Peter Walker, he's the Expert from New York.

Eddie Money
Canton Rib Cook Off 7-25-96
During my time in northern Ohio, I did a lot of shows with Eddie Money.
It's not just that he was a nice guy, but he really understood his place in the world
He was very appreciative to still have a career when so many artists of his time and of his genre just kind of away the good thing that they had.
Eddie Money always delivered to the crowd because he understood that without the fans you had nothing.

I don't know how many shows I did with him, but I know every single one of them he gave his best to the audience and afterwards he always thanked the crew for doing their best to making him do his best.
he was a real class act.
.

Peter, Paul & Mary
Blossom Music Center 8-1-96

Wash rinse and repeat.
I drove the semi to Blossom, I put up the audio system and now I'm there to be the monitor mixer for the day.
This group shows up, and the rest of the day from that point on was completely unconventional in every sense.

First off, Peter Yarrow introduces himself to me and informs me that he will not be requiring my services today.
I asked him, "Do you have your own monitor guy?".
And he replied, "We have our own thing going, you could just pack all this up, we're not gonna need any of it".
Well, who am I to argue with the talent?
I start packing up the monitor rig, it's never too early to start the loadout.

That's when my front of house guy came up to me and said, that they were planning on mixing the entire show from a homemade mixer that was about the size of a small amplifier.
The mixer was going to be down stage center on the floor, the three microphones and would just send a feed up to our mixing console and that's how they wanted to do it.

It was simply the most ridiculous thing that I had ever seen.
Their sound guy was instructed to make sure that nobody interfered with the signal path that was being sent from the stage.
He kept arguing the point with them, but as I have said many times "You can't stop somebody from ruining their own show".

They insisted they wanted no involvement from me, and I just gave them the thumbs up that I was 100% willing to not do anything for them.
If they were looking for somebody to talk them out of doing something stupid, they were talking to the wrong guy.
Not only was this mildly entertaining but for the first time ever I had the chance to not be involved with what was happening on stage.

So now I already put the monitor rig back on the truck. I've got nothing to do but wait for this thing to be over so I could take the PA out.
I certainly had zero interest in seeing one minute of the show, I was back in catering reading the paper and having coffee.
I just can't say enough, how thrilled I was to not be on stage at Blossom when usually every time I'm there it's for some 10-band extravaganza that I don't get 5 minutes of peace.
For once I could just install the PA and hang out and wait for it all to be over.

As I'm sitting there enjoying my peace and silence, somebody from the venue runs in all panicked telling me "They need you on stage immediately".
As I'm heading to the stage, I'm thinking to myself, "What could they possibly need me for?"
I have no gear out there?
At this point this had to be almost an hour into the show.
When you're a technician and you walk up to the stage during the show and you don't hear the audio system going boom, that means there's a problem.

This silence must have been going on for some time, because when I walked out on stage the audience started applauding.
There I see Peter Yarrow, laying on his belly down stage center, unplugging and plugging in that stupid gizmo of his with the sound buzzing through the audio system.
Having the audience cheer for me to come out and help this man fix this situation, only goes to show the desperation of the audience to get this thing back on track.

I didn't run out there, I casually walked to the center of the stage.
I leaned down to the guy and I said "Hey buddy, what are you doing? Can I help you with anything".
He didn't even look up and he shushed me away.
I looked at the other two, shrugged my shoulders, gave the thumbs up and I walked back to stage left.

And the best part when I got back to catering my coffee was still there.

The Sex Pistols
Nautica Stage 8-13-96
I was a stagehand for this gig so I really didn't have any heavy responsibility and for that I was thrilled.
I knew Glenn the monitor guy who had been through the Agora quite a few times.
The tour was fresh out.

What I thought was funny, was that for sound check when Johnny Rotten came on stage and talked to the microphone for the first time The first thing, he said to the monitor guy was" Why is it so loud?".
It was the last thing I was expecting to hear from the Sex Pistols.

This was one of the very few times that I was out in the audience for the start of the show.
Most of the time you go to work, show to show and you don't think much about what's happening in the moment, you're just doing the job.

But I knew this show was going to be special and it was.
They opened with the song "Bodies" and the EAW KF850 Audio system that we put in that day let everybody in the venue know what was happening up on stage.
It was crystal clear and thick all at the same time.

The band played great, they kept the tempo solid with the original recordings and it was hands down one of the best shows I ever saw there.
With a proper bass player, they were great.

Todd Rundgren
Individualst Tour, 9 shows, 8-19 to 9-1-96
In 1977 I saw Todd Rundgren headline Cleveland Stadium, in 1996 I was thrilled to go on tour with him as Todd's Monitor Mixer.

My buddy Dean was the production manager for this tour, and he put together a group of us Cleveland guys that worked together, knew each other and we were just going to go out and have fun and make it happen.

We were carrying a monitor rig, back line in a rented 24-foot truck and everyone else was traveling in vans.
The tour was just nine shows, and it was featuring Todd's latest album
 "The Individualist".

The plan was for us to leave Cleveland early on Monday the 19th because we had rehearsals in Hampton Beach NH the very next day on the 20th.
We had very little time to drive from Cleveland to Hampton Beach NH, get into the hotel, get a couple hours sleep and load in this show for the first time.

Everyone else was flying, so it was just me and Tommy the back line guy in the truck.
I go to pick up Tommy at 9:00 o'clock in the morning and the first thing he says to me, "I gotta make a couple of stops".
I'm expecting that we're going to just put all his stuff in the truck at 9:00 AM and go but that wasn't the case at all.
We had to make multiple stops around Cleveland picking up strings, sticks and drumheads that we should already have had.

We didn't pull out of Cleveland until the late afternoon, and I remember that I was pissed off about it.
It was a 678-mile ,10-hour drive ahead of us and now best-case scenario I'd get there at 4:00 o'clock in the morning.
Somewhere in western Massachusetts we pulled over to get gas, and somebody filled the tanks full of diesel.

We had to hang around and get the tanks pumped before we could move.

Getting quick service at a truck stop at 1:00 o'clock in the morning to get your tanks pumped was not on the agenda and it took forever.
We pulled into town 30 minutes before we had to load in.
I didn't even get breakfast.

At this point I've been awake a solid 28 hours and I've got to set all this up for the first time and meet Todd Rundgren.
Todd had a reputation for going through a lot of Monitor Mixers, and I had a reputation for having a high tolerance for dealing with volatile artists.

I wouldn't say exactly that we bonded on day one, but I got him everything he needed.
He liked to come around the console and dial up his own mix which I completely supported.
The guy knew exactly what he wanted he knew exactly how to do it and I was wise enough to know that I should exactly stay out of his way.

The first show went pretty good no real problems.
Portland ME was our second gig at the State Theater.
Todd was a little irritated at sound check and no matter what I just couldn't get it to sound the way he wanted it.

I was determined to figure it out what it is that was going to make this guy happy.
That night during the show, during one of the songs Todd says "Pete turn my guitar up...Pete Turn my guitar up ...PETE TURN MY GUITAR UP.....Pete if you don't turn that goddam guitar down I'm going to kill you".

There were two things that I toured with in a custom road case.
An espresso machine, and a bong.

We had a day off in Woodstock, and the next day we played The Chance in Poughkeepsie New York.
That day at soundcheck I had a fresh bong hit and a hot cup of espresso waiting for him.

Like a wild animal approaching a trap, he made several passes around the two items that were sitting on the drum riser for him. He looked over at me, I gave him the nod and he took a sip of the espresso.
"That's really good" he said.
Next, he picked up my little blue plastic bong with the lighter that was sitting next to it.
Bubble, bubble, bubble, an exhale later, everything was cool.
I did that every soundcheck for the rest of the tour and magically the guitar stopped turning itself up and down.

Because Mark Hall and I were the people that we were, our hobby was cutting out pictures of naked women and putting it on the equipment of the musicians at an angle where only they could see it. Every night the guys would come out, and there would be a new configuration to surprise them and give them continuous motivation throughout the set.

However, we didn't put any naked women on any of Todd's gear.
At one point, Todd approached Dean the production manager and asked, "What's up with the Cleveland guys and all the porn?".

By the time we get to Washington DC, Todd came up to Mark and I and said to us "Hey guys how come I don't get anything to look at?" Of course, we responded, that we would take care of that right away.

That night when Todd came out on stage, he walked down center, and on the base of his microphone stand, that only he could see from his angle, was a picture of Gary Coleman smiling at him.
He was laughing so hard; he had a hard time starting the show.

Mark Hall and I had also sent the runner out that day to bring us back a six-foot inflatable penis that we wanted to put in the dressing room.
What they came back with was a blow-up sex doll sheep, called an "I Love Uwe".
You got to work with what you got, so Mark modified the genital area with red sharpie, and we left it in the dressing room for the band.
I will note, that when the show is over, the sheep was gone.

The other fun thing about that trip to DC, was that we stayed at the Watergate hotel.
Always nice to get some letter stationary from the classy places.

We ended the tour in Cleveland at the Nautica stage which seemed appropriate.
Todd did a great job of pissing off his fans at these shows, because he refused to play any of his classic songs, he was only doing his latest album in its entirety.

Absolutely his right to do, he's the artist, his name is on the ticket.
Only one night on the tour, did he whip out some old stuff and it was amazing.
Prairie Prince was on drums for this run and he's a monster drummer.
When they went into the song "Black Mariah", all the hair on my body stood up.

Up to this point the entire tour for me, had been Todd playing all these songs I'd never heard before.
But the moment he played that song, I was catapulted back to being 14 years old and standing on the field at Cleveland Stadium June 6th, 1977.
It was Todd Rundgren's Utopia, and the stage was a Sphinx with lasers coming out of the eyes.
There was a moment when I really realized that this was the same guy up on that stadium stage 19 years earlier playing the same song.

I mean you know it walking into it, you know it factually, but you really don't know it till you feel it, till it runs through your veins like ice just waking you up.

Being on the side of the stage with Todd Rundgren when he was playing Black Mariah, was one of the most powerful moments of my career for me.

I never told Todd that I saw him in 1977, and what an impression it made on me.

Another Bad Idea
BumFuck Pennsylvania, September 1996
Some guy out in Pennsylvania who owned a construction company, had a piece of property that looked like a natural amphitheater.
It was a wide-open hillside that had 180-degree openness curve to it, with forest behind it.
Somebody got the bad idea that we should start doing shows here and that's what we were there for.

This happened to be the opening show of the venue, and there were multiple acts booked for Friday night and all-day Saturday into the night.
We had a day to load in that was the good news.
the bad news is that it had rained the entire week and it was raining when we showed up.

Water was running down that hill in little rivers accumulating to the bottom where they were going to erect the stage, and it was just a giant mud pit.

I showed up there driving the semi, with Mr. Jones, and John Conde in the truck with me.
What we saw when we drove up, was that they had built a makeshift road from the top of the hill down to the bottom where the stage was going to be.

At the bottom of that road, was the semi from the staging/lighting company and it was stuck in the mud.
They used a bulldozer to pull that truck up the hill and out of the way so they could build the stage.

Once they get the four posts and the roof system up, everyone realizes that you can't build the stage until my truck goes down there and turns around.
As deep as the mud was, for sure I only had one pass at this.

The angle of this road and the pitch of it was very steep.

I was driving a cab over tractor pulling a 53-foot trailer, and the driver's position in that truck is about 9 feet off the ground.
At that height leaning over at a 45-degree angle it was very uncomfortable.

I remember saying to Mr. Jones and John, "I think you guys should get out of the truck for this one".
I was honestly not 100% that I could do this safely.

I start to make my descent down the road, and immediately I'm sinking into the earth.
There had to be 50 people working as laborers on this site, they had multiple bulldozers and backhoes and all kinds of equipment out there.
When they realize that there's no way I could roll this semi into this soft mud they decided to build a wooden road out of logs.

I don't remember how long it took, but they laid logs down in front of my truck from where I was positioned about 70 yards down to the bottom of the hill.
As I started to roll on the new log road, the logs immediately started bunching up underneath the truck.

Now the plan is to cut the logs in half.
I don't remember if they cut those logs or had other logs that were cut in half, and I don't remember how long it took either, but it was a long time

Now we're ready to do it for the third time.
At this point, my adrenaline is rushing hard.
I'm so angry that I'm put in this position, I'm expected to perform off-road circus tricks in an 80,000-pound vehicle.

I get in the truck and start my third attempt to the bottom of the hill. the truck gets rolling, and it's a weird sensation as the entire vehicle was rocking back and forth rolling over these half split logs.
As I get rolling, I see in my rearview mirrors that everybody is running away as fast as possible away from my truck.

What's happening, is that as I'm driving over these half logs, I'm crushing them and splintering them, and they're being flung around the field like flicked toothpicks.

I had the momentum and I kept going.
I was prepared to make a wide turn when I got to the bottom so I could swing the truck around in one motion and have it facing back uphill so it would be easier to tow out and we could still unpack it.

As I'm at the bottom of the hill making my swing, the salesman for the gig Mr. Z., jumps in front of my truck waving his arms and screaming, 'NOOOO".
I locked up the brakes and the truck slid in the mud and sank to a halt.

I popped open the door of that truck and jumped out, if I would have had a weapon in my hand, I would have killed him with it.
I screamed at him "WHAT THE FUCK ARE YOU DOING? DO YOU HAVE ANY IDEA HOW DIFFICULT THIS IS? WHY DID YOU STOP ME?".

Mr. Z. looked right at me and said, "You almost drove on the grass".
I remember being frozen, completely shocked at what I was hearing.
This site was a disaster, and we haven't even started yet.
The least important thing in the entire world to me at that moment what's the grass.

We spent the next hour with a bulldozer pulling the sound truck out of the mud.
Just as my previous prediction we ended up with a semi pointing up the hill and once the stage was constructed, I backed it up against the stage and kept the monitor rig inside the truck for the rest of the gig.

The stairs leading up to the stage had eight steps to it.
Yet only six were visible because the other two were under the mud.
one of the young guys that was with the staging company lost a shoe in the mud and never recovered it.
Spent the weekend with one shoe on.

Not one human being that was a part of that production felt any mercy to send somebody out to get this young man a pair of shoes.

It was standard operating procedure for how technicians were treated.
Friday night we did the shows, it rained the entire time, and nobody showed up.
It was one of those scenarios where it was easier to introduce the audience to the band then the band to the audience.

The next day it rained every minute.
The perimeter of the hillside was a bunch of tents set up with vendors who I'm sure paid to be there only to suffer through the disappointment of being cold, wet with zero customers.

There was one tent that had a young woman in it that was selling custom jewelry.
She was shivering and huddled around a little clip light that she had.

It was later in the afternoon at this point, everything was wet, and it was getting colder.
I spent a few minutes looking at everything she had for sale, and she asked me finally if I would like to buy something.

I said yes, "How much for the clip lamp?".
I could see she was torn, because it was their only source of light and heat but at the same time, I was most likely her only sale of the day.

$5 later, I had a clip light for the inside of the truck.

I liked Mr. Z, most of the time, just not that time.
The gig totally sucked.

Bob Dole Tour
10-10 to 10-20-96
Here I was on the tour that I did not want to be on.
We were doing rallies and media junkets for Bob Dole and his running mate Jack Kemp.

I was driving the semi, and I had two other guys with me in the truck.
We would show up someplace, set up a stage, press risers, a cutaway platform for a camera, that's how you get that fancy presidential looking shot, the lighting for the stage and the audio for the site Including press feeds.
It would all throw up out of the same truck.
Dealing with people from political campaigns is always a nightmare.
Nine times out of 10 it's people that are unqualified for the position, have no idea what they're talking about, and don't have a firm grasp of reality of what time frames are.

The first night on this disaster tour we had to disassemble and assemble the stage nine times because this moron couldn't decide where she wanted the stage.
Finally, I completely snapped and strongly explained to her that building the stage isn't the only aspect of what we must accomplish.
Insult to injury of course they booked us a motel 45 minutes away from the gig.
After working all night long to get this thing up and going because she couldn't decide, now I had to drive almost an hour so I can get less sleep than the quantity of time that it took to drive back and forth.

We get back to the site it's 7:00 o'clock in the morning.
Everything is covered in dew, and it's just early morning Ohio chill in the air.
Right behind my mix position, was a tent set up with catering in for the press.
I went in there to get a cup of coffee and I was denied.
Press only.

I'm the one providing the press feed, to the press, and I'm not worthy of some watered-down piss flavored coffee and a stale pastry.
That was the standard treatment for the rest of the run.

On the 20th of October we were up in New Hampshire suffering through another one of these disasters when I got a phone call from my buddies.

It was Brad the rigger from Nautica, Chris from the lighting company and Mark Hall from the Agora.
These guys were all on tour with Jesus Christ Superstar.

They asked me if I was interested and coming out to replace the front of house sound mixer.
If I accepted the position, I would have to be in Vegas in a couple of days.
I only had one answer for them, I'll meet you in Las Vegas.

Jesus Christ Superstar
International Tour, 67 Shows 10-24-96 to 1-20-97
When I was 10 years old, one of my mom's friends gave me a double album.
It would become to be known as the "Brown album".
Jesus Christ Superstar featuring Ian Gillan on lead vocals.
I was completely blown away by this music.
The opening overture is haunting, captivating, and brilliant.
Very few pieces of music have a crescendo that builds to a finale, then drops back down into a sense of suspense.
It truly is a stunning piece of music.
I consider that to be one of the greatest pieces of music ever written.

I knew all the words to the entire album, and I could play along with most of it on my guitar
The first time I got to see the movie starring Carl Anderson and Ted Neely, I was singing along the entire time.

Now it's the 28th of October 1996 and I'm dragging my luggage through the airport in Las Vegas on my way to meet up with the national tour, of Jesus Christ Superstar.

There's a phrase that gets thrown around a lot to the point where it's lost a lot of meaning.
When dreams come true.
This was 100% my dream coming true, it's difficult to explain how deep it was for me, that I was chosen for this.
My friends who recommended me for the position had no idea that I was completely familiar with all this material.

Somehow in all the time we spent hanging out together at the Agora or backstage at Nautica, the subject of early 70s musicals never came up.
Good old fashioned Vegas corruption started from the moment I left the airport.
After I got into the taxi, gave the driver the destination he asked me the question have you ever been to Vegas before.

being completely ignorant of my situation I responded with the truth no.

That's when he took a left instead of a right and my $5 ride from the airport to the Hard Rock was now $20 as I got a unscheduled sightseeing tour on the backside of Vegas.

It taught me a valuable lesson and to this day when no matter what city I show up in if a driver ever asked me if I've been there before, my standard answer is that I live here.,

I show up at the Hard Rock and going through the stage door.
As I'm coming through the back of the loading dock dragging my luggage, I walked right into the quick change for all the dancers getting into their outfits as Harrods sex slaves.
This was the sign that I was no longer on the Bob dole tour.

After successfully getting my eyeballs back into my skull, I went and hung out in the production office until the show was over.
Loadout, I put my luggage in the bay under the bus and officially climbed the board the first tour bus of my life.

The bus was an older eagle, dark blue carrying God knows how many stories from all the previous occupants that ever slept in these 12 coffins.
Standard tour bus, front lounge then 12 bunks in the middle and a rear lounge.
After some time hanging out with my buddies and some quality bong hits, I climbed up into my bunk on the top left side and had one of the best sleeps ever.

After all my time driving all over the continent, almost two years living in a school bus, for me this was much appreciated.
Just the simple comfort, drifting off to sleep without the responsibility of getting me, everybody else and the gear to the next destination.

It was awesome

We were up in the Pacific Northwest doing one nighter, as I was learning the show from the sound designer.
One thing about Broadway shows that's important is consistency.

It was my understanding; Andrew Lloyd Webber gave this company the rights to Jesus Christ Superstar under the conditions that if the show stopped for more than two weeks that the rights would revert back to him.
He wanted to do a updated version of it in London and a subsequent tour but he couldn't launch any of that while this door was still running.
Nobody anticipated that this thing would just go and go.

With Ted Neely and Carl Anderson, the show was dramatically good. Although Carl only did the A Markets, the guy that was his understudy was fantastic.
The band was great, the cast was rock solid, the show was really good.

It was a big deal for the principals to have a new mixer come in for the show, I had no misconceptions of the expectations that I was facing.
I mixed my first show in Boise ID, and everything went great.
After that was Rapid City and then Bismarck ND, I was ready.

By the time we had a three night sit down in Minneapolis I was dialed in.

After Minneapolis we went to Charleston WV for a two day sit down. If you've ever wondered how an actor knows where to stand on stage, it's because there's a marker system like a grid on the downstage and on the sides of the stage.

Downstage it's usually an alphabet or a letter system, in the case of Jesus Christ Superstar we would lay out our own rubber floor that's called "Marley" and painted on that floor was the alphabet.

If a dancer needed to be standing at C16 they knew how to find their spot another aspect of this alphabet system is that it was easy for the lighting people to label the Footlights corresponding with the alphabet on the floor.
Without footlights, light shining up in the faces of the actors, everybody looks like a ghoul.

The lighting technician was explaining to the local stagehands to just set all the lights down in order.
They kept asking what the order was.
The technician kept saying you know A,B,C,D.
Then the guy said what's after that?
The technician said E,F,G.
I had to step in I said "Guys, guys, have you never heard the song? The ABC song is not just very popular, but it is rather catchy"
I declined to sing the song for them I had my own issues.

Everything in the audio department was labeled professionally and that wasn't working.
This tour had been on the road for so many years and played every market in the country, that now the last six months of its life left with a couple of A Market close outs and a bunch of places that this show normally never would have come to.

Nobody knew what DSL was, that stands for downstage left.
I was a one-man sound department, I put up all the speakers, ran all the cables, checked all the wireless, put all the microphones on the band of the pit and mix the show.

To maximize my personal time, I need to minimize my time putting the show together and one of the hinderance, was having professional labels that unprofessional stagehands were incapable of understanding.

That day in Charleston WV I sent the runner out for two animal book stickers
That was the day I labeled absolutely everything in my system with animal stickers.
People laugh about it but believe me when I say that I never once had a stagehand plug a bunny into a horse or a turtle into a giraffe.
My system was 100% successful.
I'm all about results.

The very next night we were doing a one nighter in Reading PA.
The show was over, we were doing the loadout, I was at the front of house mixing console wrapping up some cables.
My buddy Cody who is on the props department, yelled out to me from the stage was it OK to pick up my electrical feeder?
My response, "Sure, as long as it's disconnected."
I went back to what I was doing.

About two minutes later I look up and I see these four guys pulling on this electrical feeder that is so taught it looks like a jump rope all the way across the stage.
There was a brilliant flash of white light out of the electrical room on the stage right side.
They had pulled it out-of-the-box live.
The electrician was sitting in that room as they did it and if not for the fact that he had his back to the panel and he was reading a newspaper that's the only thing that saved his eyesight.

Couple days in Jersey, back up to Buffalo and then we headed to Boston for a week.
One of the things about our tour is that we were a nonunion tour.
All the legitimate theatrical union houses were giving us a hard time about it
My point was if you don't want me to be non-union, just bring me into your union and that solves the problem, but you can't expect me just to disappear into the vapors.

One of the interesting things every day was that since Brad was the Head Carpenter, He was responsible for the distribution of the crew every day.
Even though we averaged a four-hour minimum for our load in, I had my job down to 90 minutes.
There was no reason for me to come in the venue at 8:00 in the morning, all of my gear was in the nose of the second truck.

At 8:00 AM, the entire crew is ready to work including whoever's been assigned to the sound department.
I always had four local guys assigned to me, every morning Brad would give them the same speech, "Mr Walker does not like coming off the bus until 10:30 in the morning. Mr Walker does not want your resume, does not want to hear about how the last guy did it, does not want to know how you usually do it and does not want your opinion regarding anything".

So, by the time I'm cruising in the venue 1030 ish, there's already four guys with their arms folded that had been sitting there since 8:00 in the morning waiting for me.
We get to Boston and the crew there was 100% uncooperative on every little thing that we wanted to do.
At one point I was down in the orchestra pit and the only thing I was trying to accomplish was getting an electronic keyboard out of the case and onto a stand.

The props department who traditionally handles musical instruments refused to touch it because they demanded that since it had a plug on it that falls under the electrics department.
The electrics department came down there and said that it is true that it has an electrical plug on it however it still falls under the classification of a musical instrument therefore it falls under the jurisdiction of the props department.

This went on for 35 minutes as I stood there with my hands in my pockets, staring at the ground trying not to explode.

Eventually we got that freaking keyboard on that stand and we had five nights of shows there.

Another interesting thing about Boston was before the show Carl Anderson told me that during the show, he would cue me when he wanted me to turn off his microphone to the house but wanted me to put headphones on and listen to him and he would give me some cues on how we wanted the stage to sound.

In between mixing 430 cues during the show, paying attention to everything else then pop on the headphones to listen to Carl, was challenging at best, but he was Carl Anderson and I made it happen.

After Boston we had a couple days in Stamford CT, and we had the day off on Thanksgiving before the tour headed up to Portland ME.

Mark Hall and I rolled 20 joints and jumped on a train to New York City to attend the Macy's Thanksgiving Day parade
This was the last year, 1997 that they had the floats at the old traditional high altitude, before the windstorm that day.

We were right there at 42nd St. watching Woody Woodpecker wipe out hooked on the side of that building.
Float after float was out of control and people were running and screaming as we were smoking joints two at a time just laughing our ass off.
It was awesome

The only thing better than watching Underdog wipe out into a Calvin Klein billboard was the time we spent in Times Square's worst strip club, Runway 69 before heading back to Connecticut.

Ted who played Christ was certainly a ladies' man.
Since Mark Hall was responsible for putting together the set every day, he decided that we should customize it.
There was an elevator built into the upstage of the set and it was used twice during the show.

The first time the elevator was used was when Ted would rise and make his first appearance.

The second time in the show that the elevator was used was when the actor playing Pontius Pilot would appear with his purple cape and make a dramatic spin to face the audience.
He rode up with his back to the audience.
One of our hobbies in every town once the work was done was sending the runner out to get nonsense.

We just loved the sport of sending somebody into a store, making them very uncomfortable to have to ask for very specific publications.
We always asked for the same magazines, no substitutions would be accepted.

The list was "Foreskin Quarterly", "Latin Inches" and "The Best of Ouch".
We knew you just couldn't go down to the 711 and pick these up, you had to go into some ghetto with a neon triple X sign out front. Someplace where your feet are sticking to the floor.
Drop anything on that floor, just consider it a donation.

If the runner came back and truly had a look of horror on their face, we always made sure to throw the magazines away right in front of them.
Of course, with so many gay guys on the tour, the cock magazines never went to waste.
Occasionally we would have them get the latest issue of "Black Tail", but that was for me.

We were in Ames IA, and we set the runner out for a bunch of Hustler, Penthouse and Playboy magazines.
Also on that list was a dozen children's scissors with the rounded edges.
We spent the afternoon with the stagehands and our new fancy scissors, cutting out pictures of titties and vaginas.

After that we pasted them all over the inside of the wall that faced Ted before riding the elevator.

The set was made out of many pieces, and now these 8 feet long 6-foot-high piece was forever known as the" Titty Wall".
Ted loved it.
Because of how the cue landed in the show, He would have time just to hang out there before he went up and he really appreciated having the visual stimulation as inspiration before going on.
After a few shows went by, the guy who played Pontius Pilot had a request.
His position was that since Ted had a Titty Wall, he was gay, and he didn't have anything to look at.

We said no problem, we got you covered.
So, what do you think we did?
We send the runner for the latest "Latin Inches" and "Foreskin Quarterly" and we spent the afternoon cutting out cocks with the stagehands.

After that, the" Cock Wall" was born.
As far as cock walls go, it was tremendous.
After that we had a whole new sport every load in, and it was to find the surliest stagehand and make him hold the cock wall.

There was absolutely no reason to make somebody stand there and hold that wall in place, it was only to make them feel uncomfortable. Have no doubt, it worked every time.

In many aspects the tour was certainly a rolling Sodom and Gomorrah.
With four buses of cast and crew there was a lot of partying going on.

Another funny thing that we did was we had a 6-foot-tall inflatable penis, that was the last thing that would go into the carpentry truck. This would be the first truck opened at the next gig.

The penis was strategically rigged that when the door is opened it would fall straight down, like a tower coming at you.
it was always funny watching the reaction of the guys in the morning when that penis came out of the truck.

At one of the load ins, when the penis came off the truck it landed right in the arms of the head teamster that was standing there.
The guy was just standing there stunned and shocked holding the six-foot penis like carrying the wounded out of combat.
Mark Hall immediately approached him and said, "We gotta know what show you booked. Are we doing the X or the family show? We got to know".
It was always funny.

Another running joke that we would have with the locals, we would have discussions amongst ourselves in front of the crew if we were going to do the crucifixion scene or the execution with the runaway ox cart.

We were out in the Midwest somewhere and Cody, who was the prop guy and I had one ongoing issue that was happening every day. The one thing that we requested every day for breakfast catering, was Pop Tarts.
Not toasted strudel surprise, not some weirdo generic off brand, but legitimate Pop Tarts.
Cody and I walked into breakfast catering, walked up to the little table, there was no Pop Tarts, and without saying one word to each other we flipped all the tables and walked out of there.

For me the most special shows that we did was after we came to Cleveland towards the end of the tour.
From early on, Ted Neely liked the way I mixed the show.
Although I never told Ted that I had been listening to the show since I was 10 years old, him and I talked quite a bit about nuances and little things that he thought I was picking up on that previous audio mixers were not.

I had the blessings to do what I wanted with the show straight from Jesus, so I made some changes.

We had an actor that played a high priest named "Caiaphas".
This was the only baritone vocal part of the entire show and I think it was the 4th number in.
This guy sang it naturally one octave below what it was written for.
It was tremendous hearing this guy do it, sonically amazing.

One of the things I've always hated about shows is when the show starts the audience is already excited to be there.
There's no reason to use all the audio, all the lighting, all the everything the first instant the show starts because where do you go from there?

For Jesus Christ Superstar, I would keep the subwoofers turned off for the first four songs.
The moment his vocal line came in with, "All gentlemen, you know why we are here, we have not much time, but quite a problem here", I fed his vocal directly into the subwoofers and turned them on for the first time.

There was not one performance that the audience did not gasp.
It was such a dramatic effect, people accused me of using a special effect, using a harmonizer, using a pitch transformer but it was all him.
Combination with the audience not realizing that they haven't heard and felt low frequency for the first 15 minutes of the show, it was a stunning audio effect.

On January 19th, 1997, we did the last show in Philadelphia.

This was hands down the greatest experience of my life.
I was out on this great adventure with all my friends and these people that I loved, mixing one of the greatest scores of music that I think ever was produced in the 20th century.

Just getting to meet Ted Neely and Carl Anderson, let alone hanging out with these guys, laughing with these guys joking with them and most of all mixing their performance and bringing it to the fans, it was really special to me.

At some point in life, I'm going to write a proper book about my time with the Judas company and Jesus Christ Superstar.

There are too many people to list, and I don't want to miss anybody. The stories of this tour and of this show from before I got there till when we closed it it's certainly a story worth documenting properly.

Believe me when I say that this was the best tour of my life.

New Edition, Backstreet, Keith Sweat, 702
National Tour, February 1997
Believe me when I say that this was the worst tour of my life.

I just spent six months on the road.
After six months, 67 shows I was ready just to take some time and chill out.

The other thing about living in Cleveland is that in the wintertime there was no work available whatsoever, so I was very thankful that I had been sending my money home this whole time.
I was sending my paychecks home and keeping my per diem.
It turns out that this was a bad idea.

When I got home my ex-wife had two things to tell me.
The first thing she told me was that with some of the money that I sent home she bought me a nice recliner chair, a real lazy boy that I could kick back in whenever I was home and not working.

The second thing she told me was that we had $77 in the bank.
That was not what I sent home, that was not a lot and that was not going to cut it.
Now it was worst case scenario, I had to find employment in February in Cleveland.

I contacted one of the biggest touring sound companies in the world which happened to be in Cleveland, 8th Day Sound.
In the past I had done some work for them in the shop and had a couple gigs as a tech but that was about it.

Now that I was fresh off mixing a national musical tour and I had a Class A license, suddenly, I had a value to them.
They explained to me that they have a tour out, that is such a debacle, the show is incapable of loading out and getting to the next city on time.
The tour was adding another entire arena audio system and a lighting system to leapfrog the shows.

My mission, if I choose to accept it, is to drive the semi with an arena audio system in it with some lighting bits on the end of my truck for the next four weeks doing every other show.
I would be doing all the driving and they would get another tech with me at every show to help me hang the PA.
Oh, and I would also have to deal with 4 mixing consoles and 10 racks in front of house.
I absolutely did not want to do this, but I was broke and I had no other choice.

Two days later at 5:00 o'clock in the morning on Super Bowl Sunday, I pulled out of the 8th Day Sound shop driving the Volvo semi loaded with a Turbosound Flashlight arena audio system.

My first show was in Albuquerque New Mexico, and I had two days to get there.
But first, I had to go to Chicago to a company called "Pete's Lights" and pick up some lighting bits that they were going to put on the end of my truck. I was instructed to leave 10 feet on the back of the truck for some of their gear and that's exactly what I did.

I wanted to be in Chicago by 9:00 o'clock in the morning so they could just put their stuff on my truck, and I can go.
There was a snowstorm scheduled for that day and I wanted no part of it.
For me it was bad enough that I had to go to Chicago in the first place which was completely out of the way for me.
I get to they're shop at 9:00 o'clock in the morning as I planned it, and they are 100% unprepared to put anything on my truck.
I spend the next seven hours sitting in their parking lot wasting time waiting for these jerk offs to put anything in my vehicle.

Worst case scenario, I pulled out of Chicago at 4:00 o'clock in the afternoon during a raging snowstorm and now I'm crawling down the highway.

By the time I got to Albuquerque, I pulled in just in time for the load in.

As rough as my trip was, it was a lot worse for the lighting company. Those morons put the lightest thing they had which was the truss on the back of my truck, and they put the heavy dimmers and cable in the 24-foot truck they had rented.
Somewhere in Missouri they went over a way station and were put out of service by the DOT.
Their employer had to come down there with a second 24-foot truck split the load and they drove two rental trucks to Albuquerque.

The night before our load in at Tingly arena, they had a rodeo. Every molecule of air lingered with the tail brown dirt from the ground.
You could taste the air, and it didn't taste good.

I get a crash course in hanging the audio system and we survived the first show.
During that loadout I was approached by the owner of the lighting company who wanted to meet up with me in the morning at a local truck stop and figure out what was the appropriate items to put on my truck so their truck wouldn't be overweight.

I meet these assholes at the truck scales, and we spend hours taking stuff off their truck, putting it on my truck, driving over the scales, then taking stuff off my truck, back on that truck, over the scales again.
These guys had no clue what any of their stuff weighed.
And since it was just the two techs, the owner and me, four guys carrying a 14-foot aluminum ramp is a tough item and that's what we had to move every time we took something on and off my truck. It completely sucked.

Finally, they got it figured out, and the owner pulled out a wad of cash and was peeling a 20 dollar bill off to hand me for my troubles. Like a Kung Fu master snatching the Pebble out of the hand, I snatched that entire wad of cash from him.
him and his two guys were shocked.
I said to him "Do you really think 20 bucks is worth wasting two days of my life? Go fuck yourself" and I drove to Sacramento CA.

The production staff for this tour had to be some of the stupidest people I had ever encountered in my entire life.
It's not just that they were incompetent and clearly unqualified, but they were stupid.
Every night I was on that tour, I would watch a 20-foot set piece go into one of the trucks, come out turn back around and go back in. they didn't do it wrong most of the time they did it wrong every time.

I think the entire tour was 22 trucks of nonsense and God knows how many busses of losers just along for the ride.
The stage set was a two-story house that nobody knew how to properly assemble.
The set had three different elevators, so the talent could pop out in three different locations.
Another stupid feature of this show was that each act had to have their own" Marley floor" with their own logo on it.
That means that they had to peel up the floor in between each performance.
That's a tremendous undertaking for a good crew let alone a bunch of idiots.

On our best nights the show ran five hours.
Five hours is a long time for an audience to be punished out there. the sound system was turned up to 11 from the moment the show started till the moment it was over there was never a point where there was a soft moment or a crescendo down at all it was balls to the wall the entire time.

One of the sound mixers that we had with the band Blackstreet insisted he had to have the brand-new Midas XL4 mixing console with the full automation because in his words "I can't keep track of 6 vocals".

He said this with a straight face to me, as I was standing in front of him wearing my Jesus Christ Superstar tour jacket.

I just spent six months of my life mixing a tour with 26 vocals, and here is this grown man explaining to me that he is incapable of handling
6-vocals without automation.

The Midas XL4 is considered to be one of the greatest live sound mixing consoles of all time.
But in February of 1997 the automation software just was not up to speed and the console crashed every show.
In a time before reliable cell service, we had to have a phone line run to front of house every day so we can call the guy in England and go through the sequence of unlocking the console.
it was a tremendous pain in the ass.

By the time we got to that Sacramento we had a problem.
My boss pages me, that's how old school this was to get the page.

I called back the sound company and he says" You can't let them start this show unless they give you $10,000, they owe us a lot of money.
 I don't want you to do one more show, if you don't get $10,000 from them you have to load the show out".

I follow instructions, I go into the production office, and I said to the big kahuna in there exactly that.
I need $10,000 or I'm loading the show out.
He said, "Fuck you Motherfucker".
I said OK and I left the production office, went and got the stagehands and I start lowering the PA system out of the sky and getting ready to load it back in the truck.

The production manager comes out and he brings all his goons.
The part I left out, he had a bunch of guys pulling their guns out surrounding me and he was above and beyond unprofessional and it was shitty, and this is the way those assholes did it.
When I was standing out there with 20 stagehands suddenly, the playing field was a little more level.

it was no secret how these guys were treating me and everybody at the venue was on my side.

Now suddenly, he's got 10 grand.
So now I gotta go to this process and get the runner take me some bank and forward the money to them and just another big waste of my day like I got plenty of time for that.
When I asked my boss in the first place, since I'm driving the semi, building the show, working the show, loading it out and driving to the next city, when should I find time to be sleeping?

He said I should find some time during the day somewhere.
I don't really know when that magical time may or may not be.

I survived that and they took my laminated pass away from me which they had your name on it and they gave me a new one and it said, "Mother Fucker".
I took that pass and threw it in the garbage.
For the rest of the tour, I had a sticky every day.
The tour was above and beyond horrible.

My next gig was in Boise ID, and I was nervous about one thing and that was taking the semi over the California, Nevada border on I-80 known as Donner Pass.
To make things worse the weather sucked, and it was a full out snowstorm and the only thing that kept me going was that the prediction was that the weather was going to get worse.
There was no option for me but to keep moving.

The peak of the mountain was 7000 feet, and it was mandatory that all trucks pull over and put chains on the tires for the descent down the mountain.
This was my first time ever putting chains on a truck and boy I was nervous about this.
The process is to lay the chains down, drive over them and then attach them to the tires.
It sounds like an easier process until you're in a full Blizzard and the snows coming in sideways, it was tough.

I start my descent down the mountain, and I feel like I've got a comfortable speed.
The snow stood so deep it was eye level with me in the truck.

To make things worse it was just getting dark, and the snow was coming down heavy.
I was in the right-hand lane and there was a car about 20 yards in front of me.
I look in my left-hand mirror and I could see that there's a truck passing me.
Upon closer inspection, I concluded that it's my truck that's passing me.

Gravity is taking the trailer down the mountain faster than I want to, and now it's pushing itself sideways down the hill.
Tapping the brakes in that situation is a death sentence.
The only way out was for me to accelerate and pull the whole thing back straight again and that's exactly what I did.

Like upshifted and accelerated I almost pushed the car in front of me right off the road.
I kept a pace down that mountain that was a little uncomfortable for me.
There was actually a driver behind me that witnessed the whole thing that called me up on the CB, the trucker's channel, channel 19.

We were both in the right lane doing a solid 70 miles an hour which felt extremely fast for that pitch and a truck with the giant letters that said "Swift" on the side of it passed us doing at least 110 miles an hour.
We both watched that truck as the trailer tires left the ground as it went around the turns.
it was wild.

Within a minute he was long gone and out of sight.

About 30 minutes later, the terrain flattened out on the other side of the mountain and way up in the distance ahead we could see that Swift truck pulled over on the side of the road.
Me and the other driver that was carrying a load of toilet paper both pulled over to check on the guy.

As we were walking up to the cab of the dude's truck you could smell the remains of his brakes and all his bodily fluids.
The guy was incapable of letting go of the steering wheel, his hands were tightly gripped around it.
He explained to us that at some point he was going too fast and when he took the truck out of gear to downshift, he was never able to get his revolutions back up, was never able to get it back in gear and free wheeled it down that mountain.

Once you're out of gear, it's very difficult to recover, as this gentleman learned.

I made it to Boise ID, Bobby Brown didn't show up for his show that night.
Right when the show is about over, a limo comes through the back crashes into the back of the stage outcomes Bobby Brown and Whitney falls out the other side.
It was almost over and now it goes another hour.

The loadout was such a disaster for this show, that I would take apart the mixing consoles, I had four of them at the front of house. Then I would go out to my truck, and I would sleep for 3 hours, and then come back in the arena and then start the rest of the loadout.

They tell me during that load out, that my next show is in Las Cruces New Mexico all the way down by the Mexico border.
Now I don't know how good you are with the geography, but Las Cruces is all the way across the continent.
Driving my semi 90 miles an hour all the way across Nevada to get to the next gig on time was a nightmare.

We get to Las Cruces and during the show Bobby Brown pulls a gun out on Ralph.

They would each do their own little solo thing, somebody disrespected somebody, I don't know what happened, but he pulled a gun out on stage and pushed it into his chest, pushed him through the front doors of the set and disappeared backstage.
The band was just kind of playing alone, and then the band just stops playing, gets up and they walk off stage.
Nobody knows what's going on.

I'm at the front of house mixing console, the little phone beeps, I pick it up and they say," Hey man, shows over you better come back here we think they're gonna riot".
I was like do you want me to put some music on.
It was so weird that they just wanted to end the show like that with not making an announcement to the crowd about anything.

I went backstage and all of Bobby Brown's a security people had guns all these other people had guns.
We had two buses of security people who were just people that just got out of prison for the most part, they carried firearms, but they were not super professional security.
The first people out of the building were the venue security staff they were long gone once the guns came out backstage

With all these guns out backstage, I thought I was better off with the crowd rioting.
The crowd destroyed the place, broke the glass all the way around the building.

The next gig for me on that tour off to Oklahoma City.
I got there and the stage was being provided by the venue.
The stage was one foot high.
The standard stage for us was 6 feet high so this was a little bit shorter.

Since the production staff was unable to get to the next city on time because there were too busy in the parking lot partying with girls all night and doing God knows whatever, they always showed up at 3:00 or 4:00 o'clock in the afternoon.
I'm in the venue at 8:00 o'clock in the morning doing my job.
I hung the audio system like I do every day, you know with math. It's X amount of distance from here, Y amount of distance from there, pointing the speaker system is all a mathematical equation. The stage being one foot high doesn't concern me I put the same sound system in.

So, Skip the Details, the production manager for this thing comes in and goes "Pete when they are gonna put the other motherfucking stage on top of this motherfucker".
I said, "Skip you should learn how to get here on time and do your job".

This was the same guy that had threatened me at gunpoint just a couple weeks earlier in California and now thinks that I should be concerned about looking out for him when he's not doing his job. What a douche.

Dallas was the last show of the tour, and I couldn't be more thrilled that this fiasco was coming to an end.
I sent their runner out to a pet store to buy me $50 worth of cockroaches.
Because there's one thing that I wanted to give that lighting company, a little gift of cockroaches in their cases to take home with them.
The runner called me from the pet store and said they didn't have cockroaches, but they had crickets, I'll take them.

Every show they hung their lighting trusses in the wrong spot.
I used the tape measure; they would feel it out.
I wanted to give them the gift that would keep on giving.

50 bucks' worth of crickets is a lot of crickets.

283

I filled all their road cases so when they got back to the shop, open those things up you know they'd have crickets forever.
It was very juvenile, but I can be juvenile.

Me and my buddy Bob Cowan who was hanging the PA with me on this, got up early and got the hell out of Dallas.
It was a beautiful sunny day and we're heading up to drive to Chicago to dump this crappy lighting off the semi.
We come over this hill, and there's these brown things all over the road.
We were trying to process exactly what it is that we were looking at.
Just over the horizon that I can't see, is a tornado, an F4 that is just hit a horse farm and was flinging horses everywhere.
Refrigerators in the trees.
It looked like somebody had taken a lawn mower through the forest as far as we could see left and right was a swath everywhere that tornado had just come through.
There were tractor trailers just like ours laying on their sides all over the road.

This was March 1st, 1997, up until that point it was the worst natural disaster in the history of the state of Arkansas and we drove all the way through it.
27 tornadoes touched down in the state that day.
We were the last semi allowed through Little Rock Arkansas witnessed a tornado hit a propane factory.
Watching the flames twist up into the tornado was unreal.

Traffic had crept down to a crawl because of all the devastation in front of us and there was nowhere to go.

By the time we move to southern Illinois that night tornadoes were still being reported all through the area except this time it was dark.
The highway was completely flooded, and we were just pushing water at 5 miles an hour.
There were no longer tornado ditches on the sides of the road because everything was underwater from the heavy rains.

The worst part was when you would hear on the CB that one had just touched down at mile marker 72, we were at mile marker 71 and every time the lightning would flash our heads would whip left and right looking for the funnel.

I'm not afraid to admit that I was frightened, and it was stressful.

By the time I pulled into the parking lot at the lighting shop, it was midnight and I had been behind the wheel for 16 hours through nonstop tornadoes, hailstorms, floods and every other biblical smote and I just wanted to get this gear off my truck so I could go home.

I called the guys up to come get their gear and what do you think they told me.

They would send somebody down in the morning.

I admit that I was amped up on adrenaline, had no cannabis to chill me out, I opened the back of that truck, I dumped all their gear out into the parking lot, and I split.

To this day, I hope there are still crickets chirping in that lighting shop.

Johnny Mathis
National Tour, Spring/Summer 1997
The Johnny Mathis show consisted of Johnny, a six-piece band that traveled with him and we would pick up a 48-piece orchestra locally wherever we played.

My job was to prep the show, drive the truck, carry all the microphones, and stands for the orchestra, all the monitors for Johnny and his band, and the front of house mixing console and control package.
We almost always used local PA companies for the sound system, but the control package always came from 8th Day Sound.

The word "convoluted" gets thrown around a lot, and that is the best way I can describe the patch for this mixing console.
At some point the guy before the guy that was doing it with this guy came up with some kind of system that was just ridiculous, and nobody wanted to deal with it so it came down to me.

The show was designed with no monitor console on stage, so everything was driven from the front of house.

Most of the music for Johnny was written by Henry Mancini and the scores were just beautiful.
The first night I did a show with these guys I was just blown away with what an old school class act this thing was.
I was thrilled to be a part of it, it was a long way away from punk rock night at Peabody's.

Johnny didn't want to travel in a tour bus, he just liked sitting in the passenger seat of a Cadillac and that's how he travelled from town to town.
I drove a 28-foot truck with the audio package, the band gear and everybody's personal luggage.

Another thing about Johnny was that he insisted that everybody had the exact same hotel room as him, he felt uncomfortable having a nicer room than everybody else.

because of that we always stayed at Embassy Suites, it was great.
It was a long way away from all the Motel 6's I stayed at on the New Edition tour.

We were up in Minnesota somewhere; we had a day off, it's about 9:00 at night and I get a knock at my door.
I opened the door it's Johnny Mathis.
He says to me, "Hey Pete if you don't mind, I'd like to leave an hour early tomorrow would that be OK with you?".
Of course, Johnny no problem, anything you want to do.

Ever since then, whenever I'm on stage watching an artist have a fit over something, I can't imagine them going down to the technician's hotel room and asking him if its OK if we could leave a little early in the morning.
It's not just that Johnny was nice to me, Johnny was nice to everybody.

My favorite moment alongside Johnny Mathis, was during a sound check up in Saratoga Springs NY.
I was done with everything on stage and the conductor was rehearsing with the band and the orchestra.
From the stage I saw Johnny sitting in the audience all by himself.

Johnny enjoyed drinking tea with lemon, so I swung through catering grabbed a tea for Johnny and myself and went out there.
For the next hour Johnny Mathis and I sat together sipping tea as the orchestra rehearsed and in between he was singing along with the songs.
It was an hour of my life, that I had a private and personal show with Johnny Mathis.
Hands down the most beautiful voice ever.

Years later, I saw Johnny when I was working in New York City at a show called "A&E's Live by Request, and when he came over and gave me a hug, he was genuinely happy to see me It was a really cool moment for me that in my lifetime I got to hang out with Johnny Mathis.

I spent eight months that year doing shows with Johnny Mathis, I went back and forth between him and another crooner from his era, Tony Bennett.

Tony Bennett
National Tour, Spring, Summer 1997
This was the exact same job as with Johnny Mathis.
I carried a control package, monitors for the band but no monitor console, microphones for the band and the band's backline and personal luggage in the truck.

The primary difference here, no 48-piece orchestra.
I was driving the same truck, with the same gear, making the same money and it was a fraction of the workload.

At this point the bulk of the Tony Bennett production staff had come over from what was left over from Sinatra's team.
There was an old school production company called Altel Systems out of New York that provided audio services for all the old school rat pack tours.
Sinatra, Dean Martin, Liza, Sammy Davis Jr and of course Tony Bennett.

They subcontracted 8th Day Sound to do a bulk of the dates for them and that's what I was there for.

The vibe was just great, the hang was terrific it wasn't a lot of gear.
At the time I was going back and forth between Johnny Mathis and Tony Bennett, I wasn't with Tony Bennett I was with Johnny Mathis and Johnny Mathis was great and the most amazing guy as well, but Johnny Mathis had a six-piece band, would pick up a 48 piece orchestra so it workload wise it was a lot of work but Tony Bennett was three piece baby and then at some point they added the guitarist.
Still, it was less than 20 inputs.

One of the interesting things about Tony is that he had this piano player named Ralph Sharon that was with him forever like since the early 1950s.
I don't want to say for sure but it's my understanding that him and Ralph like just hung together and wrote the majority of all that work that he did over the years.

This was the 90s and Ralph was in his 80s at that point.

We were doing monitors from front of house, so there was nothing for me to do except just kind of hang with the guys and do what they needed before they went.

Every show, whatever show it was me, Tony and Ralph hanging out waiting to go on.

We were at this gig, and there was an old woman waving to Ralph, motioning him to come over to the barricade line.

He goes over there, she says "Remember me? I'm Dolores you used to fuck me when I was 15".

The look at this guy's face was awesome.

15? Like when was this? 1915?

My favorite Tony Bennett moment was we were doing a gig down in DC and it was some private fancy function thing and me, Tony and Ralph are standing there, stage left like we always did, and a big entourage of people come around the corner, and it's President Bill Clinton.

Bill walks right up to Tony, "Hey Tony what's happening nice to see you looking forward to the show".

Tony said, "Hey you remember Ralph, and this is Pete".

Tony Bennett just introduced me to the president; it was so surreal. Tony was 24/7 cool.

I would end up doing shows with Tony Bennett for four different sound companies and Radio City Music Hall.

Over my span of my career, I've done about 50 shows with Tony Bennett, and they were all great.

50th Anniversary USAF
Louisville Kentucky, May 1997

The sound company sent me down to Louisville KY for an event that was the opening of the Kentucky Derby and the 50th anniversary of the US Air Force called Thunder over Louisville.

Two weeks before I showed up the sun company had a team of guys that were just down there running XLR cable from tower to tower. the design for the show was 19 towers of audio, 10 on one side of the river and 9 on the other side.

I was sent down as the only audio tech and I drove the semi.
In the shop I organized the load, so I could just drive to each location, peel out the speakers, amplifier, cable trunk and then drive on to the next site with a couple of stagehands and that's exactly what I did.

After everything was in place and I fired up the entire system I discovered a catastrophic error in the design.
the towers were too close together and the sound system was throwing too far, and it was causing an unintelligible echo.

The only solution for this, was to restack all the speakers so they were facing in one direction.
I had the shop send down every kind of digital and analog delay that the company owned, and I delayed everything back to one point source location.

it was a tremendous pain in the ass, but it worked.
We hired a company in to provide a microwave transmitter for getting signal across the river.
I don't remember who baby sat the nine towers on the other side of the river, but it wasn't me.

For the opening of the show, they had all these searchlights on this bridge spanning across the Ohio River connecting Indiana to Kentucky.

Through the sound system came an air raid siren as the searchlights spanned across the sky.
A squadron of vintage World War 2 bombers came low down the Ohio River and the moment they went over the bridge, the bridge exploded in fireworks.
That's how the show started.

After that it was the largest pyrotechnics show in the world at that time and it was very impressive, but nothing was impressive as that opening.
I found a video on YouTube that the local news station had captured of the event, and they completely missed the best part which was those bombers flying over the bridge.

I've seen a lot of fireworks spectacles in my lifetime, but nothing was ever as cool as those WW2 bombers flying over that bridge.

The Bee Gees
Rock & Roll Hall of Fame Induction Ceremony, Cleveland May 1997

The sound company sent me to a local recording studio with a monitor system.
I was there to be the monitor mixer for the Bee Gees.
They were scheduled to perform at the rock and roll Hall of Fame induction ceremony, but there was a lot of talk that they may not perform, they may perform, and if they did perform, they were going to rehearse and that's what I was there for.

I didn't care either way, the pay was the same.
One of the developments that was happening at this time, was my buddy Chris from Superstar had been hired to be the production manager for a classic rock tour that was going out over the summer, and he need somebody to come out with him and lead the audio department.

It was gonna be across America for the summer with four bands and he wanted somebody with him that he could depend on.
Since there was nobody available, I took the gig.

We had shopped the audio, lighting, trucking package out to multiple companies to bid.
Only one company came back way underneath everybody else and said not only that could they do it, but they promised that they could do it in one semi not two which was a huge saving.
It just so happened that this was the same company from New York City that was doing the audio for the rock and roll Hall of Fame induction ceremony.

The owner of the sound company came to the studio to meet me with several of his guys.
Absolutely from their perspective, they had a question of who the F is this guy, and why is the client insisting that not only do I go but that I be the crew chief.

After a 5-minute conversation, we put all that away forever and I told them, see you in New York City in a couple of weeks.

The next day was the show.
I went down there with the monitor rig, took it off the truck and it sat on the loading dock the entire time.
The Bee Gees did end up performing, but they used all the sound company's gear, I only had to stay in case there was any reason whatsoever that they needed any of the stuff that I brought.

For me it was best case scenario.
I spent the entire show in catering reading the newspaper.

At a show like this, it's quite the collection of characters that are wandering around backstage.
Some old guy wearing a bunch of gold chains and an open shirt came and sat down at my table with two people that looked like they definitely worked for him.

We get to talking and it turns out, it's legendary promoter Sid Bernstein who was the guy that brought The Beatles to Shea stadium.
I love concert history and I'm always fascinated by what went into getting some of the early shows together.

I asked him, "What did The Beatles want on their rider? What did they want backstage".

He was leaning back in his chair with one arm on the table, and without flinching he said, "They wanted milk and cookies, I said you ain't getting shit, get out there and play your crappy songs".

I just busted out laughing.
looking right at this guy, I had no problem believing that he said that more than once.

The moment the Bee Gees went on, I got the stagehands and loaded my truck and split.

Summer Daze Tour, aka The Fossil Rock Tour
North American tour, Summer, 1997, 20 shows
I reach the sound company in New York City, and nobody is happy to see me.
This was the original concert production company, the one that did Woodstock, the Fillmore east and every single rock concert that I saw when I was a kid, See Factor.

See Factor was founded by Bob See, He was a pioneer in the concert lighting touring business and his inventions are all over the industry standards.
To say these guys was set in their ways is putting it lightly.
The only thing I was concerned about, is that they assured me and Chris they can get amphitheater spectacle consisting of sound, lighting and put it in one semi, I was there to see that magic trick.

I had just spent the past six months at 8th Day Sound that was such a corporate environment, you are not allowed to wear heavy metal T-shirts to the shop.

8th Day Sound had a nice reception lobby, with a pleasant receptionist sitting behind a clean desk.
The lobby consisted of some nice couches, some tables with audio magazines fanned out nicely.

The first moment that I walked into the See Factor shop, there was a guy sitting behind a grubby desk and he was kicked all the way back in his seat with his feet up on the desk, his arms clasped behind his head.
Before I could say anything to him, he said to me "What the fuck do you want?".

I was not in Kansas anymore.
When I informed him that I was looking for the sound department, he responded with "Those douchebags are in the rear of the building back in the corner".

Getting the sense that I was not about to get a tour back there I said thanks and went on my way.
The moment I walked into the lighting department, there was a guy holding a beer yelling at another guy doing lines of cocaine off a road case.
it was 9:00 in the morning.

I find my way back to the sound department, and there is a guy that looked and acted just like Louie from the show Taxi, and he seemed to be yelling at two different people at the same time.
His name was Harry, and I immediately got the vibe that not everybody was getting along with Harry.

This was going to be three guys on the audio crew, Two guys on the lighting crew.
The audio crew consisted of Wayne the Jamaican whose accent was so thick that not even other Jamaicans could understand what he was saying.
Only standing directly in front of him as he was speaking could I get 30% of what he was saying.
He was going to be the front of house tech.

In charge of all the microphones on stage and dealing with all the bands was Scott.
Scott had done many tours with the exact same system and had all of my favorite New York City stereotypes in one package.
Of Scott's unique skills, was that you could name any candy bar and he could tell you the ingredients.
it was impressive.
The lighting crew consisted of Brendan who had lots of tours behind him and the rookie Craig.
My job on the tour, was to be the monitor mixer for the stage and deal with the local crew every day.

Finally on day 2 the moment of truth comes and it's time to put this thing in the truck.
We get halfway through loading this semi, and it's clear to me that this is not going to fit.

The foreman from the lighting department comes out on the sidewalk and says to me" Looks like we're going to need a second truck".

I said to him "Looks like you need to sharpen your fucking pencil, you sold this as a one truck tour, if there's a second truck, you're paying for it".

That's when the owner of the company, Bob See came outside.

The first thing Bob did, he walked up to me and said, "Who the fuck are you?"

I explained to him that I was the client, and his people sold this show as a one truck show, so is it or is it not, a one truck show?

And that's when Bob got involved with the packing of this truck.

In my entire career, I have never encountered a truck more tightly packed with equipment than this one.

This truck was so overpacked that the driver was incapable of driving with more than half tanks of fuel because the truck was overweight.

It was the only time in my life that we ever "stacked mixing consoles".

That is unheard of in our industry, I've only seen it done once and it was on that tour.

Shockingly, they were able to close the door on that truck.

The truck limped away, and the next day we all went to the airport.

Our first show was an arena in Peoria IL.

During the show, I don't remember what act was on stage, but the intercom flashed from front of house.

Concert intercom back then worked with flashing lights, there was no beeping because who would hear it?

I pick up the intercom, and it's the front of house tech Wayne and I've absolutely no idea what he's saying.

About a minute later he shows up at the monitor console, and now he's standing right in front of me trying to say something to me and with the concert going on I can't understand a word he's saying.

He grabs me by the arm, I follow him, and it turns out one of our amp racks is on fire
We get the fire out, get the amp switched out with some spares that we had, and the show went on.

The ultimate kick in the nuts, When the first show was over, we learned that we had to transport the Pat Travers band gear.
this truck was already a puzzle, getting this gear and was going to be Mission Impossible.

The other three bands on this tour, were playing their own shows in between this one so they had buses and trailers pulling their gear.
We spent five hours on that loading dock, stuffing this equipment into that truck.
it was so bad all the labor left.
We actually buckled the roof out on the truck.

The next two shows were in arenas, and I don't remember anything special about it.
There was once a movie and then a Broadway show called "The Producers'.
The premise was that of a promoter that needed a show to take a loss, but instead the show became successful.

The company that Chris and I worked for, had nothing but successful tours.
Everything they did made money.
Somebody came up with the idea that the way they could balance out their books for the year was to have one tour that lost money.
In their minds, what a what's a better way to lose money then get together 4 aging classic rock bands, that individually are barely selling out nightclubs.
And that's what they did.

Our 4th show was an outdoor amphitheater in Council Bluffs IA.
So many people tried to get to that show, that the Highway Patrol reported that the highway was backed up 10 miles.
Everywhere we went people loved this show.

10 shows in, the halfway point and we were in Hartford CT.
My two brothers we're still both in high school, lived in New York so I had them come out to the show.

It was the first time on a big stage helping me do a set change, and the first time getting high on a tour bus.
They did both successfully.

Today my brother John is on staff at Radio City Music Hall and my brother Albert works for the largest production company in the world.
If you could survive a set change with me on stage, you could survive anything.

Early in the tour, it was a pain in the ass for us that John K. from Steppenwolf wanted to sound check at 3:00pm.
Because of the order of the show, it made things difficult.
I asked Chris if he can go and talk to John K. about it to see if we could move the schedule around.
The next time I saw Chris, He looked like a World War 2 veteran that had just survived combat.
We kept the Steppenwolf sound check at 3:00 for the rest of the tour.

Another interesting part of the tour was some of the crew members from the bands.
One of the groups had a stage manager who was a chronic masturbator.
I had seen some strange behavior in my lifetime especially from my time in the 80s, but I had never seen a human being that could cum so fast.

He would take a woman on the tour bus, they would be on the bus for less than 60 seconds, and the door would pop open, and they would reappear, usually with the woman having a very confused look on her face.
One time we were walking to dinner together, and he said, "Hang on one second guys".
He ducked behind a dumpster, we saw him pull his pants down, make a grunting noise and he pulled his pants back up and said, "OK let's go".
I have no memory of ever shaking his hand.

Another interesting sport that I had to amuse myself was torturing the guitar technician for Pat Travers.
I liked the guy, but it was his first tour and I'm all about character building.
Every day when he would check Pat's guitar, I would bounce my finger on the mute button of the channel, making it cut in and out.

I would say to the guy, "Man you better fix that, you don't want Pat thinking that you're fucking up".
At some point he did have the satisfaction that he finally fixed the problem, that was the day I stopped messing with him.

June 21st we were at Chastain Park in Atlanta.
We had a lot of challenges there, starting with being unable to hang the entire sound system, a dB limit that was designed for orchestras and a difficult jump across the continent ahead of us.

Our next show is on the 25th in Concord CA and there was no way that our bus and truck driver could get us there on time.
The only solution was that we needed Co drivers.
Chris had a Class B license, I had a Class A license, and we became the Co drivers.

After that loadout that night, I grabbed a bag of stuff out of the bus and climbed into the semi.
Our semi driver was a character named "Monkey".

The inside of monkey's truck was decorated with Polaroid pictures of women in different states of nudity.
It was like I was inside the serial killer's kill room, looking at the evidence of all his victims.

I climbed into the stinky bunk and went to sleep for eight hours as Monkey drove through the night.
When I woke up, we pulled into a truck stop, got something to eat and I took over driving.
Instead of going to sleep, monkey sat next to me and talked for the next 8 hours.
Monkey was a Vietnam veteran; he had been a door gunner on a helicopter.
One night as I was driving, he told me a story about coming into a landing zone at night to pick up a platoon that was in trouble.
He said they had just touched down, and he saw silhouette of men running out of the jungle and he pulled the trigger and his gun jammed.
He thought it was the VC, but it was the platoon they were there to pick up.
If not for his gun jamming, he would have wiped them all out.
All these years later it weighed on the guy.

Now his greatest fear was running out of Polaroid film in a moment of need.
He was one of the last of the old school "Ill trade you a pass for a blowjob" kind of guy.
All my years, I never once traded a backstage pass to a woman for sex.
I just didn't think it was sexy.

After one more cycle of him not sleeping finally I snapped on the guy, I said, "look here buddy I can't trust you to drive while I'm sleeping if you haven't closed your eyes in three fucking days".
We pulled off a random exit and into a truck stop in Albuquerque NM.

I insisted that he go to sleep, and I would go get something to eat.

We had not seen the tour bus since we left Atlanta, we had no idea where they were.
After parking the truck, I was walking through the parking lot and what do you think I see?
Our tour bus.

I snuck on the bus while everyone was sleeping and made coffee.
I grabbed a couple things out of my bunk slipped back off and went back to the truck.

We finally got to concord CA did the gig and everything was great. Our next show was in Reno NV.

One of the things about tour buses, is that they are always on the go. Just a couple months span a tour bus could have multiple groups of people living on it.

The bus that we were on was previously occupied by Rob Zombie and as many acts do, he had left behind a couple of VCR tapes.
Every bus had a collection of VCR tapes, classic bus movies.
Caddyshack, Blazing Saddles, Animal House, these were all great bus movies because after a long day you didn't have to think about it just put it in have some laughs nice and easy.

First day on the bus when we found these movies, we popped them in the front lounge TV.
The first movie started with a girl standing on the side of the road. From the angle of this camera, it does not appear that this woman is a willing participant in this motion picture.
A car pulls up, a man gets out, punches her in the face and puts her in the trunk of the car.
The next scene was so horrific, it will trouble me for the rest of my life.

The next movie was even worse.
I probably saw maybe 40 seconds of the first movie, and maybe 15 seconds of the second one.

These were legitimate snuff films, and the people in them were not actors they were victims.

I told the guys on the bus; under no circumstances did I want those videos played on this bus ever again.
Well, you know how gossip on tour travels, and it wasn't long before everyone had heard the legend of" the videos".
People wanted to come on the bus and see it and always adamant that there was no way I wanted that to happen.

When we were leaving Reno to go to Los Angeles, the Foghat bus broke down.
The band was going to fly, so we took their crew on our bus and they could just sleep in the lounges.

As soon as we pulled out of the gig, the guys from the crew kept saying to us" We need to see those videos, come on man, we've seen some hardcore stuff before, let us see it".

I looked at those guys and I remember saying to them," I want you to remember that you asked for this, and you could never Unsee this".
I showed them where the tapes were, and I went to my bunk.

I got up at like 7:00 in the morning to pee, and I walked into the front lounge and there was the entire Foghat crew all sitting up and staring in silence.
I went through the motions of making some coffee and I said to the guys "You just couldn't leave it alone, could you?".
These guys were definitely traumatized.

When we left Los Angeles, the tapes disappeared off our bus.

Next stop was Las Vegas.
The last time Chris and I were here we were both with Jesus Christ Superstar.
The place looked the same.
We only had three shows left and it had been some run.

Every night the show opened with the Pat Travers band.
Pat was the nicest guy; his band was great, and he nailed it every night.

Mixing monitors for Blue Öyster Cult on the big stages was just a dream come true for me.
I had done monitors for them several times in the past in nightclubs, but this was the element that I remember them in when I was a kid coming to their concerts.
Hits all night long and it was one of the few times in my career where I really loved every song of the show.

Scott even got to play the cowbell on Don't fear the Reaper.
As we all know, you can never have enough cowbell.

For me the stars of the show, was the original lineup of Foghat.
Lonesome Dave, Rocking Rod crushed it every night.

Steppenwolf was great every night as well.
They did all their hits except the one song they never did which is one of my favorites was "The Pusher"

Everything went great in Vegas, and we headed off to Farmington NM.

This gig was so weird.
The show was in the parking lot of a minimum-security prison.
In front of the stage down the middle of the audience was a chain link fence.
It was 18 and over on one side and 18 and under on the other. I remember the catering being so far away they had to take us there in golf carts.

Apparently not everybody got the memo that this was a minimum-security prison parking lot.
The story told to me, was that Lonesome Dave from Foghat went looking for the bathroom and wandered into the prison.

He was taking a whiz at the urinal, and there were a couple guys just hanging out.
Dave asked if they were coming to the show tonight?
One of the guys responded, "No man, we're in prison".

Like I said, the gig was weird.
That night after the show we had a problem.
The tractor pulling our truck, had mechanical issues.
This was Monkey's truck that was assigned to him by the trucking company, and he was responsible for it.

Since the first day of the tour there was one thing that Monkey would not shut up about and it was about the last day of the tour. The biggest motorcycle rally in the country, the 50th anniversary of the "Hollister Incident" in Hollister CA.

The Hollister incident was made famous by Life magazine, when in 1947 a group of motorcycle enthusiasts invaded the town of Hollister and caused a bit of a ruckus.
The movie, "The Wild Ones" Starring Marlon Brando was based on this incident.
It was the ultimate biker story.
Add to that that it was also the 50th anniversary of a motorcycle club that is known as the Red and White.

Another tractor had to come pick up the trailer, and that was the last time I ever saw Monkey.

The 4th of July 1997, we show up at the gig at Hollister CA.
Chris and I had a series of unusual questions that came our way from this promoter.
We had sent them pictures of what we considered to be a proper stage and roof system.

The stage was at the end of an oval racetrack, and immediately we had several concerns.
Concern #1 was that the stage was made from quarter inch plywood and did not have any type of roof system whatsoever.

Our crew had arrived, and there were several hundred of them, all of them were members and prospects of the motorcycle club.
I find the president of the chapter and introduce myself to him.
His name was "Topper".
I explained to him, that we can't unload anything out of our truck, because the first thing off our truck will break right through this stage.

With 30 plus guys standing behind him, he stepped right up to my face and said to me "You're a liar, you just don't want to do any work".

I said, "OK, let's do it".
I opened the doors to the truck, I had the driver back right up to the stage, we pulled out the small ramp which we call" the dance floor ramp" to fill the gap between the truck and the stage.
With all the bikers standing on stage angrily staring at us, we pulled the first thing off the truck which was two 1 ton motors per case, stacked 3 high.
The moment the casters from the motor cases touched the deck, it broke through. The entire stack broke through the stage and was instantly on the dirt under the deck.

Topper came over to me, shook my hand like a gentleman and said, "You were right, what do we have to do to make this happen".
I explained to him that minimally, we need to resurface the entire stage.
He asked me if we needed to do the entire stage, couldn't we just do parts of it.
I said no brother we are going to use every inch of this stage.
He organized some Mexicans to get the motor cases out from underneath the stage, and they organized a posse to go out and by a shit load of plywood.

The entire time this is happening everyone else is working frantically to cancel this show.

We had no cell service out there and it was impossible to get a hold of anybody.

At one point during the early negotiations of getting this show together, Topper and a couple other bikers pulled me aside from the rest of the group.
They pointed over to Chris, who at that time had a long ponytail and I had a crew cut.
They said to me, "We like you, but we're thinking about putting him inside of a tire and taking him down the road, we've done it before".

I assured the guys, that my buddy was cool, and he just had a job to do and we're just trying to do what we can to make this thing happen.
I was keeping my cool on the outside, but on the inside, I was stressed.

Concern #2 was that I had the horrifying realization that there was not going to be 10,000 people for this show, there was going to be 100,000.
We did not have enough PA to cover an area this large, even if I did have a roof to hang everything from but we didn't.
We were stacking it all up as much as we could, and I remember Scott saying to me that the way we were stacking it was not recommended by the manufacturer because of "comb filtering".

My response was something to the effect of, "First off you're assuming that we survive this, and if we do survive this, none of the audio experts in the audience will ever remember the comb filtering effect".

Another development is that since there was no stagehands there was no spotlight operators.
I remember Craig specifically saying" There is no way in the world that I'm going to run a spotlight".
The picture that I took of Craig running a spotlight that night, ended up being on the wall of See Factor for years.

Right before the show started, the president of the club again approached me and said to me, "Man you were right, you guys did use every inch of the stage", and he was right, we did.

We did pat Travers for the last time, and everything was great.
The lighting guys just stood up a couple of towers one in each corner of the stage and that was all we could do.

But the time Blue Oyster Cult went on, it was just getting dark.
This is a band that definitely works better in the dark.

Foghat came out and played a great show.

At this point, we are set up for Steppenwolf and my prediction came true and there was 100,000 people out in that audience.
There was a huge commotion in the crowd, and hundreds of motorcycles rolled across the front of the stage, every one of them driving over the audio snake.
The umbilical cord of the sound system.
I thought Scott Chris and I were all going to die of heart attacks
Watching those bikes turf the snake, we were just waiting for the entire show to go down.
Surprisingly the first group of bikes that went over the snake actually dug it into the ground.
Finally, a Rolls Royce appeared, with some naked strippers on the hood and inside was John K from Steppenwolf.
When Steppenwolf started playing the place erupted, it was a moment in time that it was the ultimate biker hoedown.

After their set the crowd demanded an encore.
I was standing behind the amps on the stage left side when John K. put his guitar on.
And my arm still stands up, what I remember what it was like to hear him play those opening chords to The Pusher.
That was the only night of the tour he played that song, and for that night with that audience it was as powerful as a rock'n'roll moment as you could ever get.

When the show was all over, the president of the motorcycle club came up to me, shook my hand and said "You were honest with me, and I respect that. We are not going to help you load the show out and I want you to respect that".
He gave me a T-shirt, supporting his motorcycle club and everybody split.

We loaded that entire show out with just us and the T-shirt guy, it was tough.
When the truck was loaded, we came to the realization that they had locked us in the site.
I instructed the truck driver, to back the truck up through the fence and that's exactly what we did.

After we got out of there we were on our way to our hotel and then airport in San Francisco.
Once we got cell signal, I checked my messages, and they wanted me to do a Johnny Mathis show loading in 36 hours later in Boston.
After this, I couldn't wait to get there.

A Chorus Line
National Tour Rehearsal, Fayetteville AR, August 1997
I had just got home from a Tony Bennett run when I got a call from the theatrical company that used me for Jesus Christ Superstar and had hired me to mix West Side Story.

They told me that they had a show that was being teched down in Fayetteville AR and they had some concerns about the audio person they had hired.
They asked me if I could jump to the airport head on down there and assess what the problem was.

I was told that the cast was gonna be there in a week and this guy absolutely was not ready.
The next day I flew to Fayetteville AR.

I remember having to go to Dallas and then take a puddle jumper from there.
We had to take a second pass at the runway, because the first time there was a cow on the runway.
After the antique plane made it to earth, I went to the center of the airport to look for a cab.
When I asked about taxi service the response was, "Jeff ought to be back anytime".
Finally, Jeff showed up and I got a ride to the theater.

I walk into the theater, and I couldn't believe what I was seeing.
This guy still had equipment in cardboard boxes.
At this point in the proceedings the entire audio system should have been up and running, not still in the IKEA stage one phase.

I was not cool, I completely laid into the guy because I didn't want to be there, and the only reason I was there is because he was a big fuck up.
We immediately stopped doing things his way and started doing things my way.
24 hours later we had an operational audio system.
The day after that, the cast showed up to start rehearsing.

There were several cast members that had been with me and Jesus Christ Superstar.
It was nice to see familiar faces and they were happy to see me as well.
I let the guy drive the first sound check with the cast and orchestra and it was a train wreck.
He was sound checking each individual vocalist for 10,15 minutes at a time.
The cast was immediately getting irritated.
I told the guy that he didn't have 10 hours to sound check every day he needed to speed this thing up.

There were all kinds of phone calls back and forth, they wanted me to take over but for me this show was so boring there's no way I would have stayed awake for it.

I stayed for the first show, it was a little rough, but the guy made it through it.
I gave him some words of encouragement, looked for Jeff and went back to the airport.

MTV Video Music Awards
Radio City Music Hall, NYC, September 1997

After the Summer Daze tour, I returned to my cycle of going back and forth doing shows with Tony Bennett and Johnny Mathis.
That was all coming to an end for me because starting in September I was going out on West Side Story.
I had been hired for this tour nine months earlier when Jesus Christ Superstar ended.
It was with the exact same production company as Superstar, going back to the same cities, the same theaters for the next year.

I had a week before I had to be in Albany for the rehearsals, when I got a call from See Factor, asking me if I would be interested in doing monitors for "The Mighty Mighty Bosstones" on top of the marquee at Radio City Music Hall for the MTV Video Music awards.
My only answer is what time do you want me there?

I was thrilled to be doing a show in New York City, and I was thrilled to be doing a show at Radio City Music Hall.
I had done monitors for the Bosstones on multiple occasions back at Peabody's, I was ready.

Inside the headliner was the Spice Girls and I was thrilled to not have anything to do with them.

This was my first big TV gig, there was a whole new audio language to learn, and I was going to learn it.
The show went great, and I met a lot of great people, and I learned quite a bit about doing shows in New York City and especially at Radio City Music Hall.

West Side Story
National Tour, Fall 1997
I met up with the tour in Albany NY to rehearse this thing at a local theatre before taking it on the road.
Being hired for this thing nine months earlier, going back to all the theaters I had been to last year, I had the approval from the sound designer to do what I wanted, and I really felt that I was completely in control of my own gig.

Brad wasn't on this tour, but Chris, Cody, Ingrid the Stage Manager and Mark Hall were on it, we still required the Cleveland connection.

I had signed up to be on this tour for one year.
Finally, I was doing the kind of shows that I wanted to do.
Mixing touring Broadway musicals was a long way away from cleaning the vomit out of the urinals at Peabody's.
The way I saw it, everything was coming up Milhouse and the only thing I needed now, was to change where I was living.

My neighborhood in Cleveland Heights had turned into it a total ghetto and I wasn't comfortable leaving my family there.
A couple days before I went on tour, my daughter was outside in the front of the house standing on the sidewalk talking to one of her friends who was straddling a bicycle.
 A girl's bicycle.

I was on the second floor of our house, and I just happened to look out the window when a car pulled up right where my daughter was standing.
A guy got out, who had to be about 6 foot 4, he walked right up to my daughter's friend, punched her in the face, took her bicycle and put it in the trunk of his car.
By the time I got downstairs, he was long gone, and my daughter's 11-year-old friend had her face shattered over a bicycle.
My family could not remain in this neighborhood with me on the road, we had to move.

With my plan of perpetually being on tour for the rest of my life mixing musicals, it didn't matter where I lived, I just wanted it to be someplace safe.

When I was driving the semi with New Edition, one of my hobbies was collecting home books from around the country.
You know those colored plastic bins that you see around truck stops, you flip open the lid and grab the local real estate homes for sale, I had them from all over the country.

After looking everywhere, I narrowed it down to the same town my father lived in, Woodstock NY.
It was a small town in the Catskills with the zero crime.
I was absolutely determined that during this tour I would save up enough money to move my family out of Cleveland and into Woodstock.

When I arrived in Albany to tech the show, I had a great attitude.
I was here for the long haul, and nobody was there to question what I was doing or how I was doing it and for me that meant everything.
I hate being micromanaged and if there's one thing that I must control in my work environment it's my method of production.

The most interesting development was when we were rehearsing the show in Albany, was the tour manager that the company had hired for this production.
This guy had never been on a tour before.
How anybody thought it was a good idea to hire somebody for a job that they have never done before, to this day still escapes my imagination.

We build and rehearse the show in Albany, and technically we had no problems.
Following my previous success with Jesus Christ Superstar, I labeled everything with animal stickers again.
I'm all about results.

The only problem the show is having in the rehearsal stage, was that the actor they hired to play the role of "Riff", who was the leader of the Jets, had a heavy British accent.
Since he wasn't a very good actor, he wasn't very good at hiding his accent.
At some point we were waiting for the show to open with," Hello governor".

The personnel of the tour consisted of 10 in the crew on one tour bus, the cast, however many jets and sharks there were, a dozen musicians on several other buses.
At one point they put the cast in sit up buses, but I don't remember when that happened.

The first indication that we were in trouble happened I think somewhere in the Dakotas, very early on in the tour.

Some of the audio cables that I had we're not long enough for certain stages.
I knew some of the places that we were going to would require more cabling, so I was thrilled when I met a guy at one of the theaters that owned a local sound company, and he had the cable that we needed in his shop.
I could get everything I needed before the loadout.
Immediately I head into the production office to get some cash, and there is the tour manager and his assistant with the telephone book.
He was holding the phone, and I heard him say, "Do you have 62 rooms for Thursday?'.
I was frozen like an alien tractor beam just grabbed me.
What did he just say?

He says over the phone, "Oh I see well thank you", and hung up the phone.
I asked him point blank, "What are you doing?"
He responded that he was attempting to get hotels for us.
Again, I'm trapped in that alien tractor beam unable to move.

I said to him," Why aren't you using a travel agency? Where is the tour itinerary for all of us? Every hotel for this entire tour should already be booked.
I should already know where I could get a package delivered four months three days from today".

Immediately I alerted the rest of the crew about this situation, and we all marched into his office carrying different tour books from different tours showing him what a tour book looks like, with all the information with all the hotels with all the venues with all the information, you know all that stuff that a tour manager does.

It was like we were touring anthropologists teaching the primitive culture something new.
As he's flipping through these little books, I said to him "Hey I need $200 to pick up some gear".
He looked at me and said" $200? We don't have that kind of money".

This was the first time, that I lost my patience with this guy and ripped into him.
I said to him, "We are rolling with four buses, 2 semis, and over 60 people, you should be sneezing $200".
I had to use my own personal money to make the buy and it took two weeks to get reimbursed.
This guy was not making friends with me.

It was early in the tour and the vibe was not the same as it was on Superstar.
On this tour instead of Brad as Head Carpenter, we had a guy who was so lazy he didn't even put the whole show up every time. During one loadout, he left the "Star Drop", on the loading dock deliberately because he was sick of putting it up every day.

I think like a lot of other victims that went through trauma dealing with stupid people I really suppressed a lot of the memories of the dumb things that this guy did.

I know at one point I gave him the name Gilligan, and that's how I referred to him for the rest of the tour.

We were in Ogden UT, and we had to cancel the show because he was incapable of getting the cast there on time.
Gilligan had booked a flight for the cast and orchestra that took them to the wrong city

At this point the cast and the orchestra we're traveling in two sit up buses.
One of the realities of being on these types of buses is that the toilets that they have are not designed for solid waste matter.
Gilligan let the cast vote on whether they wanted to defecate on the buses.
That was another day the buses had to be out of service so they could deal with a wastewater issue.

Gilligan was riding on our bus, and he came in the rear lounge and told me, Cody, and Mark Hall that he didn't want us smoking marijuana on the bus anymore.
Gilligan officially had a bunk on our bus, but the next day I removed all his items and luggage off our bus, and I put it all on the one of the cast buses.
That was the moment I kicked the tour manager off our bus.

Every member of the crew was a seasoned professional.
The show looked great, the show sounded great, and we never had any technical problems.
The only person on the tour not doing their job was Gilligan.

What was a 90-minute load in for me on Jesus Christ Superstar, I turned into a one-hour load in with this show.
I built all the stage monitors into the set and the truss systems, and I even loomed all the audio cable in with lighting.
Instead of running audio cable I would just wait till lighting was done and then go make the attachments.

For the orchestra pit, I had a boom box with a cassette tape.

On that tape was my voice giving all the instructions to build the pit. If any of the stagehands asked me any questions I would just point to the box.

Another innovation I had for this tour, was that instead of delivering any microphones to the actors, I had a tall work box on stage with several lava lamps in it that would attract the actors to it like a moth to a flame.

Every wireless microphone and pack for every actor, was in a pouch with their name and a little piece of candy.
It was like a prize for leaving me alone and coming getting your own goddam microphone.
It was shockingly successful.

My favorite innovation on this tour, was that although I carried an espresso machine with me, there was barely enough time to make it during intermission.
Intermission, and then going into a loadout that was when I really needed some good espresso.
I consulted the lighting guys, and they had an open dimmer available in their lighting rig.
Ingrid the stage manager, was nice enough to write another cue into the show.
How a Broadway musical works, is that the stage manager" calls the show on headset" and every single action of the show is related to a cue and a cue number.

At the stage manager station, she has a book with hundreds of prompts, starting with cue the orchestra, all the way to the last cue when the curtain closes.
We worked it out, that 5 minutes before intermission, Ingrid would call "Cue 402", the lighting guy would engage the button, and backstage my espresso machine would start brewing.
We would hit intermission; the curtain would close and by the time I got backstage my coffee was ready.
Since it only made two cups at a time, we always rotated who got the second cup.

When you're away from home for months at a time, simple little comforts, like that regular cup of coffee that you enjoy means everything.

Any little thing that you could do to make you comfortable doing your job is worth doing.
The front of house sound mixer for any musical always goes in one location and that is the last row of the theater.
It's a horrible place to mix from because being back and underneath the balcony does not give an accurate representation of the audio experience happening in the orchestra pit.
But those are the big money seats, and management would always side with not killing those seats and just make the sound guy work around it.

Every theater in America has what we call" balcony speakers" that are installed and depending on the quality of the theater and whatever their maintenance schedule is, sometimes those little speakers are crappy, sometimes not always working properly and I found them to be consistently unreliable from city to city.
So, judging my mix from them, was not always ideal.
We carried an audio system that covered most of the venues, just not the corners and the under-balcony sections.

One of my comforts, was that I had a rug that I'd like to put out underneath my mixing console.
This was a long show, there was lots of slow soft numbers, and I'm sitting back there in the dark just trying to stay awake for all of it.
One of the things about mixing the same show every night is that it's easy to get complacent.
You must be able to delineate the difference between are you listening to it or are you just hearing it.

Another comfort of mine is that during the show, I wore Bunny slippers.
If you're thinking of like big fuzzy white Bunny slippers with the big ears on them, that's exactly the kind I was wearing.

I spent hours behind that mixing console and I just wanted to be comfortable and sit there with my Bunny slippers.
The truth is, is that most times nobody ever noticed.

I'm walking in the theater when the rest of the audience is, and you know how it is it's crowded, who's looking down at people's feet?

We were someplace in Texas, and we were only there for one night. After the show was loaded in, we didn't sound check so there was no reason to be in the theater, we were just hanging out on the bus.

Finally, we're getting close to showtime, and the different crew members were drifting off the bus and going into the theater to do their thing.
I was the last one off the bus.
Walking through the stage door, some guy places his hands on me and says to me, "You cannot come into this theater wearing those things",
referring to my Bunny slippers.
I said, "Oh yes I can, you don't get to choose my wardrobe".
He was the manager of the theater, and he had security escort me out of the building.

OK, no problem.
I went back on the bus, went to the back lounge, put on some AC/DC and I started doing bong hits.

A few minutes later, Gilligan appears on the bus.
He tells me to take those slippers off, come inside, the show is ready to start.
I said no.
The issue over my footwear is so stupid I declined capitulating.
This wasn't a big deal till two other adults made it a big deal, nobody in the world cared about this and now I'm not budging.
I turned the music up, loaded another bong hit and ignored him.

He disappeared.

A few minutes later he reappeared back on the bus with the update that the theatrical manager would now allow me back into the building, with my Bunny slippers.

The show is supposed to start at 8:00 PM.
Now it's 8:20 PM.
If that dumbass never would have stopped me, I would have been sitting at my mixing console with my feet on my rug as most of these people came in and found their seats.
Now I walk into the venue, walk right up the aisle to the back of the house, every single patron in the theater saw my Bunny slippers and I got an applause.
The show sounded great that night.

We had a few more shows around Texas and then we had one night in Corpus Christi.
Same as always, we get the show up and everybody in the crew just disperses for the day.
Some people went to see a movie, some people went to a local mall, anything to kill time because since we didn't sound check we didn't have anything to do till showtime.
I was finishing something up in front of house when Gilligan appeared.

Gilligan said to me" I need to talk to you".
I said OK, start talking.

He put his hands on his hips like he was about to announce a great proclamation.
Gilligan tells me, "Pete, I've decided that the business doesn't need people like you anymore, and I'm firing you. I'm giving you the option of leaving today with no pay, or you could stay another week at half pay and train your replacement".

I caught him a little off guard because I started laughing.
I said to him, "Does management back in New York know you're firing me?".

He replied, "No Pete I make my own decisions out here".
I just couldn't stop laughing, because I knew that the people in New York we're looking for a replacement for him, that he was the one that was about to get fired.

I asked him if I could have some time to consider his generous offer and he said he wanted my answer by the end of the day.
Immediately I went to the production office to call New York, and I saw his wallet sitting on the desk next to the phone.
So instead of calling New York, I pulled one of his credit cards out of his wallet and booked myself a flight back home.
As I walked out of the production office with my flight confirmation in my hand, I saw the runner sitting there in the hallway reading a book.
I said to the runner, "Hey can you give me a ride to the airport?", they said sure no problem.

I grabbed my case from stage left that had my bong and my espresso machine, got my luggage off the bus and I left my rug behind.
Before anyone came back from what they were doing, before lunch was even over, I was already at the airport.
I didn't say goodbye to anybody I just vanished.
There was a part of me that was so pissed off about this whole situation.

Now I admit that I picked on him and I was a total dick.
But my viewpoint at the time was that this gig was supposed to be so easy, and everybody was a professional except him.
I'm incapable of mentally recalling all the little stupid things that this guy did on a day-to-day basis, I just pushed them down the memory hole

I was not the only one on the crew not getting along with Gilligan, but him and I butted heads the most because I refused to give him an inch. From the beginning he was just so resistant to listen, not just to me but to anybody else on our crew and for that I had zero respect for him.

God knows that I have been in situations where I was in over my head, and in those situations, I knew the thing not to do was butt heads with the people that knew what they were doing.
That's not what a leader does and that is not the best way to get results and at the end of the day this business is all about results.

Called the New York office from the airport right once I was going to get on the plane and told them that their boy had fired me.
Although they insisted that I should go back to the theater, and they would work it all out I was no longer interested in playing along.

This was early December at this point, and we had been on this tour for three months with nine more months left to go on it.
Gilligan understood that I was in the process of buying a house, he had to sign some paperwork for me as my immediate employer representative for my bank loan, so he knew that firing me right then and there was a tremendous kick in the nuts to me.

The person that I felt the most for at this juncture was the woman that he had hired to come in and replace me.
She landed at the airport I took off from about an hour after me.

As told to me by my friends on the tour after the fact, he had assured her that I would stick around for several weeks training her to mix this show.
She had some club sound experience and her only time ever mixing a musical was that she did the high school production of West Side Story.
This was not a high school production.
This was 30 vocals plus an orchestra, as far as being an audio mixer, it doesn't get more complex than this.

Gilligan absolutely threw her under the bus.
I can't imagine how intimidating it was for her to walk up to that mixing console and be expected just to step right in.
They had to cancel the show that night.

The next show they loaded in but couldn't get the audio system functioning and had to cancel that show as well.
After that audio would take 8 hours to load in every day when it was taking me one hour.
Full sound check with the orchestra and every member of the cast every day after that.
I guess that's why the business doesn't need people like me anymore.

Before getting on that plane in Corpus Christi TX, I made one more phone call.
I called See Factor in New York City and ask them if they had any upcoming work available.

They told me that they had a big show at Madison Square Garden next weekend and asked me if I would be interested in being the monitor mixer for it.
I told them, I'll see you next week.

Jingle Ball
Aerosmith, Sarah McLachlan, Lisa Loeb, Fiona Apple, Hanson, Savage Garden, Chumbawamba, Backstreet Boys, Allure, The Wallflowers, Celine Dion.

Madison Square Garden, NYC, December 9th 1997

Every show I ever did has led me up to this moment.
All those shows at Peabody's, the rib cook offs, the WMMS radio shows all of it headed up to this.

This would be my first show at the world's most famous arena Madison Square Garden.
The biggest difference between this show and everything I had ever done up to this point, far as multiband festival Is that I would not be alone on stage doing goddam everything.

There were four guys to deal with all the bands microphones, we had enough stuff so every band had their own individual setup, and I didn't have to go on stage for anything, I could just stay behind the monitor console.
First time ever.

The plan was for me to have five consoles lined up on the side of the stage, 4 Ramsa 840 monitor consoles and 1 Yamaha PM4000.
The "A2's" were responsible for all microphone inputs had the plan that every input was going to land sequentially across all five consoles.
There was only one group that was going to have their inputs split across two consoles, and that was Hanson, and we really didn't care.

The plan for the show was for there to be two stages.
the mainstage at the end of the room where it usually goes and then a smaller cocktail style stage on the other side.

The lead sound guy from the audio company had a convoluted plan to have multiple systems hanging and he would turn them on and off depending on what band was playing.

It sounded so horrible that I make the claim that to this day you could still go to Madison Square Garden, stand in the center of that room and if you're listening closely, you can still hear some of the echo from that show still bouncing around the rafters.

This was going to be a brutal day no matter how you looked at it, we were loading in at midnight.
By 8:00 AM I already had eight hours of work behind me.

11 AM we were ready for our first sound check.
How we communicate in the concert business for sound checks is that we use a Talkback system.
The mixer at the front of house console has a microphone with a switch, and I keep that through all the speakers on stage so whenever he wants to talk to the band, he could just hit the switch, talk to everybody up there including talking to the technicians when we're going through a sound check.

Another thing about doing sound checks, is it saves a lot of time if we all do it at the same time.
For a show like this there's three different mixers confirming every microphone.
The front of house, the monitor mixer, and the recording truck.
We have the drum tech sitting behind the drum kit ready to start going through the drums with all the mixers.
At this point, somebody must call it, and it's traditionally the front of house mixer.

We are all waiting.
And we're waiting.
Finally, through all the speakers on stage comes a sound, "Kkkkkkkkkkkkkccccchhhhhh".
Me and the other A2s couldn't figure out what was going on.
I'm checking the inputs, put my headphones on and again we all hear, "Kkkkkkkkkchhhhhh".

It turns out that what we are hearing, is the front of house mixer Harry, attempting to say the word "Kick".

He was so loaded up with cocaine, that his jaws were all locked up. All clenched up.

We get to the next input, which was snare.
All we had coming through the Talkback was, "Sssnnnn sisssnn". Couldn't even say snare.

We had to send somebody out there so they could talk and let Harry push the buttons.

Even though the crew was gacked out of their minds on cocaine we got through the day with no problems at all.
Until we got to Aerosmith.

Growing up I was a huge Aerosmith fan.
I bought the album "Rocks" on the day it came out and I saw them live 11 times.
For me, to be on stage at Madison Square Garden, we're about to soundcheck Aerosmith, I was almost shaking I was so excited.
I was exhausted from being up for almost two days at this point, but I was so thrilled not only that I was going to be here for an Aerosmith soundcheck but that everything was just going so well with all the gear we had no problems at all, everything was just great.

The lead A2 for this show was Sean Kelly, who was hands down one of the best in the business.
We do the set change, get Aerosmith in position, our last sound check of the day and I could see that Sean has a serious look of concern.

He had the ends of a cable in each hand, connecting these two together is what he needed to make happen to continue with this Aerosmith sound check.
There was supposed to be a connecting piece that we called "a butt", but he didn't have it, we didn't have it, and it wasn't happening.

There were only two bands that day that had a monitor mixer Aerosmith and Hanson.
The Aerosmith guys are pissed, and now we've got this huge delay in everything. I don't even remember how long it took or how it got resolved but it put a real cramp on the day.

For the most part I don't remember any hiccups in the show.
I did find it funny that the drummer from Hanson kept yelling at the monitor guy, who was at that time a few years older than me.
I was surprised that he was going to take that from a 9-year-old, I told him he should go up there and take away his juice box.

During the Aerosmith set I was right there at the monitor console holding back the biggest smile of my life.
I was just taken back to what it was like being a teenager watching these guys and being so excited about it to currently being on stage with them, I could never describe what a feeling that was.

After Aerosmith, we put up the last band, The Wallflowers.
I was the monitor mixer for The Wallflowers, and we were a couple songs into their set when a guy tapped me on the shoulder and asked if he could stand with me.
It was Joe Perry.
I said, "Yeah Joe no problem" and I went back to what I was doing, paying attention to what's happening on stage.
Couple minutes later standing on my right side was Steve Tyler, he said "Hey man sounds good up here".

I spent the rest of The Wallflowers set hanging out with these two guys that I idolized in the 70s.
Without hesitation I could say that the coolest rock'n'roll moment I ever had was hanging out with Joe Perry and Steve Tyler at the monitor console during a sold-out show at Madison Square Garden.

When the show ended Joe thanked me for letting him hang out at the console, it was surreal.
The loadout was long and brutal, but I was still running high off the energy of hanging out with Aerosmith in Madison Square Garden.

Escape from Cleveland
December 1997

After the show at Madison Square Garden, I went back to Cleveland to pack everything I owned.

The entire time I was out on West Side Story I was in the process of buying a house and finding myself immediately unemployed was a problem.
After the MSG show, See Factor told me if I come to New York, they will give me all the work I wanted.
Just a year earlier, I was driving the semi and doing the show for $175 a day.
In NYC they were offering me $250 a day and I didn't have to drive anything.

My father had an apartment on the Lower East Side of Manhattan. Back in 1968 he was a squatter in some building on E 4th St., the city of New York promised him that if he left the building so they could tear it down, at some point they would provide him with another apartment.
Or he can go to jail, I think those remained the options.

Flash forward to 1985, he gets a postcard to his Woodstock PO Box, and it says contact us your apartment is ready.
He went from living in a van down by the river in Woodstock to a brand-new apartment building on the Lower East Side.
The same apartment that I would move into to live and work in New York City.

I was on a tight window, because they wanted me back in New York right away but the house I was trying to buy in Woodstock wasn't available yet.
I didn't want to come to New York without moving my family to Woodstock first.
The auction for the house I wanted was happening on the 2nd of January 1998, and I had to be out of the house I was in back in Cleveland on the 26th of December.

There was a one-week difference, and even then, I wasn't guaranteed that my bid on the house would be the highest.
So, I gambled, I put all my stuff in a truck and with my wife driving the Jeep like a caravan we made the pilgrimage to Woodstock.

I kicked in the front door of the house and moved all my stuff inside of it.
This was going to end one of two ways, me exiting in shame with the Sheriff's Department or me winning the bid for this house.
Thankfully, law enforcement never had to be deployed.

The same day I moved all my furniture into the house, I went to the bus station went down to New York City and went on a gig.

Looking Back

After moving to New York City, I would work for See Factor for 2 1/2 years doing a series of epic shows around the city and around the country.

In the summer of 2000, I was invited to become a member of the International Alliance of Theatrical Stage Employees Union Local One in New York City, and I was hired on staff at Radio City Music Hall. I would spend eight years on staff at Radio City before moving over to Madison Square Garden.

After five years as the audio lead for the stagehands at MSG in the theatre and the arena, I left to do predominantly television concert events which is what I still do to this day.

Now every time I go to work, it could be the biggest show in the world on that day, 50,000 people in the audience broadcast to a billion people around the world.

Going to concerts with my friends in the 70s, being on the road with my own band in the 80s, working my way up through the nightclubs, theaters, and arenas in the 90s all prepared me for New York City.

I knew that if I could make it here, I can make it anywhere.
Who knows, maybe even someday, I could be an Expert from New York.

ROADIESNROCKSTARS.COM

334

Printed in Great Britain
by Amazon